shattered anzacs

DR MARINA LARSSON is a Melbourne historian who has held lecturing positions at La Trobe and Monash universities. In 2008, she received the Australian Historical Association's biennial Serle Award for the study upon which this book is based. Marina has published and presented on war and repatriation history, and her research interests include disability history, public history and the history of the family.

Dedicated to Katie and Archie

marina LARSSON

shattered anzacs
living with the scars of war

UNSW PRESS

A UNSW Press book
Published by
University of New South Wales Press Ltd
University of New South Wales
Sydney NSW 2052
AUSTRALIA
www.unswpress.com.au

© Marina Larsson 2009
10 9 8 7 6 5 4 3 2 1

This book is copyright. Apart from any fair dealing for the purpose of private study, research, criticism or review, as permitted under the Copyright Act, no part may be reproduced by any process without written permission. Inquiries should be addressed to the publisher.

National Library of Australia
Cataloguing-in-Publication entry
Author: Larsson, Marina.
Title: Shattered Anzacs: living with the scars of war/Marina Larsson.
ISBN: 978 1 921410 55 0 (pbk.)
Notes: Includes index.
Bibliography.
Subjects: Australia. Army. Australian and New Zealand Army Corps.
Disabled veterans – Australia.
Families of military personnel – Australia.
War neuroses – Australia.
World War, 1914–1918 – Veterans – Australia.
World War, 1914–1918 – Economic aspects – Australia.
World War, 1914–1918 – Social aspects – Australia.
Dewey Number: 362.4086970994

Design Di Quick
Cover Patient in a cane wheelchair, No. 1 Australian Auxiliary Hospital, Harefield, England, c.1916, Australian War Memorial negative number P02402.013. Mother with pram, c.1910–20, State Library of Queensland negative number 184156. Unidentified child walking in bare feet, c.1915–51, National Library of Australia negative number nla.pic-an24507652. A soldier's welcome home, Adelaide, 1918–19, Australian War Memorial negative number, P05328.001.

 This publication has been supported by La Trobe University www.latrobe.edu.au.

contents

Acknowledgments   7

Abbreviations   9

Notes on sources   11

Introduction: Family stories   15

1 War wounds as family wounds   29

2 Returning to family life   61

3 Making ends meet   90

4 Family relationships   120

5 Families and mental hospitals   149

6 Tuberculosis: The 'family disease'   178

7 Burnt out soldiers and the 1930s Depression   206

8 Postwar death, grief and memorialisation   234

Conclusion: The shared legacies of war disability   265

Appendix 1: Recruitment methods for oral history informants 273

Appendix 2: Profiles of oral history informants   275

Notes   282

Bibliography   302

Index   314

acknowledgments

I have many people to thank for their support during the writing of this book. I extend particular thanks to Diane Kirkby for her exceptional guidance and ongoing encouragement and to Katie Holmes for her generous and perceptive advice. I express my heartfelt gratitude to my colleagues at La Trobe University and elsewhere for their camaraderie and wise counsel: Richard Broome, Janet Butler, Natasha Campo, John Cashmere, Cathy Coleborne, Deb Dempsey, Jim Hammerton, Rachel Jenzen, and Tanja Luckins among others. I gratefully acknowledge Lucy Chesser, Julie Dillon, John Hirst, Ken Inglis, Lee-Ann Monk, Bruce Scates, Alistair Thomson and Bart Ziino for reading and commenting thoughtfully on the manuscript at key points during its preparation.

The assistance of archivists has been vital to this project. I thank the staff at the National Library of Australia, the State Library of Victoria, the Mitchell Library, the State Library of South Australia, the Public Record Office Victoria, the City of Sydney Archives, the Vision Australia Archives (formerly the Royal Victorian Institute for the Blind), the Red Cross Archives (Victorian, New South Wales and National branches), Returned and Services League, the Tubercular Soldiers' Association Archives, the Royal Australasian College of Surgeons Archives, and the Legacy Archives (Melbourne). I also thank Helen Brinsmead at the Department of Veterans' Affairs for her role in providing access to the repatriation case files of disabled soldiers.

I owe a special debt to the eleven children of First World War disabled soldiers who shared their stories with me in oral history interviews. This book has been immeasurably enriched by the contribution of Beverley Broadbent, Betsy Burchett, Margaret Cramond, Keith Falconer, Mavis Floyd, Joyce Muir, Beryl Nelson, Diane Nicholas, Mary Reddrop, Gwen Summers, and Joan Wishart. Their stories add a dimension to this book that was simply not available in the written archives. Listening to these men and women has prompted me to think more deeply about war as a family experience.

I wish to acknowledge the support of the Commonwealth Department of Veterans' Affairs, which provided a grant to assist the publication of this book under the Australian government's commemorations program *Saluting Their Service*. The Department has not participated in the research or production or exercised editorial control over the work's contents, and the views expressed and the conclusions reached herein do not necessarily represent those of the Commonwealth, which expressly disclaims any responsibility for the content or accuracy of the work.

The publication of this book has also been assisted by the Serle Award. Generously established by Mrs Jessie Serle, this biennial prize commemorates the contribution to Australian History of her late husband Geoffrey Serle. I thank the Australian Historical Association for presenting me with the award in 2008, and Mrs Serle for her continued support of emerging Australian historians.

Finally, I would like to thank my own family for their support and faith in me: Margaret and Bernard Jansen, and Katie and Archie Somerville.

abbreviations

AIF	Australian Imperial Force
ANZAC	Australian and New Zealand Army Corps
APD	Australian Parliamentary Debates
APP	Australian Parliamentary Papers
ARCS	Australian Red Cross Society
AWM	Australian War Memorial, Canberra
CSB	Closer Settlement Board
CSWM	Centre for Soldiers' Wives and Mothers
LSA	Limbless Soldiers' Association
ML	Mitchell Library
NAA	National Archives of Australia
NLA	National Library of Australia
PTSD	Post-traumatic Stress Disorder
RSL	Returned and Services League (previously RSSILA)
RSSILA	Returned Sailors' and Soldiers' Imperial League of Australia
SLNSW	State Library of New South Wales
SLV	State Library of Victoria

SLSA	State Library of South Australia
SSFA	Sailors' and Soldiers' Fathers Association
TB	Tuberculosis
TSA	Tubercular Soldiers' Association
TSAS	Tubercular Soldiers' Aid Society
UMA	University of Melbourne Archives
VA	Voluntary Aid
VD	Venereal Disease
VPRS	Victorian Public Record Series

notes on sources

USE OF PSEUDONYMS

Pseudonyms have been used to refer to ex-servicemen and their family members named in 'closed' Department of Repatriation medical files, those of the Victorian Department of Lunacy, the Tubercular Soldiers' Aid Society, as well as legal records relating to divorce cases. My access to these files was conditional on this undertaking. In some instances, pseudonyms have also been used to conceal the identity of people mentioned in 'open' files which contain sensitive information. One of my oral history informants, 'Joyce Muir', requested that a pseudonym be used because of the sensitive nature of her story.

QUOTATIONS

Quotations from archival sources are used as they appear in the original text, complete with misspellings and grammatical errors.

FIRST WORLD WAR MEDICAL RECORDS

The National Archives of Australia (NAA) holds the service records of personnel who served in the Australian forces during the First World War (series B2455). Copies of these files are available digitally on the NAA's website (www.naa.gov.au). In addition to this, the NAA also holds the repatriation medical files of Australian ex-servicemen from the First World War in several series. These are often not individually listed on the NAA online collection database, but may be requested. Please contact the NAA for more information.

WE ARE THE MAIMED!

In Flanders' fields we do not lie,
Where poppies grow and larks will fly.
Forever singing as they go
Above the bodies row on row,
Of those whose duty it was to die!

We are the maimed. Death did deny
Its solace. Crippled, blind we try
To find on earth the peace they know
In Flanders' fields.

Forget us not! As years go by,
On your remembrance we rely,
For love that sees the hearts below
Our broken bodies. Else we grow
To crave the peace with those who lie
In Flanders' fields.

Tassie Digger, February 1921

INTRODUCTION

family stories

> Our cup of sorrow has
> been filled to the brim.
>
> Father of a disabled soldier, 1926.[1]

On Anzac Day 1921, Australians paused to commemorate the heroism and sacrifice of the nation's soldiers during the Great War. In Melbourne, the streets echoed with the footsteps of 25 000 returned men who marched from Princes Bridge to the Melbourne Cricket Ground for an open-air memorial service to honour the 'great dead and the noble living'. Among the marchers were a number of disabled soldiers who hobbled along awkwardly with the aid of walking sticks, marched with arms that hung limp at their sides, or bravely faced the crowds despite disfiguring wounds. The *Herald* declared that the disabilities of these men were the 'price of victory' and represented the sacrifices they had made on the battlefield.² During the commemorative service, official speakers honoured the 'fallen', acknowledged the grief of their bereaved families, and recognised the valiant struggles of physically and mentally scarred veterans. Missing from these speeches, however, was any acknowledgment of the impact of war disability upon the family members of disabled soldiers. On this and subsequent Anzac Days, speakers praised damaged ex-servicemen for 'bearing their heavy burden with quiet courage' but the grief, loss and sacrifice of their family members were consistently overlooked.³ War disability transformed the lives of thousands of Australian families who welcomed home a 'changed' man. Yet they received little public honour or recognition, and the meanings of the burdens they carried as a result of their loved one's disablement were submerged beneath the surface of the nation's public commemorations.

This book reveals the hidden history of Australia's 'shattered' Anzacs and their families after the First World War. It brings to light the shared lives of disabled soldiers and their kin who struggled with the consequences of physical and mental war disability during the 1920s and 1930s. It explores how families collectively responded to disablement and makes visible the largely unrecognised impact of ex-servicemen's impairments on their kin. Importantly, it celebrates families' capacity for courage, resilience and resourcefulness in the face of the profound challenges that confronted them as the years passed. The effects of war disability reached far beyond the individual soldier, deep into the lives of his family members. Even before Australia's young recruits arrived on the battlefields of Europe, the possibility of disablement weighed heavily on the minds of concerned family members, and the news that a loved one had been 'incapacitated' came as a distressing shock. After soldiers were invalided home, families were called upon to manage the often devastating emotional, economic and social effects of disablement. Wives and mothers nursed ailing veterans, households learned to live on meagre pensions, and many relatives spent years visiting veterans in 'Repat' hospitals and mental institutions. As ex-servicemen aged and their health deteriorated, the demands on family members increased and thousands were left to mourn the premature deaths of men who finally succumbed to their injuries. For these families, the trauma of war did not end in 1918 – instead the aftermath began.

FAMILY HISTORIES

Thousands of Australians have a 'shattered Anzac' in their family history. A generation grew up after the First World War with fathers, grandfathers and uncles who returned from Gallipoli, the Western Front and the Middle East with irreparably damaged bodies and deep psychological scars. Family members of disabled soldiers became intimate witnesses to the devastating impact of war on the human mind and body. Even today descendants have vivid memories of the toll of war upon their families. In 2007, Bernard Long recalled his childhood with a physically impaired father:

> Dad was in World War I serving three years on the Western Front. Every day of our lives we lived with that reality as he faced war's impact: washing out the great gouge in his leg from shrapnel, the dent in his chest, and always the non-being of his right arm, shattered and amputated – another piece of shrapnel. Phantom pains would sometimes wrack him for hours. He never whinged. He got on with living. His pre-war life as an orchardist had been destroyed ... Occasionally, as he sat on the border of his magnificent garden musing on the mysteries of his chooks, you would see a flicker of sadness. But that was all.[4]

For families like the Longs, the effects of war disability shaped daily life and kin relationships in deeply-felt and ongoing ways. Yet the experiences of these families have largely remained unheard outside their own kinship networks. Such stories are typically shared *within* families: they are rarely the concern of historians. By contrast, this book lays bare the struggles and negotiations of ordinary Australian families whose lives were forever transformed by the return from war of disabled men. It argues that these families' experiences need to be acknowledged and integrated into our historical understandings of the First World War and its aftermath, for although disabled soldiers sustained and bore the wounds of war, their family members too shouldered considerable burdens as a consequence of their loved one's disablement. By using the family as a lens through which to understand disablement, this book bears witness to the interconnectedness of the lives of soldiers and their kin, and broadens our understanding of the social groups wounded by war. It calls us to reconsider the Great War as a conflict with deeply personal legacies for both combatants and civilians, which touched the lives of successive generations of Australian families after 1918, well into the twentieth century and beyond.

THE COST OF DISABILITY

By the end of the First World War, every second Australian family was bereaved by the death of a soldier killed overseas.[5] Yet the number of Australian families left to support a 'disabled digger' was significantly greater than those who mourned the 'fallen'. By Armistice Day in 1918, disabled soldiers overwhelmingly outnumbered the war dead. Of the 324 000 soldiers who took to the field, 60 000 were killed and about 150 000 were wounded.[6] Medical advances in the early twentieth century, such as the development of antiseptics and new surgical techniques, meant that the death rate among the wounded was low in comparison to previous wars. Better survival rates, however, resulted in a proportionally higher number of disabled soldiers. By 1920, about 90 000 Australian ex-servicemen were receiving war disability pensions, and during the following two decades the total number of pensioners fluctuated between 25 per cent and 33 per cent of the returned soldier population.⁷ At the outbreak of the Second World War, over 77 000 veterans of the First AIF (Australian Imperial Force) were still living with a war disability. Three were dying each day from their wounds.⁸

Soldiers of the Great War sustained a staggering range of disabilities inflicted by the new techniques of modern warfare. Machine guns, heavy artillery shells and explosive bullets literally shattered men's bodies. Although the limbless soldier became an iconic wartime image, fewer than 3300 of Australia's disabled soldiers returned without a limb.⁹ In reality, most injuries did not involve missing body parts, but took the form of invisible internal damage to organs, bones, muscles, and other bodily systems. Soldiers also experienced respiratory problems due to poisonous gas, and conditions such as shell shock and tuberculosis arising from the traumatic and squalid conditions in the trenches. Despite the enormous range of war disabilities, and the high prevalence of men with multiple wounds, accurate medical statistics are unavailable. In its official data, the Repatriation Department counted each veteran according to his 'primary' impairment and failed to keep a tally of their 'secondary' ailments.¹⁰ It is to the everyday lives of ex-servicemen, rather than the statistics, that we must look for the impact of war disability in all its diversity.

Within families, the term 'disability' was rarely used during or after the war. Ex-servicemen and their kin tended to use more colloquial descriptors: 'he's got lung troubles', 'he's changed', 'he gets nervy', 'he's having a mental turn', 'his knee's gone bad', 'it's the shrapnel in his chest'. Such explanations spoke of the fluctuating reality of men's conditions without inevitably pathologising them, and also pointed to the local impact upon their kin. By contrast, the guiding legislation of the Repatriation Department, the *Australian Soldiers' Repatriation Act*, was organised around two highly medicalised administrative categories, 'incapacity' and 'disability', which subsequently become key concepts in the modern welfare state's management of disabled people.¹¹ Repatriation officials measured ex-servicemen's damaged bodies against the fixed and enforceable boundaries of these classifications, without reference to any social or familial context. Conditions not clearly attributable to war, such as alcoholism, and those explicitly excluded from the Act, such as self-inflicted wounds and venereal disease, were not always officially deemed to be 'war disabilities'.[12] Within this book, I use the term 'disability' inclusively to denote any physical, mental or psychological impairment sustained or aggravated during a serviceman's period of enlistment, whether or not it was officially recognised. Given that impairment constitutes merely one dimension of disability, however, I also use the concept to signify veterans' social disablement as a result of external factors, such as employer discrimination.[13] By adopting an integrated model that recognises both the physical and social dimensions of disability, we can productively shift our historical gaze between disabled soldiers and the cultural worlds in which they lived, to understand better how servicemen and their families experienced, embodied and negotiated disablement and its consequences.

War disability touched the lives of families in very different ways. In some instances its impact was massive and traumatic, while in other cases disablement more subtly affected the rhythms of daily life. Families' experiences varied according to the nature and extent of their soldiers' disabilities, as well as structural factors such as class, wealth, rate of pension, place of residence and family size. Yet, most disabled servicemen did have one thing in common – the family was the cornerstone of their lives. I use the term 'family' to refer to the people with whom soldiers had, or could be expected to have interdependent relationships, by virtue of their connections through blood, marriage, domestic circumstances or affection.[14] In the early twentieth century, there were strong social conventions around marriage as well as a cultural expectation that family members commit to the long-term wellbeing of their household and maintain invalid relatives. In times of sickness, crisis or unemployment, families became a vital source of welfare because state welfare provision was much less comprehensive than it is today. Family relationships were also the emotional foundation of many people's lives. After soldiers had been wounded, the strength of their familial bonds often became more pronounced. In 1915, Alfred Derham wrote fondly to his family from hospital, 'I think of you all very far away and the circle of people that matter narrows down very small. One meets almost nobody who can even come a little way into that niche in ones affections however strong the ties of comradeship'.[15]

Upon their return from war, the family became a key site of repatriation for disabled soldiers. Although the Repatriation Department was officially responsible for the pensioning, medical treatment and rehabilitation of veterans, in reality much of the practical and emotional burden of care fell to kin, particularly wives and mothers, within the domestic sphere. In homes across Australia, ex-servicemen became dependent upon the unpaid economic and emotional labour of family members. In 1940 Mrs Violet Aiken reflected on life with her husband Harry. 'My husband [was] a long sufferer from his war injuries … & was nursed … day and night in our own little home here by myself.'[16] While disabled soldiers like Harry Aiken could depend on the support of their families, other men were not as fortunate. Disability caused some families to pull together, but a number was simply unable to cope with their 'changed' man. In some instances, marital relationships broke down and families separated under the strain of living with a chronic invalid or 'mental digger'. Some families stayed together with the support of charitable agencies which supplemented the assistance of the Repat: others ultimately relinquished their relative to institutional care. War disability tested the resourcefulness and resilience of families, and proved the undoing of some households.

DISABLED SOLDIERS AND THE ANZAC LEGEND

The impact of war disability reverberated through disabled soldiers' families, leaving no one unaffected. Yet these family stories are largely absent from Australia's dominant collective memory of the Great War

– the Anzac legend. To most Australians, the national memory of war revolves around the birth of the nation at Gallipoli, the 'supreme sacrifice' of the 60 000 war dead and the commemoration of their sacred memory. Indeed, the image at the heart of the Anzac legend is not a disabled soldier, but a youthful, able-bodied man with a magnificent physique, before he had been wounded or made immortal through a courageous death.[17] Similarly, families have traditionally not featured in public commemorative narratives of war. Even today, Anzac Day services typically emphasise the importance of mateship over family relationships. Official speakers make little mention of the dependence of disabled ex-servicemen on their kin, the domestic sacrifices of wives and mothers, or the personal cost of living with a war-damaged man. The Australian War Memorial also tends to overlook families' experiences as it displays the nation's histories of war, despite its brief to commemorate Australians' service and sacrifice arising from past conflicts. Although, in recent years, there has been greater recognition of the 'family fallout' of physical war disability and post-traumatic stress disorder (PTSD), these stories remain at the periphery of public memory.

In the shadow of conflicts in Vietnam, Iraq and Afghanistan, public awareness of the personal cost of war for veterans and their kin has been increasing. Yet historians have been slow to ask questions about the family lives of 'broken' soldiers of the First World War. In Australia, some scholars have certainly acknowledged the familial impact of disablement, but few have provided any sustained analysis.[18] Rather, most have adopted a soldier-centred approach examining disabled soldiers' rehabilitation and pensioning, exploring their political identities and critiquing their treatment by the Repatriation Department.[19] Overseas studies similarly display more interest in veterans' relationships with the state than with their own families, and a recent spate of theoretical work which interrogates cultural representations of 'the body' has served to turn historians' attention further away from damaged soldiers' experiences and relationships within the family sphere.[20] Historians have tended to overlook the role of families in the lives of disabled soldiers in order to tell 'national' stories about veterans' political identities as citizens within the modern body politic.

The history of war disability, however, is not self-evidently a national story: there is also a family story to be told. Soldiers' repatriation was a profoundly human experience. It was a complex, shared and daily process involving not only the servicemen who returned, but also the kin to whom they returned. Soldiers were not lone historical agents, but men whose lives were entwined with those of their kin. Placing the family at the centre of historical analysis opens up new possibilities for writing histories of 1914–18 and its aftermath. A family model demands that we come to terms with the profound impact of that conflict on soldiers and civilians, as well as its deep, lasting – and sometimes scarring – effects upon the households and communities to which they belonged. It is only by admitting to the devastating effects of war on the private lives of Australian families that the true cost of war for the nation can ever truly be understood.

INVISIBLE FAMILIES

Yet writing about disabled soldiers' family lives is no easy task. As historian Jay Winter notes, although we know that it was often family members who shouldered the burden of caring for disabled soldiers virtually all of this work went unrecorded.[21] In Australia, the Repatriation Department archive richly documents soldiers' medical treatment and rehabilitation, yet it does not record the private caregiving work of their families. This is because the Australian repatriation system was based on a formal administrative relationship between the government and the individual soldier, not his family unit.[22] Apart from paying families a fortnightly pension, the Department was not responsible for the welfare of families, nor was it obliged to 'care for the carers'. Indeed, in 1919 one government report even dismissed the need for family support, declaring that 'there is no reason why a disabled man need not be a useful and self-supporting citizen instead of a possible burden to himself, his relations, and the community at large'.[23] The Department conceptualised war disability as an individual problem for the soldier breadwinner to overcome, rather than as an issue which affected the wellbeing of his entire family. Despite the vital role of kin, repatriation officials commented infrequently on the lives of those who were classified as veterans' 'dependants'.

This reluctance to acknowledge families' experiences of war disability is also evident in public domain sources, such as newspapers. Under wartime censorship regulations, stories about the private sufferings of returned soldier 'cripples' were not welcome because they potentially damaged recruitment campaigns. We rarely read extended commentary about relatives' shock and grief upon meeting their 'shattered' loved one. Such discussions necessarily raised anxieties about veterans' loss of independence, which was central to the male breadwinner ideal and image of self-reliant military manhood. Moreover, to acknowledge families' domestic burdens and sacrifices threatened to usurp the primacy of soldiers' battlefield sacrifices within Australia's collective memory of war. Accordingly, a heroic narrative emerged within public commentary, which foregrounded the successes of the nation's 'brave disabled warriors' in rehabilitation and employment, rather than their reintegration into their own households. Paradoxically then, at the same time that thousands of families negotiated their new lives with their 'changed' men, the dominant image of the disabled soldier was a valiant and cheerful individual on a journey towards 'manly independence' depicted in the absence of family relationships.[24]

This popular image of the 'familyless' disabled soldier, together with the individualistic focus of the Repatriation Department, serve to cloak the reality of the lives of veterans and their kin. To gain a glimpse into the domestic realm, we must read 'against the grain' soldiers' medical files, official literature and public commentary for traces of their 'dependants' as whole people. The fragmentary nature of archival evidence does not mean that the role of kin in the lives of disabled soldiers was not significant. Rather, it is a powerful testament to the lack of official and public recognition they received for their sacrifices. By focusing on families' experiences, *Shattered Anzacs* has much in common with recent studies of death during the First World War.[25] This rich literature casts soldiers' family members as the key protagonists and considers the impact of grief and loss upon the bonds of kinship. It encourages us to consider the histories of families who gave of themselves not only as a consequence of death, but also disablement. Disabled soldiers' family members did not experience the devastating finality of death. Yet, like bereaved families, they did experience forms of loss and grief which they never could have imagined before their loved one went to war. In the Australian context, those who mourned the dead did so in the absence of a body: kin of the disabled lived in the presence of a 'broken' body.

ORAL HISTORIES

Today, the elderly children of First World War disabled soldiers are the only living link to the experiences of these families. Between 2004 and 2006, I spoke with eleven children of Great War veterans who lived with the daily impact of their father's war disability on their lives. These interviews sit at the heart of this book. They attest to the shared family nature of war disability and reveal private emotional experiences that are simply not evident in written sources. Although these men and women could not speak on behalf of their parents, their 'child's eye' perspective remains valuable. Indeed, many of them observed that their fathers often remained silent about their war experiences. Yet they were willing to open up and talk candidly to me about the effects of war disability on family life. Some spoke proudly of their fathers' war wounds, drawing upon the Anzac legend to affirm the purpose of his war service. Others fashioned their memories in relation to ideals about family loyalty and personal stoicism, as well as political discourses about the injustices meted out by the 'Repat' and the failure of the Soldier Settlement Scheme. Some shared anti-war and pacifist beliefs developed in response to their fathers' experiences.

In the stories of these informants, we can also hear a desire to make sense of the impact of war disability upon their childhood, as well as adult lives. Some blended their accounts of the 1920s and 1930s with stories of their husbands or other relatives who had been disabled during the Second World War. Others looked back to the 1960s when their own sons faced conscription during the Vietnam War and the possibility of death or disablement. As we spoke, it was clear that these men and women, aged in their seventies and eighties, were engaged in a 'life review' process. Through the selection, omission, ordering, highlighting and repressing of certain events, they constructed memories that offered them a sense of identity and subjective 'composure' in the present.[26] The significance of a disabled father in their childhoods was mediated by the changing meanings that war disability had held for them throughout the subsequent decades. In telling their multi-layered stories, however, they insisted that their fathers' pain had also been a family burden, and one that continued to resonate across generations.

LIFESPAN HISTORY

These oral histories also alert us to the changing nature of families' experiences of war disability. The condition of veterans' impairments fluctuated, and carried different meanings for men and their kin as they aged and as their roles within the family changed over time. Because of this, *Shattered Anzacs* is structured around a 'life span' approach to the history of war disability.[27] It measures the passing of both chronological time and 'corporeal' time. While the Repatriation Department measured time in a bureaucratic manner, according to the fortnightly distribution of pensions and monthly medical assessments, families' sense of time related more organically to the improvement or worsening of veterans' conditions, as well as the changing structures and resources of households as the years passed. Accordingly, each chapter explores an aspect of families' experiences as soldiers and their kin aged and the social and economic worlds in which they lived underwent transformation.

Chapter 1 contends that families' burdens began well before soldiers were disabled and returned to Australia. It examines the anxiety of kin at the prospect of their loved one's disablement, and analyses how they negotiated their concerns through their correspondence after he had been wounded. Chapter 2 examines how families responded to their 'changed man' upon his return to Australia. It explores the challenges faced by households during the initial stages of soldiers' reintegration into civilian life. Chapter 3 demonstrates that many families of disabled soldiers faced significant financial burdens as incapacitated breadwinners struggled to earn an adequate 'family wage' through pension or employment income. Chapter 4 investigates the emotional impact of war disability upon soldiers' family relationships. It examines the practical and emotional labours of kin, such as home-based caregiving, and reveals the personal demands of war disability on family members. Importantly, these two chapters reveal the official neglect of family units by the Repatriation Department, which focused on the provision of benefits to individual veterans rather than attending to the collective welfare of their households.

Chapters 5 and 6 explore the familial dimensions of two of the most prevalent war disabilities – shell shock and tuberculosis. Chapter 5 examines the experiences of families who were unable to care for 'mental diggers' within the home and sought institutional treatment for them, and chapter 6 considers how tubercular veterans and their kin battled against infection within the home. Chapter 7 examines the effects of the 1930s Depression on the family lives of 'burnt out' soldiers, many of whom were suffering increasing health problems. Finally, chapter 8 investigates how kin responded to the postwar deaths of returned men who died from their disabilities years after discharge. It suggests that their experiences of loss and grief were disenfranchised within Australia's national commemorative traditions which honoured soldiers who had made the 'supreme sacrifice' on the battlefield, to a greater extent than those who died at home after the war. This lack of recognition was one of the final burdens carried by disabled soldiers' family members.

War disability had a ripple effect within families that extended beyond the soldier. In 1936, Mrs Emma Vawser reflected on almost twenty years of caring for her son who had sustained serious injuries on the Western Front, and lamented the day when his wounds finally took their toll: 'My son, Percy Vawser enlisted in South Australia on July 1st 1915 & returned after the Armistice ... [he] was twice wounded also he was three times in hospital suffering from ear trouble and shock ... his war experiences brought on a slow trouble & after years of weakness he was called Home on May 23 1935'.[28] Soldiers, like Percy Vawser, were not isolated individuals when they journeyed to war, nor when they were invalided home or died in repatriation hospitals on Australian soil. They were members of families whose experiences and interests were fundamentally connected to those of their kin. War disability had a transformative impact on combatants as well as their civilian kin, who were often deeply affected by the demands made upon them. *Shattered Anzacs* offers a window onto the interdependent lives of disabled soldiers and their families, and calls us to acknowledge their neglected role in official accounts of 'healing the nation' after the First World War. It is a history of disablement as well as an exploration of the power of relationships to shape experience. By bearing witness to the experiences of damaged ex-servicemen and their kin, it restores the family story of war disability to Australia's history of the Great War.

CHAPTER 1

war wounds as family wounds

> I am all the time picturing you in the Hospital
> with all sorts of wounds for I know you have not
> told me everything I must know.
>
> Rose Keast to her son Jim Keast, August 1916.[1]

In October 1917, William Tooney wrote to his daughter, Edna, from an Australian military hospital in Dartford, England after being seriously wounded in the leg at Ypres. 'Daddy was wounded for the second time' he explained, 'but do not worry my dear girl, as I am doing splendid, & may be coming home to Australia in a few weeks'.[2] In subsequent letters from Blighty, William was optimistic about his recovery and shared his relief with his family at having survived the ordeal of wounding. He described the shelling of his unit and how he hobbled along the trenches past large numbers of dead, finally reaching the safety of a field hospital. For William, being wounded rather than killed was a form of deliverance, as he reminded his family from his hospital bed, 'I am still in the land of the living'.[3] William had escaped death, yet he knew that his injuries could lead to permanent disablement. But it took him five months to raise the possibility of long-term physical impairment with his family. In February 1918, he finally disclosed his fears, lamenting that the doctors 'cannot do any more for me', and announced his concerns that he would be 'a cripple for life'.[4]

During the First World War, wounded Australian soldiers like William Tooney were faced with the daunting task of writing to their families to describe their injuries and impairments. Aware of their relatives' likely distress, they often downplayed the severity of their wounds, and reassured kin that they were in the best of health despite their ordeal. Some never revealed the extent of their disabilities until their return home. For those at home, news of a loved one's injuries came as a shock when the official telegram arrived. The wounding of a husband, son or brother serving overseas was a traumatic experience for homefront families. 'It is an awful anxious time for me knowing you are so ill' wrote Ethel Goddard to her husband in October 1916.[5] Family members were often frustrated at not being able to offer personal comfort to their loved one, and experienced considerable anxiety about the physical and mental damage he had sustained. The letters between wounded soldiers and their kin offer an insight into how families managed the emotionally charged task of discussing injury and disablement in each other's absence. Importantly, this archive of correspondence reveals that the burdens of sacrifice carried by the families of disabled soldiers began long before they were reunited.

Most histories of war disability commence with disabled soldiers' homecoming. This one, however, begins well before incapacitated servicemen were invalided back to Australia. From the moment they departed for war, Australian soldiers began a parallel journey with their families as they both imagined, anticipated and reacted to war injury and impairment. In very different ways, wounding had direct consequences for soldiers overseas at war, as well as for those from whom they were separated. On the battlefront, soldiers made enormous personal sacrifices as they risked their lives and suffered painful and traumatic wounds away from their kin. On the Australian homefront, families made sacrifices of a different order. They read the casualty lists with dread, bore the shock of telegrams and waited for letters from their wounded loved one, hoping for news of his recovery. Their fears were compounded by the vast distance between them. 'How awfully anxious you must be – it is all so far away!' wrote Ethel Clarke in 1915, as she comforted a friend whose son had been wounded.[6] Although those at home were not directly harmed by enemy fire, their bond with their soldier meant that his injuries had significant emotional consequences for them – his war wounds became family wounds.

THE PROSPECT OF DISABLEMENT

After the outbreak of war in August 1914, many young Australian men were stirred by feelings of patriotic duty, and discussed with their families their desire to enlist in the AIF. While some men joined up without consulting their kin, the decision-making process was often family-based, and the prospect of disablement figured heavily in such discussions. At stake was the interconnected economic and emotional future of households, should a man return 'damaged'. Mothers and fathers were key protagonists in these deliberations as over 80 per cent of the AIF was unmarried and 52 per cent was aged between eighteen and twenty-four.[7] Moreover, about 15 per cent needed a letter of permission from their parents to enlist because they were under the age of twenty-one. This requirement saw heated exchanges between sons eager to 'do their bit' and parents concerned about war disability. Some parents forbade their sons to go to war, while others reluctantly gave permission and hoped for the best.[8] In some instances, families encouraged their sons not to enlist because of existing health problems. Gordon Mackay was over twenty-one when the war broke out, but his family begged him not to enlist because he had a weak heart as a result of childhood rheumatic fever. After receiving white feathers in the letterbox, however, Gordon joined up in May 1916. The family was horrified, and his brother wrote a letter informing the army of his vulnerable health, but he was officially declared 'fit' and sent to the Western Front.[9] While such direct family intervention in the enlistment process was not common, the Mackay family's interventions demonstrate the degree of anxiety some families felt about how the long-term health of their relatives would be affected by war service.

Young men's motivations to enlist, or not, were complex, and the possibility of disablement was one of numerous factors they considered. During the war, 40 per cent of Australian males between the ages of eighteen and forty joined up, yet many more chose not to serve, including 50 per cent of all single eligible men.[10] Men enlisted for a variety of motives, both noble and pragmatic, including a sense of patriotic duty, the desire for adventure, and the wish to escape unemployment or domestic troubles. Some were carried along by a tide of popular excitement about the war and gave little thought to becoming a casualty themselves. As one soldier recalled, 'We realised of course that we might be killed or wounded but never thought much about this'.[11] Others were moved by a sense of duty to their countrymen at the front, including the wounded. These emotions were exploited by official recruiting posters which depicted injured Anzacs swathed in bloodied bandages calling from the trenches for reinforcements with a look of urgency in their eyes – 'is it not "up to me" to take his place and avenge his injury?'[12] Disabled soldiers not only featured on posters, but became spruikers on the recruiting platform, drawing attention to the cowardice of the stay-at-homes. At one Melbourne rally in May 1916, Sergeant Ball made a 'pathetic appeal to send more recruits "to the boys out there"' and girls rushed forward to shake the hand of the 'still cheerful hero'.[13] Yet there was an uneasy response from the men in the crowd, who were perhaps more disturbed than motivated by Sergeant Ball's blindness and 'shattered' arm.

Stylised images of wounded soldiers often featured on recruiting posters to motivate civilian men to enlist. Norman Lindsay, WE Smith Ltd, *The Last Call*, photolithograph on paper, 50.4 × 34.2, c. 1914–18, Australian War Memorial, ARTV00043.

Men who remained at home cited a fear of death and disablement as well as a complex array of personal and situational reasons, including family responsibilities, pacifism, and business commitments. When asked in 1916 about his intentions to enlist, Charles Bazeley of Kensington in Melbourne made his position clear:

> I have been three years preparing for my marriage and can't see my way to keep up the mortgage payment on my house ... especially if returned and discharged maimed in a few months without any provision being made, as is happening to so many.[14]

Other young men were advised not to enlist by relatives who had witnessed the horrors of war first hand at the front. 'Don't let Alby or Tom join' wrote Henry Palmer to his parents after being wounded in August 1916.[15] While some families proudly sent all their sons to war, a number negotiated a compromise and agreed to send all but one, to minimise the impact on the family if he was killed or maimed. Families' decisions reflected a desire to reduce the emotional cost of death and disability as well as the potential economic consequences.

Given the centrality of the male wage to the survival of households in early twentieth-century Australia, the financial implications of enlistment were a crucial consideration. Families had to decide whether they could survive on army allowances during the war, and needed to consider the long-term economic consequences should relatives be killed or maimed. Married soldiers with large families, or those supporting parents, risked leaving their dependants without a breadwinner, while single disabled men were in danger of losing their future employment and marriage prospects. Men and their sweethearts, as yet unmarried, were faced with the choice of a hasty 'war marriage' or delaying the union because of the risk that 'he may return crippled'.[16] The government was aware that prospective recruits might be discouraged by the possibility of injury, and it advised official recruiters to 'use all your powers of persuasion' to convince men of benefits, such as pensions, that were available to disabled men after their return.[17]

Recruiting pamphlets formed the basis of collective decision making in many households, and allowed families to evaluate the government's promises in the light of their concerns. Leaflets advertised the rate of the war disability pension, but the extent to which this reassured households depended on each family's particular circumstances.[18] In 1914, the average male wage was £2/15/1, although some skilled workers earned up to £4, or more in the professions. On overseas service, an AIF private with a wife and one child was paid about £2/12/9½ per week, which included allowances paid to his dependants.[19] This was financially appealing to men on below-average incomes, but it did mean a drop in income for higher wage earners. The government promised a war disability pension of £2/15/0 per week for a totally incapacitated man, his wife and child, which was reduced on a sliding scale for men with partial disabilities.[20] Given the apparent similarity of army pay and the war disability pension, and promises that the war-disabled would be provided with vocational training and employment assistance, new recruits may have felt reasonably certain that if they returned disabled, at least their family's financial future would be no worse than during their service at the front. Moreover, men were not only enticed to enlist by official repatriation schemes, but comforted by a more general belief that disabled soldiers would be honoured and 'taken care of' within civilian society.

The embarkation of soldiers from Australian shores was a moment of great emotional significance for families. Harold Hinckfuss recalled that at a church service the Sunday before he left, his mother claimed to have seen a light over his head as he was being blessed, and took it as sign that he 'would be all right'.[21] At ports and railway stations across Australia, soldiers' departures were occasions for the public celebration of Australia's commitment to the war, and bands played

PENSIONS GRANTED
BY THE
COMMONWEALTH GOVERNMENT.

The following Pensions are payable to a member of the A.I.F. on ground of total incapacity:—

	£	s.	d.	
Private	3	0	0	per fortnight
Driver	3	2	0	,,
Bombadier	3	6	0	,,
Corporal	3	8	0	,,
Sergeant	3	9	0	,,
Q.M.-Sergeant	3	11	0	,,
Sergeant-Cook	3	12	0	,,
C.S.-Major	3	14	0	,,
Lieutenant	4	0	0	,,

The wife of an incapacitated member is entitled to a Pension at HALF the rate granted him.

In the case of the death of a member of the Forces, the following rates of Pension are payable to the widow:—

	£	s.	d.	
Private	2	0	0	per fortnight
Driver	2	3	0	,,
Bombadier	2	9	0	,,
Corporal	2	12	3	,,
Sergeant	2	13	9	,,
Q.M.-Sergeant	2	16	0	,,
Sergeant-Cook	2	17	3	,,
C.S.-Major	2	19	6	,,
Lieutenant	3	10	0	,,

The children of deceased members receive Pensions as under:—

	s.	d.	
For the first child	20	0	a fortnight
For the second child	15	0	,,
For each subsequent child	10	0	,,

Orphans.—Where both the member of the Forces and his wife are dead, every one of their children is entitled to Pension at the undermentioned rates:—

	s.	d.	
Up to 10 years of age	20	0	a fortnight
From 10 to 14 years of age	25	0	,,
From 14 to 16 years of age	30	0	,,

The children of totally incapacitated members are entitled to the same rates of Pension as the children of deceased members.

Pensions are also payable to other dependents if wholly or partially dependent upon the member of the Forces during the twelve months prior to his enlistment.

HOW TO JOIN THIS TOUR.

To participate in this unique offer, you must be between the ages of 18 and 45, have a minimum height of 5 feet 2 inches, and be able to expand your chest to 33 inches.

If you can meet these requirements fill in the application form hereunder, and post it to the Organising Secretary, State Recruiting Office, Sydney.

I hereby offer myself for enlistment in the Australian Imperial Force for active service abroad, and undertake to enlist in the manner prescribed, if I am accepted by the military authorities.

Age............ Height............. Weight............

Occupation..

Signature ....

Postal Address ....

....

....

Date..

William Brooks & Co., Ltd., Printers, Sydney.

This leaflet, 'Free tour to Great Britain and Europe', provided potential recruits with details of death and disability pensions to reassure them about joining the AIF. State Recruiting Committee, NSW, c. 1914–18, Australian War Memorial negative number RC02289.

rousing tunes such as 'Australia Will Be There'. These farewells were also a time of great sadness for families because of their impending separation from loved ones, and the knowledge that they may never see their soldier again. As troopships prepared to depart, wharves were crowded with thousands of relatives and friends in various emotional states 'some hysterical, some laughing, some crying, shouting, singing and calling "Good Luck"'.[22] Soldiers and their families often communicated with each other between ship and shore in the remaining time they had together. For many, the paper streamers thrown between soldiers and their families constituted their last moments of connection. As the troopships drew away from port, the ribbons tightened and snapped, severing soldiers' physical union with their families. These streamers became symbols of the ties that bound them together, and many kept the broken remnants as a souvenir of their last contact with their kin. Some families would return to these ports only months later to welcome home loved ones who had been physically or mentally disabled.

HOMEFRONT ANXIETY

After farewelling their soldiers, the possibility of disablement weighed heavily on the minds of family members, along with the dreadful prospect of death. Ruth Derham started dreaming about her brother, Alfred, shortly after his departure: 'I dream about you every night & always just before I wake up & it is beastly'.[23] Although the battlefront and the homefront were two distinct worlds, soldiers and their families still 'inhabited the same world of war', connected by the emotional bonds of kinship rather than each other's physical presence.[24] The inexorable distance between them only exacerbated their concerns for one another. On the homefront, some mothers developed 'war strain' because they lived with the 'ever-present anxiety about the future and what sad news may come any day to their doors'.[25] In 1916, Rose Keast described the worry of one friend who 'like all the rest of us mothers I suppose [is] imagining all sorts of dreadful things happening to our dear boys'.[26] Families often had little accurate information about their soldier's whereabouts which only increased their sense of powerlessness. In desperation, some women turned to fortune tellers, who, for a fee, used their supernatural powers to determine whether the absent soldier was wounded, ill or dead.[27] By remaining active in their relationships with their soldiers, even through practices of dubious efficacy, kin attempted to reduce the disempowering effects of fear. In 1917, one enterprising manufacturer capitalised on relatives' sense of helplessness by selling steel vests that could be posted to the front. The makers of the 'Armor-Vest' claimed that the body-covering deflected bullets and bayonet thrusts, and asked worried families 'are you going to protect your soldier boy?'[28]

Newspaper casualty lists became a daily reminder to families of the dangers their loved one faced. The first lists were published on 2 May 1915 after the landing at Gallipoli, and from that point on, reading them became a ritual for families, who scanned them with feelings of hope and fear. As the number of dead and wounded rose in mid-1915, the casualty lists became longer and newspaper circulation numbers increased.[29] Although journalists advised relatives to 'refuse to entertain thoughts that may depress them', these catalogues of loss resonated with the grief of each man's family, and brought the reality of death and injury into homefront households.[30] As the casualties steadily mounted, Isabella Walker wrote, 'How harrowing it is to read daily of the heavy list of casualties, it makes our hearts ache for the many parents whose houses are desolated by this cruel war'.[31] Those who read the casualty lists not only looked for their own soldier's name, but the names of soldiers in their extended family and friendship networks.

If the casualty lists were a source of anxiety, the optimistic feature articles that accompanied them may have provided some hope to families who feared the wounding of their sons. During the war, newspapers were replete with stories of 'plucky' soldiers cheerfully overcoming their injuries through their courageous determination and superior medical treatment. Despite 'frightful wounds' men nonchalantly puffed on cigarettes 'between the twinges of pain', one-eyed soldiers stumbled valiantly through the trenches to deliver vital messages, and those paralysed in the spine were 'able to run'.[32] These insistently positive articles were a product of wartime censorship which banned the publication of 'gruesome details' about the wounded on the grounds that it would undermine the war effort and disturb relatives.[33] In the mainstream press, wounded soldiers came to symbolise vigour and vitality rather than invalidism: advertisers of commercial health products even used testimonies from such men to promote their remedies. The extraordinary resilience of wounded Australians, notes historian Peter Cochrane, became a legend within the Anzac legend.[34] Homefront newspapers presented soldiers' families with a contradictory mix of reportage. The casualty lists reminded them of the possibility of disablement, yet patriotic commentary insisted that wounded soldiers were ennobled, rather than crippled, by their injuries.

THEATRES OF WOUNDING

On the battlefields of Europe, soldiers lived each day with the terrifying possibility of wounding and disablement. From April 1915, Australian soldiers experienced the horrors of modern warfare for the first time, with unprecedented casualties. 'I can tell you it was by no means pleasant to see the boys getting blown up and cut to pieces' wrote William Peach from the Dardanelles.[35] In the first two weeks of the Gallipoli campaign, more Australians were killed than during the nation's entire involvement in the Boer War. By the December 1915 evacuation, 19 441 men had been wounded and 63 969 had succumbed to illness.[36] The AIF then shifted the bulk of its troops to the Western Front where soldiers endured appalling conditions in the trenches and were subjected to heavy shelling, grenades and machine gun fire which often resulted in multiple traumatic injuries. In 1917, one Australian nurse despaired that 'the boys are so frighteningly mutilated it would not be possible for one person to dress them'.[37] The wounded quickly developed infections due to micro-organisms in the fertile manured soil, and gassed men died an excruciating death, or survived with agonising burns to their eyes and lungs. On the Western Front, 136 727 Australians were wounded – more than six times the number wounded during the Gallipoli campaign – and 213 053 fell victim to illness.[38]

One of the defining features of modern trench warfare was the enormous psychological toll it exacted from combatants. 'Our nerves are quivering with the shock of shells' wrote Ray Jones to his parents from the Western Front in 1916.[39] Some men experienced psychological trauma as the result of a shell bursting in close proximity or being buried by a bombardment. In 1917, William Clayton wrote to his sisters describing men 'lifted into the air' by shells, who emerged from their ordeal with the 'greatest difficulty in speaking'.[40] In the trenches, the random destructive power of heavy artillery engendered feelings of powerlessness which could precipitate men's descent into mental distress. Desperate for relief from the frontlines, some soldiers inflicted wounds on themselves. On the Western Front, 701 Australian soldiers damaged on their own bodies, most shooting themselves in the hand or the foot.[41] Others feigned illness or shell shock as a means to get home, or at least to buy them some respite away from the trenches.

WRITING ABOUT WOUNDS

In their correspondence home, soldiers raised the possibility of war injury and disablement, but they typically took care to reassure their kin about the dangers they faced. 'I don't want any wounds, if I can keep as well as I am now' wrote Henry Palmer from Gallipoli.[42] At the front, soldiers tended to write cautiously about the carnage around them and convey their fears about death or injury in a restrained fashion. Their circumspection can be partly attributed to censorship regulations, under which they were prohibited from mentioning details of military significance, and forbidden to include information that might damage homefront morale. In addition to this, as historian Michael Roper has argued in the British context, the content of soldiers' correspondence was also influenced by the knowledge that it potentially transmitted anxiety into the family home.[43] There is evidence that Australian soldiers, too, self-censored their letters to shield their families from the unpleasant aspects of war. Some years after his discharge from the army, Lindsay Ross admitted that he deliberately composed his wartime letters to 'cheer-up' his parents, believing it was 'not advisable to write morbid letters' that caused worry.[44] Soldier correspondents typically understated the dangers of war as they negotiated a delicate balance between honestly sharing their experiences with kin, and potentially traumatising them.

Although there were limits to what could be said in a letter from the front, written correspondence was the primary means by which Australian soldiers and their families maintained their relationships. Letters were an 'instrument of emotional union' that sustained the dynamic affective bonds holding their families together.[45] Letter writing was an important activity for soldiers. The majority of men in the AIF were volunteers, not career soldiers, and writing home allowed them to reconnect with their civilian selves and provided them with a comforting link into their familial worlds. Soldiers most commonly addressed their letters to their mothers, who acted as the 'principal bridge' to their sons and shared their correspondence with other relatives.[46] Families cherished and regularly re-read correspondence from the front. Even heavily censored letters and generic field postcards were treasured. For, as historian Martyn Lyons notes, the significance of a soldier's correspondence lay not only in what was written, but the mere fact that it existed.[47]

Soldiers, too, eagerly waited for letters. Family correspondence reminded men of their homefront relationships and the hopeful future they could look forward to on their return. Soldiers bitterly resented delivery delays and missing letters. During the war, the postal system between Australia and Europe was strained by the escalating volume of mail. Letters took one month, if not longer, to reach the front, and sometimes men received their letters in large intermittent batches. Soldiers experienced the epistolary silence as a loss of intimacy and personal connection, as Corporal Mayne wrote to his wife and children in 1916, 'I am grieved at not receiving any letters from you'.[48] Letters from home shored up soldiers' emotional resolve to survive. They reminded men, however, that their kin also lived in fear of battlefield disablement. In October 1916, Ethel Goddard wrote to her husband plaintively, 'Charl, do take care of yourself for your little wife & childrens sake as we do want you to come home just as you went away'.[49]

Families first heard of their soldier's wounds not through a letter, but via an official telegram. The news of wounding, rather than death, meant that their loved one was still alive. Yet it could still come as a shock. Family, friends and neighbours rallied around distraught households which had received a telegram. In October 1916, a stream of visitors descended on Ethel Goddard's Melbourne home, all assuring her that they would pray for her seriously ill husband.[50] Similarly, the Derhams received numerous letters of sympathy after their son Alfred was wounded at Gallipoli. 'I trust you will all bear up in this time of grief and trial' wrote one friend.[51] The sympathy of relatives and acquaintances often reflected their own fears, as one of Mrs Derham's friends confided: 'I can realise so freely how very anxious your mother-heart must be over your wounded soldier-laddie'.[52] After receiving the telegram, families eagerly waited for a letter from their soldier that would confirm or contradict the official advice and tell them how he was coping. Until they received a letter from their wounded loved one, families lived in a kind of emotional no man's land in which the stark and unsatisfying words of the official telegram were the only link to their boy.

Wounded soldiers were acutely aware of the distress the official telegram brought into the home. Mindful of the postal delay, some men initially sent a cable to ease the worry of their families: 'Well – love – Alfred'.[53] During their recovery, many wrote to tell their families about their injuries in more detail. Each man had a different story to tell according to the nature of his wounds, where he was hospitalised and the expected length of treatment. Some soldiers wrote home within hours of being 'hit', while others put pen to paper several days, or even weeks afterwards. Men wrote from hospitals close to the battlefront, in Lemnos, Alexandria and France, as well as from the safety of Britain. Military hospitals offered soldiers a relatively peaceful environment, away from the danger of the trenches. Lightly wounded men often had only a short stay in hospital before being sent back to the front. For the seriously wounded, however, recovery was often a slow business involving weeks or months of treatment. For these men, letter writing often became an activity that punctuated the monotony of convalescence. 'I have lots of time on my hands nowadays' Jim Keast wrote to his sister from Blighty, 'so I can answer [your letters] straight away'.[54]

Although the distance between wounded Australians and their kin was a source of anguish for families, their separation has resulted in a particularly rich and sizeable correspondence archive. The literacy rate among Australian troops was high, and they depended exclusively on letters to communicate with their Antipodean kin while in hospital.[55] In contrast, although British, French and German soldiers were active frontline correspondents, they relied less on letters after being invalided to military hospitals within visiting distance of their families. The Australian archive, however, is somewhat unbalanced, because considerably fewer letters written by family members have survived. This is because homefront correspondence was easily lost in battle, or subsequently destroyed in the belief that the news it conveyed was not historically significant. The limited availability of relatives' letters makes the experiences of kin more difficult to uncover, and means that we must look to soldiers' letters for reflected accounts of the feelings and actions of their family members. We must also be aware that while many wounded soldier patients were active letter writers, others stopped or slowed their correspondence because they were physically incapable or emotionally unable to write about their losses. This archive, then, represents the endeavours of only a proportion of the wounded.

HOSPITAL LETTERS

In their first letters home, wounded soldiers typically played down the extent of their injuries and appealed to their families not to worry. Men anticipated their family's shock at receiving the official telegram. 'Now I'm in hospital I expect you will hear that I've been killed, missing or a thousand other things', wrote Les Chandler in August 1917.[56] Soldier patients were keenly aware that letters containing bad news had the capacity to ignite panic among those at home, and accordingly constructed narratives to manage the perceived distress of the recipients. In October 1918, Jim Lord declared to his family in shaky handwriting, 'Don't worry about me as I am all right. My wound is not serious although my right arm is well punctured & I won't be able to use it for a good while. I am in excellent health & cheerful'.[57] Men's first letters had a dual purpose: to impart factual information about their injuries in the light of the official telegram and to allay the distress of kin. Importantly, they marked the start of an epistolary relationship which saw wounded men construct letters with extraordinary care to protect and manage the emotional needs of relatives, as they negotiated their anxieties about disability and its associated losses, at a distance.

From the other side of the world, family members wrote to their loved ones with a deep sense of powerlessness. In October 1916, Mrs Ethel Goddard frantically composed a letter to her husband: 'I really do not know how to write to you. I feel so dreadfully worried & upset about your illness'.[58] Families' frustration was compounded by the lack of official news they received about their soldiers. Telegrams provided only a standardised rudimentary description of soldiers' wounds and incorrect telegrams were alarmingly common. As families waited for further news of their injured sons, their anxiety was compounded by reports of mistakenly dispatched cables and mixed-up surnames. For some, the wait for accurate and detailed information was agonising. 'It is awful for me not to know what really is the matter' wrote Ethel, who was not informed for several weeks that her husband had tuberculosis.[59] Worried family members commonly visited or wrote to the Base Records Office to make further enquiries, and some experienced a cruel shock after receiving conflicting advice.[60]

Not all battlefield wounds and diseases led to lasting disability, but disablement was the main axis around which the anxieties of soldiers and their families revolved. Indeed, some men feared mutilation more than death.[61] Understandably then, during treatment and convalescence, wounded soldiers continued to compose optimistic letters that cautiously imparted information about their recovery. 'You must expect an alteration in my face a bit', wrote Roland Edwards about his facial disfigurement in 1915, insisting that he was in good health 'except for this knock, so don't worry'.[62] Severely disabled soldiers typically expressed hope about their rehabilitation. In January 1917, Vincent Blevins reassured his mother about his future with an artificial arm: 'you would be surprised to see the way they fix you up with legs and arms here. I believe there is one soldier who lost both his legs and they dolled him up with two artificial ones, and now he is walking about London as large as life, with just one stick'.[63] If medical treatment could not restore bodily function, soldiers often used humour to demonstrate to their families that they were in good spirits and coping with their disabilities. Eric Beament informed his parents that the left hand was a 'most lucky place' to be wounded, humorously observing that he was 'now cooked for piano playing'.[64]

In some respects, soldiers' reassuring hospital correspondence is not dissimilar in quality to their battlefront letters. Both from the trenches and their hospital beds, men tended to minimise the trauma of war and downplay their own suffering. And yet the optimistic tone of wounded soldiers' letters is often less attributable to official censorship than their frontline correspondence. Letters from hospitals in Britain at least, appear to have been subject to almost no censorship. 'While in France I couldn't write in too much detail, but now here goes', wrote Jim Keast from a Sheffield hospital in August 1916.[65] Despite this, wounded soldiers' letters are characterised by enormous self-restraint. One practical factor that may have encouraged their continued circumspection was an awareness that postal delays affected their capacity to communicate information about their injuries in a timely manner. Men wrote from hospital knowing that their condition or prognosis may have changed by the time their letter reached its destination, and were cautious about providing unsettling information which family members would be unable to clarify. As a consequence, clear and optimistic statements of enduring emotional value became key components of their narratives.

Although the tone of wounded soldiers' letters was overwhelm-

A wounded Australian soldier, who has lost both hands, writes a letter using the stumps of his wrists, while convalescing at the No. 1 Australian Auxiliary Hospital, Harefield, England. Undated photograph, Australian War Memorial negative number H16947.

ingly hopeful, some men did disclose their fears about disablement to their kin. For soldiers who had been wounded multiple times, the task of maintaining an upbeat mood was particularly difficult in the face of being sent back to the frontline yet again.[66] Twice wounded, Ernest Poppins was mindful of not upsetting his family, but he did not always hold back from sharing his concerns. After being gassed and machine gunned in March 1918 he told his mother, 'of course you know that after that gas I will never be the same. I think my lungs are affected'.[67] Ernest's letters reveal an inner struggle about the extent to which he should share his own anxieties about his wounds. Throughout his letters, he moves between alternating periods of candour and circumspection, but is ultimately careful not to place too heavy a burden of worry upon his parents. Ernest's letters point to the dilemma of disclosure faced by all wounded Australians. How much should they reveal and conceal in their letters? One of the disadvantages of written correspondence was the lack of immediacy and openness usually associated with face-to-face interactions. Yet some men used this to their advantage, and consistently deployed silence or exaggeration as a strategy to shield their families from discomforting news.

EPISTOLARY SILENCES

The silences in wounded soldiers' letters, by their very nature, are difficult to identify and amplify. It is clear, however, that men's cheery descriptions sometimes appear to be concealing traumatic experiences. In a letter to his parents in January 1918, Ray Jones insisted that despite suffering nerves and deafness, he had 'never been better in my life'.[68] Men's insistence on their wellness is difficult to interpret, but one genre of hospital correspondence suggests why men constructed such hopeful narratives that pushed the boundaries of belief. Letters written by nurses on behalf of patients who were physically unable to write offer a powerful insight into soldiers' decisions about the inclusion and omission of content. These letters were usually composed collaboratively through a process of dictation, although nurses often took the lead and broke the news of injury to homefront kin in their own words. They sometimes reveal a discrepancy between men's experiences of wounding and disablement, and the way they wished it to be represented to their family members.

Such a disjunction is evident in William Worth's first letter home after wounding. In May 1915, Worth was shot in the neck at Gallipoli and became paralysed from the neck down. Unable to move his arms, William asked a nurse, Sister Narelle Hobbes, to write a letter to his mother in Wagga Wagga, making it 'as O.K. & bright & hopeful as you can'.[69] 'Don't tell her about my old limbs', William implored, insisting that she downplay the extent of his injuries. Although William had instructed her to understate his condition, the letter she penned was frank in its revelation that he had been 'rather badly wounded'. Like other nurses in her predicament, Hobbes perhaps believed that 'half-facts' were cruel, and would not prepare William's parents for his eventual return. She sensitively explained that William's right shoulder blade had been shattered, that he was suffering 'partial paralysis of the whole body', and that he was slightly deaf.[70] She informed Mrs Worth of her broken pact of secrecy with William, and warned her not to mention his paralysis in her return correspondence – 'be as cheery as you can', she advised.

The Worth/Hobbes letter reveals a clear difference between William's experience of disablement, and the account he wished to be conveyed to his family. His desire to suppress the truth undoubtedly reflected a myriad of concerns. He was conceivably only just dealing with his own distress and disbelief at his paralysis, and did not know how to inform his parents about his severe impairment. His letter may certainly have reflected his own hopes about his recovery, but it is more likely that he sought to hide his disability until he had come to terms with it. He conceivably felt shock and guilt that his decision to enlist had resulted in such far-reaching consequences for his family. His reticence may have related to deeper anxieties he held for his future as a husband, breadwinner, sexual partner, and father, as well as the knowledge that he may be financially dependent on his parents for the rest of his adult life. While not all men sustained impairments as severe as William's, his desire to remain silent about them reflected a more general unwillingness among men to share their physical and emotional vulnerabilities with their families.

We know little about how Mr and Mrs Worth reacted to Narelle Hobbes' forthright letter about William. There is evidence, however, that family members sometimes had mixed feelings upon receiving conspicuously cheerful letters from their soldier. Some were openly suspicious of the overtly positive tone. 'Although you say you are fine, I don't believe you. I know you too well for that', wrote Eric Evans' sweetheart, Dot.[71] In some instances, wounded soldiers' letters, rather than comforting family members, only served to heighten their anxieties. Rose Keast wrote to her son, 'I know you only tell me the bright side of things but you know it takes a mother to read between the lines'.[72] Kin of the wounded lived in fear of receiving a 'died of wounds' telegram. 'There are too many stories like that being told, and it's hard to listen to them', Dot anxiously wrote.[73] In an era before antibiotics were available, the threat of wound infection and opportunistic secondary illnesses meant that not all wounded soldiers survived. Over time, however, family members could be reassured by a series of letters testifying to the writer's health. In November 1916, after a month of regular letters from her husband, Charles, Ethel Goddard declared '[I have] a new life knowing you are getting strong'.[74] The various stages of emotional adaptation evident in hospital correspondence suggest that soldiers and their relatives began the process of adjusting to disability many weeks and months before they were reunited.

HEROIC NARRATIVES

Wounded soldiers' reluctance to reveal their own trauma and distress was informed by Edwardian codes of manliness which dictated that men refrain from openly sharing their feelings or showing signs of emotional weakness. Self-control was central to both soldierly and civilian constructions of manliness, and the forbearance of pain and stoic endurance was at the heart of the 'muscular Christianity' promoted by the Edwardian middle classes.[75] Soldiers' emotionally restrained correspondence style demonstrated to those at home that their manliness was intact, even if their bodies were damaged. The authoritative tone of their letters showed to the family that were in control of their wounds and bodies. The withholding of information was further proof of their command over the self, as the chivalrous protection of women was held to be a core manly virtue. Indeed, some young men declared their responsibility for enlistment, relieving their parents' guilt: 'You used to say … that if anything like this happened to me I would blame you for letting me go to war … all I can say [is that] you did not know your own son. The loss of a leg is not very nice, but then, again, I must be thankful I never lost my life'.[76] For wounded men, manliness lay in the transcendence of suffering through an inner code of dignity, courage and determination. The premium placed upon self-control perhaps explains why so few shell-shocked soldiers appear to have written to their families from hospital. For a man to admit that he had lost control of his emotions was tantamount to admitting unmanliness. In 1918, William Bourke informed his wife in a postcard that 'I am still going strong' after being hospitalised in Britain for shell shock.[77] Notably, he made no mention of his 'shameful' nervous breakdown in the firing line.

In their letters, wounded soldiers adopted various strategies to reassure their families by demonstrating their manly forbearance and fortitude. Some re-worked their experiences into heroic narratives that reminded their readers, and themselves, of the purposefulness of their injuries. In 1916, Fred Hocking transformed his experiences at Pozières into an adventure story. He described being shot while crawling through the mud as 'bullets whistled past me & men were falling everywhere', and declared 'it's marvellous what a man will do when his life is at stake'.[78] Some wounded men expressed their eagerness to return to the Western Front and face the enemy again.[79] Jim Keast encouraged his parents to respond to his wounds with patriotic pride rather than anxiety. 'I'll be able to wear the Gold Stripe now Mum given to all who have been wounded in battle.'[80] He was particularly pleased that his wound 'isn't serious and yet it will leave a scar (for serving King & country)', and imagined that his father would be 'puffing out his chest like a pouter pigeon'.[81]

As men composed their letters, some may have been influenced by the heroic accounts of war they had read in their youth, while others may have modelled their letters on newspaper reports they had read before their departure. The cheerfulness of some wounded soldiers' letters may also reflect the patriotic culture of optimism evident in military hospitals. In England, upbeat hospital magazines were circulated to soldier patients to boost their morale, and offered them a positive framework within which to understand their wounds and disablements. At the Bishop's Knoll Hospital, the editors of *Coo-eee!* promoted 'the right spirit of cheerfulness' among convalescent soldiers.[82] Such magazines reassured wounded men that their injuries were valued as a 'premium' sacrifice to the nation, and that they should 'consider [their] disappointments lessened'.[83] While not all wounded soldiers were convinced of the patriotic value of their disablements, some may have found the bright and hopeful language of hospital magazines instructive as they composed letters for a homefront audience.[84]

The translation of battlefield wounding into heroic narratives allowed soldiers to write in a manly persona. Yet it also had therapeutic dimensions. In 1917, Jim Roberts used his time in hospital to compose a diary retrospectively for his family, a practice not uncommon among men whose convalescence was protracted. His daughter Mary Reddrop reflected that this process was 'very healing for him' because it allowed him to retell the traumatic story of being wounded as an active protagonist rather than a vulnerable combatant. She wryly observed that he cast himself as something of a hero in the narrative: 'There's a lot of boyish vanity in there, and showing his leadership qualities even when he's wounded ... he did well in it!'[85] Jim's story of being wounded at Armentières was an adventure, but it was also an account of reaching relative safety when his commanding officer 'put his arms around me like a father' and conveyed him to a motor ambulance while men around him were 'smashed to a pulp'.[86] Mary believes that the writing process also helped Jim to come to terms with the distressing loss of a dear friend who died after receiving wounds in the same incident. Wounded soldiers' heroic stories of injury served a variety of purposes for men and their kin. In some instances, family members may well have suspected a degree of licence in the story telling. The very act of reclaiming a traumatic incident as heroic, however, was a comforting indicator of their loved one's emotional resolve.

The courage and bravado evident in some wounded soldiers' letters led some proud homefront parents to submit them for newspaper publication. On 2 May 1915, Vyner Jones wrote a glowing account of his 'baptism of fire' at Gallipoli to his father, and lyrically described being wounded while 'laying in a lovely bed of daisies'.[87] The letter was written in an upbeat and patriotic tone, and reassured his family that he considered himself 'very lucky to only have a bad leg'. A month later, Vyner's father proudly handed the letter to the *Albury Daily News* and it was published under the headlines 'Stories of Heroes/Albury Boy's Thrilling Narrative/How Vyner Jones Was Wounded/"While Lying In A Lovely Field of Daisies"'.[88] Each year, family members like Mr Jones, acted as homefront agents for the wounded, passing hundreds of letters out of the private sphere into the public domain, which subsequently became part of the popular written record of war. These selectively published personal epistles were evidence of the Anzacs' remarkable resilience, and inspired new recruits who in turn were wounded and wrote home. Through the act of disseminating soldiers' correspondence to wider audiences, families transformed their feelings of anxiety into patriotic pride. In their public form, these letters became a resounding testament to the strength of families' relationships, and allowed kin to feel part of a larger community whose sons had been wounded.

NARRATIVES OF SURVIVAL

While some wounded soldiers emphasised the heroic circumstances of their wounding, others provided their families with lengthy accounts of their transport to hospital and medical treatment. Through the telling of their journey from battlefield to hospital, soldiers constructed narratives of survival without dwelling on their own suffering. In 1917, one wounded soldier described being lifted out of the chaos of battle: 'I called for help, and within a few moments was sailing for home on a stretcher shoulder high, face bandaged up in a shell dressing and happy as any Australian going home on leave'.[89] Clive Lynch described having a 'pound of meat' blown out of his shoulder in 1916, but offered his wife little reflection on this traumatic experience. Instead he gave a detailed account of his transportation to London by train and ship: 'The whole system is perfect. The trains have cots and every medical & surgical convenience'.[90] By composing letters about their deliverance from danger, wounded soldiers provided their families with an account of their experiences that foregrounded their survival: their wounds were a sign that they had not been killed.

Some soldiers posted wound-related artefacts home to share their relief at having escaped death. After being injured in the arm, in June 1915, William Randall wrote to his father, Edward, advising him that an unusual package would arrive shortly: 'I sent you the sleeve of my tunic home for you to have a look at. It is a wonder I did not lose my arm. It [the arm] is still a bit stiff, but I expect it to be quite well by the time I get back to the trenches'.[91] William's blood-encrusted sleeve was proof he had prevailed over the guns of the Turks. It was an object with extraordinary emotional power. Taking on the shape and smell of his body, as well as absorbing his sweat and blood, William provided his kin with an intimate sensory experience that affirmed he was alive, and 'reached out' to them through this symbolic remnant of his uniform. For men and their families, survival was something to be celebrated and the souveniring of wound trophies was not uncommon. In 1916, Nurse Anne Donnell observed in her diary that soldier patients were 'awfully interested' in the bullets extracted from their bodies during surgery, and that she routinely collected them for the men.[92] Jim Keast was one such patient, and intended to give the piece of shell inside his arm to his father as testament to his ordeal. 'If it is worth it when I take it out', he proudly told his mother, 'I will have it made into a pendant for Dad's watchchain'.[93]

Wounded men not only sent their families trophies of their survival, but photographs which also became visual evidence of their wellbeing. Some professional photographers conducted sessions at military hospitals, and created portrait postcards for a few pence which men could send home. In January 1917, an Australian soldier, Private Hugh 'Paddy' O'Brien of Tumbarumba, had his photograph taken while a patient at a convalescent depot in Weymouth. Neatly dressed in his 'hospital blues', his hat sits atop his freshly bandaged head as he looks confidently into the camera with a faint smile on his face, proudly demonstrating to the viewer that he can stand with the use of crutches. On the reverse of the card he wrote: 'Best love from what's left of Paddy/Not broken but badly bent'.[94] The identity of the recipient is unclear, but we can surmise from his statement 'Best love' that he was possibly writing to his mother, wife or girlfriend. Through this portrait postcard, Paddy consciously constructed a tableau of wellbeing for someone at home, thereby providing visual verification that he was on the way to becoming 'whole' again. The image allowed homefront relatives to 'see' Paddy's injuries, which they had thus far only been able to imagine. For until kin received a photograph, their damaged soldier and the extent of his wounds only existed in their mind's eye.

Just as soldiers enacted their manly intactness in their correspondence, wives and mothers wrote with a strong sense of feminine nurturing responsibility towards their soldier boys. When men left for war, they moved out of the realm of the family into the care of the army. Through their letters, however, women continued to perform their familial roles as carers, which for many meant 'mothering

This portrait postcard was sent home by Private Hugh 'Paddy' O'Brien in January 1917 as he recovered from wounds to the neck, face and back. Australian War Memorial negative number P04166.008.

at a distance'.[95] In 1916, Rose Keast affirmed her devotion to her son after he was wounded, ever fearful that she may lose him. 'You are never out of my mind' she wrote, 'I see you always I never thought when I was rearing you up that I would have to part with you to be a soldier and suffer such hardships as you do'.[96] Wives and mothers alike were frustrated in their desire to comfort their wounded man personally. Suspecting that he may be in a vulnerable emotional state, they used their written words to reassure him. To this end, they too concealed potentially upsetting news and presented a positive image of home. Before heading back to the front, Jim Keast suspected that his mother was concealing her ill-health from him. '[She] isn't as well as she tries to make out' he wrote knowingly to his sister.[97] Keast's letter also reveals that although men's correspondence was often shared within families, they sometimes wrote candidly to individual kin, entrusting them with more detailed accounts of their worries.

HOSPITALS: A HAVEN IN A HARSH WAR

Wounded soldiers were aware of their families' concern that they were left in the care of strangers. Accordingly, some men reassured their families that hospital was 'almost like home' and encouraged them to take comfort in the kindness they were receiving from the nurses, Voluntary Aids (VAs) and other patients who became their surrogate families.[98] In October 1916 William Peach wrote to his mother about his new home at the Norfolk War Hospital: 'The sisters are a fine lot of girls, and all the other chaps in this ward are very nice fellows. We have a real good time among us'.[99] He regaled her with stories of pillow fights on the ward, and the abundance of delicious food that was fattening him up. Hospitals were a haven in a harsh war. Comforts such as clean sheets and hot baths were a welcome change from the hellish conditions of the trenches. A sense of relief pervades the letters of men with 'holiday wounds'. 'It was the best bit of luck I've had for a long time' wrote Harold Evans to his parents and sister, of his wounded left hand.[100] Those who required more lengthy treatment reminded their families that at least they were away from the dangers of the firing line. In May 1916, Lindsay Ross informed his mother from a London hospital that it was 'almost "great" to be wounded', and three months later wrote 'don't worry – I'm not in the battle of the Somme (worse luck)'.[101]

While most wounded Australians were forced to rely on letters to describe their experiences of wounding and recovery, a significant minority of the AIF were British-born and were called on by their relatives during visiting hours.[102] Robert Antill migrated to Australia at the age of sixteen in 1913, and found himself back in the 'old country' after being wounded at the Dardanelles in 1915. From King George's Hospital, he wrote to his mother and father in South Tottenham: 'Will you please come and see me, I am here in London, just fancy being home in dear old London'.[103] Soldiers like Robert were the envy of Australian-born men who missed the emotional succour of family. In 1916 one of Robert's Melbourne-born friends, William Eckhardt, took the liberty of writing to Mr Antill requesting a visit: 'You can tell Mrs Antill that I would only be too pleased for someone to come and see me as I have no friend at all in England … so it is very lonely for me'.[104] Some Australians were fortunate enough to establish close relationships with – or even fall in love with – kindly Britons, who provided friendship and support during their stay in hospital, and may have even seen it as their patriotic duty to 'adopt' a wounded dominion soldier.

THE PROSPECT OF RETURN

The correspondence between wounded Australian soldiers and their families during the First World War helps us understand how war wounds were also family wounds. Soldiers were wounded within the bonds of kinship. From the moment they enlisted, young men became soldiers of the AIF; however, they also remained members of families. They trained, fought and sustained wounds not only as combatants but as much-loved sons, husbands and brothers, whose families worried deeply about their wellbeing. Despite the distance between homefront and battlefront, soldiers' wounds and impairments had enormous emotional resonance for those at home. The process of adjustment involved both men and their kin, who cautiously negotiated their anxieties around disability and its attendant losses for a significant period of time before their return – sometimes up to a year. To this end, soldiers carefully presented their families with reassuring narratives that affirmed their manly capacity to cope emotionally with their injuries, sometimes to the point of incredulity. Paradoxically, while letters were an 'instrument of emotional union', they were also an instrument of concealment. The ways in which soldier patients encouraged their relatives to respond to their disabilities with optimism also suggests that their letters were instruments of instruction. By demonstrating their own capacity to cope with their losses with dignity, they provided an emotional template to guide family reactions to their 'changed man' upon his return.

Thoughts of home were never far from the minds of wounded Australian soldiers. For soldiers whose wounds resulted in permanent disablement, their war service ended prematurely and they were 'marked for Aussie'. But the prospect of returning home incapacitated was daunting for some. 'I don't envy any of them who are going back disabled for years or life', wrote Charles Baker in his hospital diary in August 1918.[105] Some men anticipated a relationship of increased dependence on their family members. 'You are getting old enough now to look after Daddy', William Tooney warned his daughter, perhaps foreseeing the need for nursing and domestic assistance.[106] On the homefront, family members looked forward hopefully to the return of their man. Wives and mothers imagined the day that they would be able to personally nurse their loved one. 'Never mind old Darling when we get you home we will make you well', wrote Ethel Goddard to her husband.[107] While some families looked forward to the return of men with light injuries and ailments, other households prepared themselves to welcome sons and husbands with severe physical and mental impairments. The next chapter examines how families responded to their loved one after they were reunited with one another in Australia, and considers how they negotiated the challenges they faced as they recommenced their shared civilian lives together.

CHAPTER 2

returning to family life

> I met my brother on his return from
> the war. He was not the same man &
> was incapable of doing anything.
>
> Edwina Leonard, sister of Jim Leonard, March 1929.¹

On Saturday 2 December 1916, the hospital ship *Karoola* arrived at the docks in Port Melbourne. On board were four hundred wounded soldiers invalided from England, an 'extra large' number compared with previous arrivals. The trench warfare of the Western Front had exacted an enormous toll from the AIF, and many aboard had been injured at Pozières five months earlier. The *Karoola* received a warm homecoming after it docked, and its cargo of wounded soldiers soon became the focus of a series of patriotic rituals which had been enacted many times before.² On the pier, women of the Welcoming Committee presented the soldiers with fruit, chocolates, cigarettes and flowers. A fleet of motor cars, organised by the Automobile Club, conveyed the men along a well-worn procession route from Port Melbourne through the city's main streets to the barracks and Red Cross Rest Home on St Kilda Road where they were reunited with their families. A military band led the parade, and its rousing music announced the arrival of the wounded. Several thousand onlookers gathered, and the *Age* reported that the crowds were larger than usual, boosted by Saturday morning shoppers who enthusiastically cheered the procession of 'warriors'.[3]

That same cloudy Saturday morning, the Hargreaves family went to meet the *Karoola* to welcome home their son John. Inspired by the Gallipoli campaign, eighteen-year-old John had been granted permission by his parents to enlist in the AIF in July 1915. In late October 1916, the family received official notification that he would be returning to Australia as a result of wounds he had received on the Western Front. John's father, Richard, attempted to seek more information about the nature of his son's condition, but Base Records claimed they were unable to state the reason for his return.[4] The Hargreaves family spent six anxious weeks waiting for John to return without any reliable information about the extent of his injuries – was he slightly wounded or would he return as a 'cot case'? As the arrival of the *Karoola* drew nearer, the family decided that they would all undertake the long train journey from Ararat to Melbourne together, travelling in a party which included John's father, step-mother, younger brother and two sisters. Their hopes of meeting him upon disembarkation, however, were disappointed. By the time they arrived, John had already been conveyed to the Caulfield Hospital, as the *Karoola* had docked one hour earlier than expected. The family proceeded directly to Caulfield, and was ushered into a quiet room to meet their tall, dark-eyed John.

What they saw devastated them all. John had fallen into a 'mental stupor' as the result of being buried by a shell at Pozières. He lay completely frozen on his bed and stared out into space with his eyes wide open, unable to speak. The patriarch of the family, Richard Hargreaves, was so distressed by the state of his eldest son that he ran out of the room crying.[5] John appeared unable to recognise his family members, although he did squeeze the hand of his favourite younger sister, Teddy. The family was informed that during the journey to Australia he had been hand-fed by the cook on the *Karoola* to keep him alive. After the ship docked, John had been immediately transferred to the Caulfield Hospital because of his condition, and missed the 'hearty reception' in Melbourne's city streets. This soldier's welcome home took place away from the public spotlight, and was a subdued and intensely private family affair.

RETURNING TO THE FAMILY REALM

The Hargreaves family reunion suggests that there are two stories to be told about the return of disabled soldiers to Australia. The first tells how 'brave disabled warriors' were welcomed home by a grateful nation eager to reward their heroic sacrifices.[6] The second reveals how thousands of war-disabled men made the transition into the family realm, and how they and their kin together responded to the challenges of newly acquired impairments. These stories, of course, are not mutually exclusive. Historians, however, have typically been more interested in telling a 'public' story of soldiers' return, and have focused upon aspects of repatriation that highlight the experiences of these men within the body politic. They have neglected to ask what it meant for a disabled soldier to return to the 'private' realm of the home, and rarely explored the process of transition into the domestic and familial sphere. Accordingly, the dynamics of disabled soldiers' return to family life, the resumption of kin relationships and the quest for a marriage partner have often been overlooked. Yet, disabled soldiers were not only individual combatants patriotically welcomed home by the nation, they were also sons, husbands, brothers, sweethearts and fathers who returned 'home' to take up their places as members of families.

This chapter examines the transition of disabled soldiers back into family life in Australia between 1915 and the early 1920s. The first part explores disabled soldiers' return to their families of origin and considers how they negotiated the challenges of disablement. The second part investigates how disabled soldiers courted prospective wives and established their own families, given that impairment was deemed by some to be an impediment to matrimony. When family members first met their disabled soldier upon his return, they often described him as a 'changed man'.[7] During their transition back into civilian life, disabled soldiers began a complex process of physical and emotional adjustment and social reintegration. This involved adapt-

In late 1916, John Hargreaves (top left) was invalided home to Melbourne in a 'mental stupor' after suffering severe shell shock at Pozières. He is pictured here in 1917, a couple of days after Christmas, with his father, Richard (top right) and siblings Edna 'Teddy' (bottom left), Doris (middle) and Eric (back).
Photograph courtesy of Joan Wishart.

ing to their bodily and mental changes, finding a suitable place within business or industry, as well as coming to terms with the loss of pre-war hopes and expectations they had once had for their adult lives. They also re-entered their local communities and resumed relationships with family and friends. Yet, it was not only disabled soldiers who embarked upon a journey of adjustment and reconciliation to disablement. After meeting their 'changed man', family members commenced a new phase in their own process of adaptation, accommodation and transformation, negotiating disability and its meanings for the first time in the physical presence of their soldier. Families' experiences varied greatly, depending upon the nature of their soldiers' impairments and the circumstances of the household. In some instances, the return of a disabled soldier profoundly changed the lives of family members, while for others adjusting to war disability was a less demanding endeavour.

There are few historical sources that offer insight into families' practical and emotional adjustment to war disability in Australia. Ironically, we know more about how families responded to their soldier's impairments before he was repatriated home, because of the correspondence generated during their separation. Once reunited, however, letter and diary writing usually ceased. Men and their kin had little need to document their feelings upon meeting one another and going through the process of domestic adjustment. Moreover, in newspapers and official publications, disabled soldiers' transition into the family realm and the involvement of kin in the adjustment process received scant attention. There was a great deal of commentary on disabled soldiers' rehabilitation and employment prospects, but historical evidence of families' experiences, particularly the emotional aspects, remains elusive. Nonetheless, by carefully synthesising documentary, photographic and oral history sources, it is possible to gain a sense of the first stages of family life after the return of a disabled soldier, and to examine the burdens of sacrifice families faced once they had been reunited on Australian soil.

INVALIDED HOME

Between the outbreak of war and the end of demobilisation, 102 324 sick or wounded soldiers were repatriated back to Australia. Some men were invalided home within weeks of firing their first shots.[8] The first hospital ships carrying Australian soldiers home arrived from German New Guinea and Egypt in early 1915. These early transports tended to carry men suffering from tropical illnesses, injuries from training accidents, venereal disease and pre-existing health problems. The first large contingent of wounded Australians arrived in Fremantle on 9 July 1915 aboard the *Kyarra*, after Australia's first large-scale military engagement on the Gallipoli Peninsula some two months earlier.[9] From that point onwards, growing numbers of sick and wounded soldiers returned to Australia. Between 1915 and 1918 the number of men invalided home increased almost five times, rising from 6184 in 1915 to 31 148 in 1918. The single biggest evacuation occurred between January and March 1919 when 28 192 men were finally repatriated.[10] Unfortunately, the demobilisation of such large numbers of medically unfit men coincided with the outbreak of the 'Spanish flu' pandemic, and some succumbed to the disease before they made it home. As a measure to prevent the spread of infection, all soldiers aboard hospital ships were quarantined for two weeks before being reunited with their families.

Australian recruits embarking for the battlefields of Europe had been farewelled as god-like heroes with magnificent physiques, but they returned as men whose bodies were all too mortal. Some bore visible wounds or missing body parts, while others suffered invisible damage. A number carried shell fragment in their bodies. Others escaped injury but were chronically debilitated or underweight through the stress and strain of service. Many servicemen bore psychological scars and exhibited mentally disturbed behaviour, while prisoners of war typically returned home with health problems due to the privations of captivity.[11] About two-thirds of all sick or wounded soldiers were invalided home on medical grounds, the remaining third recovered from their wounds in England and were demobilised as 'fit' men.[12] For disabled servicemen who sustained permanent impairments, the long sea voyage back to Australia was a time of contemplation as they considered their futures as 'incapacitated' men. In September 1918, one disabled soldier aboard the *Karoola* described how men 'sit about and swap yarns, or talk of the future, or think quietly each of his own home and friends and prospects'. 'We are different men', he declared, 'we each have our own private problems, hope and longings'.[13]

MEANINGS OF HOME

For many soldiers, home was the apex of their journey to war, as historian Bart Ziino has observed.[14] It was only upon returning that the consequences and meanings of their experiences were revealed, both within the nation for which they had fought, and within the households from which they had been separated. 'Home' was a place where soldiers had been assured in 1914 that the purposefulness of their injuries would be recognised and rewarded. Aboard ship, the extent to which the government's promises would be met weighed heavily on the minds of those permanently unfit to carry on in their former trades or occupations. Disabled soldiers hoped for generous pensions and benefits, and completed repatriation paperwork during their journey home. Some men, however, worried that the repatriation system was not delivering all that had been promised, especially in the later years of the war. 'They tell us the returned men get a rough time when they get back to Aussie', Charles Baker wrote in his diary in September 1918, as he anxiously contemplated his future with a leg injury.[15]

'Home' was also an emotional destination, a safe and familiar haven in which disabled soldiers hoped to convalesce from the trauma of injury with the support of their families. Men anticipated the moment of reunion when they would meet their loved ones face to face. One nurse reported the excitement of a patient aboard the *Karoola*:

'Oh, Sister, do you think that mother will be there to meet me? I want to see her before anything else in Australia'.[16] Some disabled soldiers, however, were worried about their transition back into family life. For many, prospective financial and emotional dependence upon parents or relatives was a concern, while others despaired about their capacity to become a husband and father. As disabled soldiers returned from war, they reflected upon their futures with mixed feelings. Journeying along the Australian coast, some were reminded of their earlier keenness to reach the battlefront as they crossed paths with troopships full of new recruits heading towards the war.

Disabled soldiers' first encounter with 'home' upon Australian soil typically involved public rituals of welcome, which greeted them at the docks. Upon disembarkation, they were warmly welcomed by official parties and conveyed to an appointed place to meet their kin and start their transition back into family life. The 'walking wounded' made their own way off the ships while others were conveyed in stretchers or 'crated' by special cranes onto the wharf. As they left their floating hospitals, some disabled soldiers were unsure about how the welcoming parties and their families would react to their injuries. While mildly wounded men were in a position to reassure kin that they had sustained only minor or temporary damage, those with more permanent impairments conceivably anticipated their homecoming with some apprehension, because it represented the moment that their loved ones would be confronted for the first time by the damage they had sustained during their war service.

For some, leaving the ship was emotionally difficult. William Gamble recalled the cheering crowds upon his arrival in Melbourne, but also remembered that his head wounds disturbed some of the spectators. He had a large hole on the left side of his skull, a partially paralysed face and a missing eye. He later wrote, 'A young lady of [the] group must have been impressed, as I passed by she remarked, "What a shame, and such a fine looking fellow too" ... I realised ... that what claim I may have had to reasonable looks went with my left eye'.[17]

For Gamble, the attention of onlookers increased his anxiety about how his injuries would affect his relationships with others, particularly women. Their stares made him realise how much he had physically changed and that his sense of identity, based on 'good looks', had been forever altered. The young lady's ill-chosen words reminded him that his injuries had rendered him an object of pity, rather than admiration. Indeed, some disabled soldiers anticipated the pitying gaze of the crowd and deliberately avoided the spectacle of welcoming ceremonies altogether. WJ Voss, a blinded soldier, arrived in Australia in 1918 aware of motor cars 'waiting to convey us to the station through streets lined with cheering crowds'. He described the official wharfside welcome as an 'ordeal' which he 'mercifully escaped' by jumping into a taxi with three others.[18]

FAMILY REUNIONS

Family members of the wounded travelled to meet their loved ones with feelings of hope and trepidation. Official notification of a soldier's return could be a cause for joyful celebration. After the 1918 Armistice, one mother recalled kneeling down and thanking God because this meant that her two wounded sons were to come out of the war alive – 'no more war worry!'[19] Relatives were grateful that their loved one had survived. Many, however, did not have a realistic idea of his wounds, and were anxious about the extent of his disablement. Official telegrams provided only general descriptions of servicemen's injuries, and, as we have already seen, soldiers often understated their condition in their reassuring letters home. Similarly, censored newspapers and cinema newsreels tended to downplay the unpleasant aspects of injury, and depicted the maimed as plucky individuals who bore their wounds with cheerful fortitude. In the later stages of the war, larger numbers of wounded men returned to Australia, and families commonly encountered disabled soldiers first-hand within their communities. Yet, as kin tried to imagine the condition in which their

These photographs capture the emotions of relatives waiting for and meeting their wounded soldiers at the Anzac Buffet, Hyde Park, Sydney. Australian War Memorial negative numbers H11576 (c. 1918), H11575 (c. 1915) H11574 (c. 1915).

returning to family life

own soldier would return, many were not fully prepared for his altered physical or mental state.

Families' experiences of meeting their disabled soldier as he disembarked from a hospital ship varied according to the information they had received and their emotional preparedness. In Sydney, family members waited anxiously in the Anzac Buffet near the wharf at Woolloomooloo, the same place from which many had farewelled their loved ones. Space was limited at the Buffet, so only two tickets were issued to representatives of each family to meet their soldier and have refreshments before accompanying him to waiting relatives in the Domain gardens.[20] Photographs show family members watching with unwavering concentration as they tried to catch a glimpse of their wounded soldier in one of the cars driving towards to the Buffet. Their faces suggest concerned anticipation, quietly tempered excitement and, for some, relief.

The moment of reunion was filled with emotion. In May 1917, the *Sydney Morning Herald* reported that 'Women with children in their arms ducked under the banners and rushed at a car wherein was a husband, son or brother. The child would be pitched into the returned soldier's arms, while the mother sprang on the step of the moving car and flung her arms round the neck of the returned soldier'.[21] Some family members displayed their feelings openly as the stress of waiting for their soldier to return ended. After one ship docked in Melbourne in December 1918, the *Argus* reported that 'ordinarily staid and undemonstrative men kissed their sons with unrestrained fervour, while tears of joy lined the faces of the majority of the women as they rushed forward to meet their boys'.[22]

One can only imagine the extraordinary first moments of these meetings. As they met their soldier, family members began to reconcile the flesh and blood of their wounded man with their knowledge and imaginings of his condition. During their first interactions together, men's impairments became evident to kin who may have been surprised or confronted by them. Blinded soldiers could no longer see their family members. Deafened men had trouble hearing their relatives' words of welcome. Men with jaw or mouth injuries struggled to speak. Families of shell-shocked men were confronted by men whose personalities were transformed. Soldiers with serious physical injuries were no longer the able-bodied lads they had once been. Some men were on stretchers, never to walk again, while others leaned on crutches or walking sticks. Despite their physical and mental changes, however, kin welcomed loved ones home in the knowledge that at least they had arrived safely.

After their official welcome upon disembarkation, some disabled soldiers were whisked away by ambulance to military hospitals, mental institutions and convalescent facilities, to return home at a later date. Others were well enough to make their way directly back to the family home. In their home towns and suburbs, wounded servicemen often received an additional reception, which was for many the real welcome home. Men from rural Australia typically returned home by train, and were met at the station by their families and the local welcoming committee, which provided cars to drive them to their homes. Communities staged gala ceremonies for the returning wounded in church and town halls, patriotically decorated with flags and flowers. Local politicians gave rousing speeches lauding the honourable nature of their injuries. In January 1918, one Warrnambool councillor declared 'it had been a joy to welcome the boys, and to see the cheerfulness and fortitude with which they bore their wounds and disfigurements'.[23] Some soldiers were presented with medals inscribed with the word 'wounded'. Communities pledged their support for invalided men – 'It behoves us all to do our duty to them to see after their welfare and do all in our power to assist them'.[24]

Public welcoming ceremonies, both at the docks and in local communities, reaffirmed the promises made to recruits that men would be 'looked after' if they returned incapacitated. The government's guarantees of generous pensions and benefits engendered a strong sense of entitlement among returning disabled soldiers. 'Of course I shall get a pension' Jim Lord informed his mother in 1919, as he considered his future with a seriously injured right arm.[25] Upon their return, disabled soldiers were provided with booklets outlining the benefits available to them, including disability pensions, war service homes, settlement upon the land, travel allowances, and loans for re-establishment in business. Official repatriation literature promised disabled soldiers a future brimming with hope and opportunities, and they were offered full social and industrial integration through rehabilitation and employment programs. During the war, the rehabilitation and re-training of disabled soldiers received enormous public attention as they became 'respectful and useful members of society'.[26]

READJUSTING TO FAMILY LIFE

As disabled soldiers contemplated the challenges of becoming 'men and citizens', however, they and their family members also began the process of readjusting to war disability within their home environments. The majority of disabled soldiers returned to the homes of their parents, as the AIF was overwhelmingly composed of young, unmarried men. The remaining minority of married men were accompanied home by their wives, many of whom had not seen their husbands in years, and, in the case of hasty pre-war marriages, had spent very little time with before enlisting. Disabled soldiers themselves often found that they had returned to 'changed' households. One of the most common changes occasioned by war was the death of other soldier relatives. Men sometimes arrived home to find grief-stricken families mourning the loss of loved ones killed at the front. It was not uncommon for parents to experience multiple losses through death and disability if a family had sent more than one son to the war. As one parent observed in 1921, 'while some families are mourning their dead others are divided between their duty to [their] returned living and battered boys … and their dear dead'.[27] In December 1917, Reginald Eager, a shell-shocked soldier who 'suffered greatly' at the front, returned to a home environment strained by grief.[28] His sixty-seven-year-old widowed mother, Mrs Fanny Eager, was already caring for her daughter whose husband had been killed, and the child of that marriage, all of whom lived in a small three-bedroom house. Reginald was discharged into the care of Fanny even though he was 'quite a wreck' because he claimed he could 'not stand further treatment' at Randwick Hospital. He joined a household in mourning, in which every member, from youngest to oldest, had been touched by death and disability.

In some instances, disabled soldiers had no wife or parents to welcome them home. Such men often returned to the homes of siblings or extended kin who took responsibility for their care. In July 1917, Miss Lynch of Stanmore took in her brother who had been wounded in the back, head and eye.[29] He had enlisted as a 'very powerful man' but was unable to do anything but 'light work' upon his return. James Lynch was a widower with three children, and his injuries and low earning capacity prevented him from establishing an independent household. James and his sister established their own household in which she was the domestic manager, and took on the responsibilities of raising James' youngest child in the absence of their mother. To lighten Miss Lynch's load, two older children were sent to live with their maternal grandmother in the country. The Lynch family's living arrangements were shaped by James' economic dependence. Their household was split in two so that he and the children could be provided for adequately. In the longer term, the marriage prospects of female relatives, such as Miss Lynch, were diminished by their ongoing responsibilities to disabled soldier relatives and their dependent children.

As households adjusted to the arrival of their 'changed' man, there was much to discuss. Disabled soldiers, however, were often reluctant to talk about their war experiences and some men were guarded about the details of their impairments. One soldier 'bravely kept all knowledge of his sufferings from his relatives and friends' even though a 'shadow of death' hung over him.[30] Men were particularly hesitant about sharing their mental and emotional turmoil, and 'suffered in loneliness' with 'secret fears hidden even from wives and mothers'.[31] Their silence, perhaps, reflected a broader unwillingness of returned men to discuss their war experiences lest they burden kin with their distressing memories. Yet, given that war disability was an immediate reality that raised practical questions for family members, kin were understandably interested in talking about the implications of their loved one's impairment.

After William Gamble returned home, his father, Samuel, asked him how he envisaged his future with only one eye and a disfigured face. Samuel Gamble feared his son's exclusion from social and industrial life, being 'so young and ... knocked about'.[32] William responded: 'I told him, I said "Look Dad, I went to the war meself". I said, "I asked you to let me go, and you agreed. I got this meself and I'll carry it meself". I said "You can forget all about it."'[33] William had a staunchly independent outlook and intended to respond positively to his impairments. He insisted that he would not become a burden on his parents and aimed to become as self-reliant as possible. After this initial discussion, William's parents saw that he was coping well with the transition back into civilian life, and their anxiety lessened. His mother declared that 'if any one of my three boys ... had to come home with what you've got, I'm glad it was you'. Although the Gambles were initially worried about their son's future, their fears were allayed once it was clear that he had a reasonable chance of leading an independent life. Indeed, by 1925 Gamble was married with one child and was satisfactorily supporting his family with a job at the Victorian Railways.

NEGOTIATING DISABILITY

Settling into the rhythm of family life, a process of adjustment began not only for returned men, but also their kin. The practical, emotional, and social demands upon family members varied greatly depending upon their loved one's disabilities. Families like the Gambles may have at first been shocked by the changed appearance of their soldier, but realised that he was at a comparative advantage over men with severe functional impairments. The knowledge that a loved one could still physically and mentally function was a relief for families fearful of losing a breadwinner. Injuries that were serious, but not incapacitating, could even be a source of humour for family and friends as they encouraged their soldier during his convalescence. In November 1918, Mrs Simpson of Kin Kin, Queensland wrote to her son Roland about a disabled soldier, 'Perce' Cooper, who had returned to the district. 'Perce' had been seriously wounded, yet his injuries were not debilitating. 'He has two holes in his neck you could put your finger in', wrote Mrs Simpson, 'His wife told me he used to whistel through them just the same as with his mouth, & hold matches to it & blow them out but he can speak now which he couldn't when he arrived home still he looks well otherwise'.[34] For such families, the physical recovery of their soldier became the focus of their first months together, and their households were able to overcome collectively the challenges that faced them with relative ease.

The family members of more severely disabled men, however, often carried heavier burdens. In mid-1917, Mrs Louisa Hogan commenced a regimen of hand-feeding her son. Frederick had returned home with his 'lower jaw shot away' and was unable to use his right arm.[35] Each day, Louisa prepared liquid meals for him until he died in May 1918. The adjustment and accommodation process within each household was different. Families of shell-shocked soldiers had to become accustomed to psychological symptoms, such as sleeplessness, headaches and memory loss. Kin of bedridden men had to get used to the idea that their soldier was a permanent invalid and, in some cases, no longer resided at home but in an 'Anzac Hostel'. Relatives of men whose wounds required constant medical attention found that their lives were organised around visits to the hospital, operations and relapses of health. 'Practically ever since my arrival [in Melbourne]', declared war bride Edie Hyslop in 1919, 'my husband has had to have medical aid & advice'.[36]

One of the most difficult adjustments confronting family members was responding to psychologically changed men. In 1920, Miss Bennett noted that she had observed a 'remarkable change' in her brother, Timothy, since his return, and that he alternated between being very morose and excited in his manner, especially when he spoke of the war.[37] Like Timothy Bennett, some men had 'definite' mental impairments that affected their outlook on life, while others had no clear disability but had returned broken in health and nerve. In some cases, physically disabled men became so despondent about their impairments that they slid into a mental depression and became 'absolutely indifferent to their own futures'.[38] To ease their pain, a number sought solace in alcohol while others became dependent upon the drugs (including heroin) they had been prescribed in hospital. Such veterans often found it difficult to make the transition back into civilian life. Some withdrew from social contact, while others expressed their frustrations publicly, disrupting public events, participating in drunken brawls, and committing violent crimes.[39] Their 'disorderly' behaviour affronted public sensibilities, but it also had consequences for their families. Parents despaired over the antisocial tendencies, alcoholism and vulnerability of their soldier sons. 'A terror must lurk in the heart of every mother whose boy's resistance to [alcoholic] temptation has been temporarily or permanently lowered' wrote one father in 1919.[40] Parents, who had not shared their son's experiences at war, struggled to understand their loved one's predicament and his inability to make a successful transition to a 'normal life'.

DISABILITY AS A LOSS

War disability was often experienced by soldiers and their family members as a loss. While bereaved families of the war dead mourned soldiers who had been killed overseas, families of the war-disabled faced a different kind of grief. Their soldier had not been taken by death, but had returned home with diminished physical or mental capacities. As Elsie Frank declared of her son, Walter, who returned in 1918: '[he was] all out of order – quite a different boy prior to enlisting'.[41] Families mourned not only the immediate effects of impairment, but the loss of expectation and hope that they had once held for their boy. As sociologists have observed, acquired physical or mental impairments in young adults can occasion a 'total and abrupt' disruption to life and require a complete reconstruction of one's physical self, identity and personal world.[42] Parents of disabled soldiers feared that their sons' marriage prospects and employment opportunities would be reduced, and their status would be diminished in a society which privileged able-bodiedness. Even before the end of the war, there were reports of maimed soldiers having to stand in crowded railway carriages.[43] Wives had to readjust their dreams and expectations about future married life, and come to terms with their husband's lost earning power and the dependence of the family on a pension. Within households, milestones in young men's lives became reminders of their health problems. Walter Frank joined up in 'splendid health' as an eighteen-year-old, but faced his twenty-first birthday gasping for breath as 'chest troubles' due to the effects of gas set in.[44]

The ways in which families initially responded to their sense of loss varied and depended upon a range of factors. Experiences of previous or concurrent losses, existing financial resources, the number of family members willing to share the load, as well as their innate emotional resilience, all had a part to play. As disabled soldiers returned to Australia, their kin could turn to a patriotic culture of stoicism for comfort. Official and popular literature regularly encouraged relatives to look beyond their 'private sufferings' and to find strength in the 'glory of wounds' their sons had incurred in their country's cause.[45] Personal codes of forbearance particular to the Victorian generation arguably also shaped the emotional responses of the middle-aged parents of disabled soldiers. When I spoke with Beverley Broadbent, she emphasised the apparent emotional toughness of her grandmother who welcomed home three war-disabled sons and mourned the death of a fourth. Reflecting upon her capacity to cope, Beverley commented, 'I think they were stoic, much more than we are, we're softened, we've had it easy'.[46] Similarly, Margaret Cramond believes that her grandmother found the courage to cope with her sons' physical losses (one was gassed and the other lost a leg) by understanding them as part of her patriotic duty. 'In that generation, people were more fatalistic' she observed, 'and also perhaps more patriotic, they thought they were all doing their bit for their country'.[47] It is difficult for historians to comprehend fully the inner emotional lives of disabled soldiers' family members. Their feelings were invisible and largely undocumented, and can only be hinted at in the testimonies of their children. It is clear, however, that while some successfully reconciled themselves to their 'changed' men, others struggled with the adjustment process.

Some kin, particularly wives and mothers, found the shock of a war-disabled loved one too great to endure. As historian Tanja Luckins reminds us, a number of women were unable to overcome their war-related losses, and collapsed physically and emotionally.[48] In May 1918, the distraught mother of a severely disabled Rutherglen soldier committed suicide, unable to cope with her son's extensive physical wounds and psychological scars.[49] Similarly, after the return of her severely wounded husband in July 1917, Mrs Frances Parker of Forbes experienced a nervous breakdown and was admitted to the mental hospital at Parramatta for six months.[50] Private Stephen Parker returned to Australia 'with loss of left leg & left hand useless'. Prior to the return of her husband, Mrs Parker had already been devastated by the return of her brother who was badly gassed and 'coughs up clotted blood constantly'. The disablement of both her husband and brother traumatised Mrs Parker and overwhelmed her capacity to cope. The collective future that she imagined for her family before the war had been radically transformed. Her husband, formerly a shearer, faced a life of serious physical limitation that would touch all aspects of their lives together. She became his primary carer, and her two sons lost a father and an uncle who could take an active physical role in their lives. The return of two disabled men to the Parker family highlights the complex demands placed upon relatives. In this case, as Mrs Parker's brother and husband struggled with their own impairments, she carried a double burden of adjustment.

BROKEN MARRIAGES

War disability tested the marriages of women who had promised to stand by their husbands 'in sickness and in health'. Many stayed in their marriages, despite the difficulties they faced. Other women, however, saw no future in their relationships and chose to leave. After the war, there was a significant jump in the divorce rate.[51] In some instances, war disability contributed to the breakdown of ex-servicemen's marriages, but the available evidence makes it difficult to determine to what extent it was a precipitating cause. Prolonged separation and the associated freedoms that this brought for men and women affected the marriages of all returned men. Moreover, many couples resolved their difficulties through separation, thereby avoiding the high cost of divorce and stigma, and left no documentation from which we can discern their motives. Similarly, in cases of formal divorce, court records can be difficult to interpret, as claimants had to construct their stories around alleged cruelty, adultery or desertion to ensure a *decree nisi*. Nonetheless, it is clear that some women abandoned their marriages as a consequence of war disability, and left their husbands to petition for divorce. In 1921, Joseph Cutts, a one-legged ex-serviceman, filed for a divorce on the grounds of desertion, after being left by his wife who declared 'you're only bloody half a man, you're no good to me' and refused to live with him.[52] In another case, Henry Wood filed for a divorce on the grounds of adultery. After his departure for the front, Wood's wife commenced a relationship with his brother. Upon his return, 'unable to speak owing to shell shock', she told him 'he was not wanted'.[53]

Some marriages faltered because of a malady contracted by soldiers away from the trenches: venereal disease. During the war, almost as many Australian soldiers caught venereal disease as died on the battlefield. In 1919, it was publicly announced that 55 000 AIF soldiers – or 17 per cent of Australia's army – were officially estimated to have contracted VD during the war.[54] In the early twentieth century, venereal disease was notoriously difficult to treat and had extremely serious consequences: it was one of the major causes of permanently incapacitating invalidity for Australians less than forty years of age.[55] Some Australian soldiers enlisted with an infection, while others contracted it while stationed in Australian training camps, or succumbed in Egypt, France or even during their convalescence in England. Far away from family, friends and sweethearts, dominion soldiers were particularly at risk of contracting VD if they chanced sexual relations with unfamiliar partners. In April 1918 Mrs Gertrude Brown found herself 'in very great trouble' because her husband had contracted 'a certain complaint which is very dangerous'.[56] Similarly, Mrs Bessie Trevan's husband was invalided home after losing his leg, but she soon learnt that he also had venereal disease.[57] Both women sought divorces on the grounds of adultery, and declared that it was impossible to live with their husbands again. The plight of these women demonstrates how the physicality of war and its associated activities, made its way into the family home, transcending the body of the soldier and touching the lives of kin.

DISABILITY AND DESIRE

While some disabled soldiers returned to married life, most were bachelors. These single damaged men, who had enlisted 'in the prime of their manhood', were faced with the challenge of courting prospective wives.[58] Between 1919 and 1921, there was a sharp increase in the number of marriages in Australia, as men returned home and started families. By 1933, 17 per cent of returned men remained unmarried, only slightly less than the 20 per cent of males aged 30 to 59 in the general population who remained bachelors.[59] Although statistics on marriage rates among disabled soldiers were never recorded, we know that impairment presented an obstacle to matrimony for a number. Some postponed marriage until physical ailments had stabilised, while others remained bachelors as a result of their disabilities.[60] Yet, disability was not necessarily an impediment to marriage, and men with a variety of physical and mental impairments married, including the blind, shell-shocked and double amputees.[61] By 1921, the number of pensions paid to the dependants of disabled soldiers surpassed those paid to disabled soldiers themselves, which can largely be accounted for by marriage and the arrival of children (see table 2.1). In Australia, most public commentators encouraged disabled soldiers to seek a spouse. In April 1921, Melbourne's *Truth* asked, 'Why, it is asked, should a disabled man not marry if he can find a woman capable of bringing happiness into his life, and to help compensate him for the loss of sight or limbs? ... We have disabled soldiers here in [the] thousands. Are they to be condemned to a life of celibacy?'[62]

Table 2.1 Between 1918 and 1922, the number of disabled soldiers' dependants increased significantly.[63]

Year	Number of pensions: disabled soldiers	Number of pensions: disabled soldiers' dependants
1918	40 702	32 154
1919	71 512	59 581
1920	90 389	86 448
1921	79 491	93 995
1922	76 249	102 046

In the public domain, discussions about war disability and matrimony took place within existing debates about marriage. Before the war, marriage had been a topical subject because of widespread anxieties about the declining birth rate and the perceived decrease in the white population. Within these discussions, the robustness of the Australian stock had also come under scrutiny, and the eugenically minded feared that the 'unfit' were out-breeding the 'fit'. After the war, these concerns became more acute, given that 'so many of our most virile and most productive' had been lost through death or permanent disability.[64] In mainstream commentary, however, disabled soldiers were not typically represented as a eugenic danger. Although veterans with classic conditions of 'racial decay', such as tuberculosis, insanity and venereal disease, were viewed with definite eugenic suspicion, soldiers with physical injuries which were not hereditary were portrayed as innately robust and fit men. 'A one-armed or a one-legged husband will in the future be a husband to be proud of', declared one writer for *Australia To-Day*.[65]

In the early twentieth century, marriage was thought to be the natural destiny of every healthy man. Many felt strongly that disabled soldiers' battlefield sacrifices should not preclude them from marriage and its attendant social, sexual and emotional advantages. Marriage was especially important for disabled soldiers, because of the unpaid support that a wife could offer. Devoted wives could make an enormous difference to veterans' quality of life by compensating for the loss of sight or limbs and ensuring that men's practical and emotional needs were met. This was especially so for men with conditions that rendered them dependent. 'Every young blinded adult of the male sex very badly needs a partner who can look after him' noted one rehabilitation expert.[66] The Repatriation Department, however, was strangely silent on the subject of disability and marriage, and made little contribution to these discussions. Rather than pronouncing on personal matters, it preferred to focus on responsibilities within its jurisdiction, such as veterans' rehabilitation and pensions. Discussions about marriage were left largely to commentators in the popular press.

In magazines, tabloid and local newspapers, there was considerable pressure exerted on young women to desire soldiers who had given the 'great and glorious gift' of their health for the nation. Journalists emphasised the masculine appeal of men injured while undertaking 'brave and warlike deeds', declaring that wounds even made soldiers 'more eagerly desired' by marriageable young women.[67] For some, marrying a disabled soldier came with some prestige and social status. In 1919, Poppy of Richmond declared that 'I am married to a soldier with an arm off ... and I am proud'.[68] The marriages of wounded soldiers were often celebrated in the suburban and regional press. In January 1917, the South Melbourne *Record* reported the marriage of Bertie Prentice who had lost both his eyes at Gaba Tepe. His 'warrior's bride' wore a bridal train made with fabric he had brought back from Egypt.[69] Such reports confirmed that physical disability was no impediment to a man taking up his marital duties, and also demonstrated that women should consider sharing a future life with a disabled husband.

While journalists emphasised the appeal of disabled soldiers, some ex-servicemen were anxious that their impairments lessened their attractiveness as husbands. In January 1918 one limbless soldier, 'OSO', wrote to the *Everylady's Journal* in a quandary about whether he should propose to his sweetheart.[70] He feared rejection because he was 'maimed and different to other fellows', and suspected that she was 'measuring up' his physical attractiveness against other men. 'Domina' reassured OSO that most women regarded the sacrifices of wounded soldiers with respect and compassion, and suggested that he declare his love and explain to his sweetheart 'what [he had] gone through'. Domina suggested that if the proposal was rejected, he should 'forget her as quickly as may be', declaring that any woman who spurned a soldier 'marred and spoilt in his physical beauty' was 'no fit wife for him'. For the predominantly female readership of the *Everylady's*

Journal, this was a powerful message that soldiers' war disabilities should be viewed as honourable scars of sacrifice, not as unsightly disfigurements. Yet, the extent to which women actually adopted this advice is difficult to measure.

We do know, however, that some women did have concerns about marrying disabled soldiers, particularly shell-shocked men. In December 1917, 'EB' wrote to the *Everylady's Journal* asking whether she should continue her relationship with her fiancé who had been changed by war in 'every fibre of his being'.[71] 'Domina' urged EB to dedicate herself to the care of her fiancé, declaring that 'allowances should be made' for wounded soldiers: 'Can there be anything in this world too great to do for the man – such a man!' She warned EB that breaking off the relationship was tantamount to rejecting the woman's share of the war: 'Think of this wounded soldier – wounded, body, soul, and spirit – as you would think of a little child … [and] with your most tender care win [him] back to happier ways, to brighter thoughts, this returned broken man'. Such commentators suggested that disabled soldiers' helplessness awakened a spirit of 'mothering' in young women, and urged them to embrace their feminine role as nurturers and healers.[72] As the *League* magazine noted in 1922, many returned men were reclaimed by marrying 'the right woman'.[73]

Within the context of these public debates, disabled soldiers' experiences of finding a spouse and embarking upon marriage varied. Some married in England during their convalescence, and were among the 15 000 Australian soldiers who returned home with a British bride or fiancé.[74] The nursing relationship allowed close bonds to develop, and some soldier patients courted nurses or Red Cross volunteers in military hospitals in Blighty. Keith Falconer's father proposed to his mother, Mary Ann, while she worked as a VA on his ward. Frank's head had been 'blown open' in France, and Mary Ann was a first-hand witness to his recovery, nursing him back to health after a steel plate was inserted into his skull. She knew that he suffered from chronic headaches, and perhaps suspected that he may have health problems in the future. But despite any misgivings she may have had, they married in England and began a new life in Australia.⁷⁵

Other disabled soldiers married sweethearts or women they had met after their return home. In his autobiography, *A Fortunate Life*, Albert Facey described meeting Evelyn Gibson while convalescing in Perth, after being invalided home in November 1915 with a crushed right leg and internal injuries.⁷⁶ Evelyn visited him regularly at the repatriation hospital and the two struck up a close relationship. Upon his discharge, Albert was informed by the medical board that they 'couldn't guarantee that I would live more than two years'.⁷⁷ This came as a shock, as he had already secured the permission of Evelyn's parents to propose to her, and she had accepted. 'I felt very sad', wrote Facey, 'as I couldn't expect a girl to marry me under such a cloud'. Albert discussed his prognosis with Evelyn, and she decided to go ahead with the engagement because the board's ominous assessment was not a foregone conclusion. They married in August 1916. Albert recalled that the wedding was a small, quiet affair, permeated by a sense of sadness, as two of his brothers had been killed during the war.

While Evelyn's parents gave their permission for Albert to propose, some parents were adamant that their daughter not marry a disabled soldier. Joan Wishart's grandparents expressly forbade the marriage of her mother, Caroline, to John Hargreaves, the shell-shocked soldier whose story opened this chapter. The couple met in 1917 soon after Hargreaves' release from Royal Park Military Mental Hospital, and their courtship took place in Melbourne's Flagstaff Gardens. As their affections grew, Caroline broke off her engagement to her fiancé, a soldier serving at the front. Her parents were horrified, and made it clear that they did not approve of Hargreaves 'because they thought he had some sort of severe psychiatric disability'.⁷⁸ Against her parents' wishes, Caroline ran away to marry John in 1919. Joan reflects that despite the protestations of Caroline's parents and John's psychological vulnerabilities, there was an 'overwhelming feeling between the two of them' that inexorably drew them together. Such was the strength of family disapproval, however, that the wedding ceremony was conducted without Caroline's parents and other key relatives in attendance. No photographs of the occasion were taken, and accordingly descendants have no visual record of the event.

While many women married disabled soldiers for love, there is evidence that some women may have settled for 'second best' when they accepted a proposal from an incapacitated man.[79] At the end of the war, the pool of marriageable men in Australia had shrunk, and by the early 1920s some commentators claimed that there was a 'surplus of shes'.[80] In the quest for a husband, war widows competed with young single women, and English war brides became the target of anger from Australian women who feared that there were not enough men to go around. Although, at this distance, it is difficult to identify women's personal motives for marriage, some with limited marriage options may have married a disabled soldier more out of necessity, or a desire not to remain unmarried, than love. Others may have hoped to 'lean on [the] benevolence' of the pension system or gain a pension after the death of the soldier from his injuries.[81] Whatever their reasons, a generation of young Australian women married disabled soldiers of the Great War, and through their marriage vows, committed themselves to caring for their husbands "til death do us part'.

JOURNEYS INTO THE DOMESTIC SPHERE

When disabled soldiers were invalided 'home' to Australia, they returned both to the nation and the family realm. They disembarked from hospital ships as individuals whose impairments were honoured and celebrated in the public sphere. They also arrived as members of families who were reunited with their kin and made the journey back into the domestic sphere. After a long period of cautiously discussing their loved one's wounds in their letters, and imagining his disablements, families finally met their 'incapacitated' man. From the moment they were reunited with one another, disabled soldiers and their families began a complex process of transition to living with war disability. Yet official commentators and newspapers rarely reported on the process of family adjustment. Although the question of marriage received some attention in public discourse, the repatriation of disabled soldiers was overwhelmingly represented as a national question of pensioning, retraining and employment for the nation's 'brave disabled warriors', rather than as a journey back into the family realm as sons, husbands and fathers.

Yet, for thousands of families across Australia, the return of a disabled soldier signalled the beginning of a shared process of adjustment and reconciliation within the privacy of the home, which involved his kin. During the first weeks and months, as incapacitated veterans passed from the care of the army into the familial realm, the extent of their dependence became apparent and families gained a sense of the practical and emotional burdens they were to carry. Within some households, it became clear that war disability posed few challenges and the demands upon kin would be negligible. In other cases, the immediate emotional impact of war disability was devastating and families' futures were radically transformed by the arrival of their 'changed man'. Across the spectrum of disabilities, however, one thing was certain: adjusting to war disability was not just the task of soldiers as individuals, but an endeavour which involved entire families.

The reconciliation of soldiers and their kin to disablement did not end after the first few months of being reunited, but was an ongoing process of adaptation. As the Prime Minister observed shortly after the Armistice, some homes would forever 'look upon the scars of war on … their dearest and best'.[82] For many households, the disablement of a loved one had lasting consequences which reached into almost every aspect of family life and demanded ongoing sacrifices of kin well into the 1920s and 1930s. The following two chapters demonstrate how families negotiated the consequences of war disability in partnership with one another as the years passed.

CHAPTER 3

making ends meet

> I have done my very utmost to make
> the pension go as far as possible, but we
> have not been able to pay our way.
>
> Mrs Iris Mead to the Tubercular Soldiers'
> Aid Society, April 1928.[1]

In June 1922, Mrs K Dare of North Sydney wrote to the treasurer of the Citizens' Returned Soldiers Benefit Fund administered by the City of Sydney. Mrs Dare's husband had been 'a fine healthy man' prior to enlistment, but had returned from the war a 'broken up wreck' and was now 'ill & weak at the Parramatta Asylum'.[2] He had contracted bronchitis at the Dardanelles and had been 'in & out of different homes' and was most recently an inmate of the Waley Home at Picton, a Red Cross convalescent home for shell-shocked men. He was granted a pension of less than 50 per cent for his 'lung and nerve troubles', and the family, including two children, faced a perilous future on a meagre war pension of 14/6 a week. Given the regular hospitalisation of her husband and his continued ill health, Mrs Dare was left with the responsibility of preventing her family's descent into destitution. The family lived together in one rented room, and she had 'been obliged to pawn everything I have to keep things together', sacrificing even the blankets on her own bed. Mrs Dare lived with constant anxiety about the decline in her husband's health and his possible death, stating 'I really do not think my husband will see the Winter through'.

War disability could and did have dire economic consequences for soldiers' families. The financial burdens shouldered by the Dare household were considerable. Mr Dare's parlous mental state, his unemployability and the lack of an adequate war pension spelled financial disaster for the whole family. Such poverty was not uncommon among the families of disabled soldiers, yet the Repatriation Department seldom acknowledged this. Official rehabilitation literature championed the recovery of individual men and boldly asserted their capacity to become 'self-supporting citizens'.[3] Mrs Dare's patriotic fund application prompts us to look beyond this rhetoric. It provides a window onto the personal struggle of a disabled soldier. Importantly, it locates that struggle squarely within the context of his family, revealing that the relatives of disabled soldiers were centrally involved in the economic maintenance of their households. Mrs Dare was a skilful domestic manager. She was responsible for making ends meet and took the initiative to generate additional income, in this case by composing a letter that would maximise her chances of charitable relief. Her letter shows how the economic burdens of war disability were shared and negotiated together by disabled soldiers and their kin.

This chapter examines the economic consequences of war disability for families. It investigates veterans' capacity to become breadwinners, and considers the strategies adopted by their families to achieve financial stability during the 1920s. Rather than analysing the flow of pension benefits from the state to individual servicemen, as many historians have done, it examines how families collectively managed the micro-economies of their households on a day-to-day basis.[4] For many disabled soldiers, inadequate pensions and employment difficulties meant that becoming a family breadwinner was an unachievable dream, and thousands found themselves in a position of profound financial dependence on state and charitable organisations. Paradoxically, some men became reliant upon the economic support of family members who were officially classified as their 'dependants'. The financial consequences of an invalid breadwinner demanded a collective family approach to the household economy, in which wives, parents and other relatives played a key part. Although the Repatriation Department championed veterans' capacity for 'manly independence', their families' survival actually depended on the economic interdependence of kin.

The impact of war disability upon household economies was diverse. Families' financial outlook was mediated by a range of factors, including the precise effect of a man's disability on carrying out his trade or profession, whether he received a pension, his social class, the ability of household members to work and their financial resourcefulness. As these determinants changed over time, so did the family's economic prospects. While some families were able to attain a reasonably comfortable financial position, others found themselves in straitened circumstances. The case files of the Repatriation Department offer an insight into how veterans and their kin survived financially. As Stephen Garton notes, however, families experiencing economic hardship are over-represented in this archive.[5] We must therefore acknowledge the case files which contain no evidence of veterans' financial distress: these are usually thinner and typically contain only a medical discharge record. 'Thin files' constitute about 25 to 30 per cent of disabled soldiers' case records, and can be interpreted as evidence that these men and their families did not suffer economic adversity.[6] In some instances, the paucity of documents may be a clue to pre-existing wealth, successful employment, an adequate pension or the financial support of other family members. While it is important to recognise the economic hardship and resourcefulness of families in poverty, we must also bring to light the experiences of families who not only struggled, but prospered financially.

THE ECONOMIC IMPACT OF WAR

In the early twentieth century, the male breadwinner's wage was the backbone of most Australian household economies. The 'household economy', however, depended on a complex mixture of income-generating activities and domestic practices that minimised expenditure. Although a professional wage was usually sufficient to maintain a middle-class household, the financial survival of working-class families often hinged on the wages of wives and older children, and a strict budget. Women were typically the domestic managers of the home. They were charged with the responsibility of carefully managing the purse-strings by shopping frugally, preparing thrifty meals, making clothes, and in some instances, earning cash in the non-formal economy by taking in laundry or child-minding.

During the war, the economic pressure on soldiers' wives and mothers intensified because enlistment often meant a drop in household income. At a time when a weekly working-class wage was between £2 and £3, the army paid a wife and child about £1/18/9½d while their breadwinner was at the front.[7] Many families struggled to maintain the standard of living to which they had been accustomed, especially middle-class households. In the absence of a civilian breadwinner's wage, soldiers' dependants adopted various financial strategies to manage their limited income, such as replacing good quality cuts of meat with 'snags' and turning to extended family networks for material aid.[8] Financial survival was a daily challenge for some, and a number of households became reliant on regular payments from patriotic funds for the duration of their soldiers' war service.

After the war, the economic struggle often continued for families of disabled soldiers. Many had high expectations of financial assistance from the government, having been reassured that they would not be disadvantaged because of their breadwinner's incapacities. During their first few months in Australia, many disabled soldiers had good reason to be optimistic about their financial outlook. Veterans were often placed on a fixed pension for six months while they regained their health, and were provided with vocational training and educational opportunities. Most returned men had an allotment of deferred army pay which usually accrued at the rate of one shilling per week, and they received a war gratuity payment of 1/6 for each day served overseas.[9] Through the War Service Homes scheme, they could apply for loans of up to £700 to build new homes.[10] They were also eligible for loans to purchase household furniture, set up a business and purchase trade tools. Repatriation benefits, loans schemes and savings initially eased disabled soldiers' economic transition back into civilian and family life. By the early 1920s, however, disabled soldiers often found that their deferred pay had run out and loan repayments had become unmanageable. Some found themselves in a poverty trap because their pension rate was reduced due to improved health, but employers were reluctant to take on workers whose physical and mental condition was less than optimal. Despite the government's promises that disabled soldiers would be financially provided for upon their return, many were unable to generate a sustainable family income, either within the pensions system or the labour market.

PENSION TROUBLES

Most disabled soldier families relied on pension support to some extent. For the kin of totally or severely incapacitated men, war pensions were the cornerstone of financial survival. Australia's war disability pension system was structured according to the 'family wage' principle established by the Harvester Judgement in 1907.[11] This landmark determination confirmed the primacy of able-bodied men as breadwinners and defined women as their dependants. The repatriation system adopted this model, and disabled soldiers were paid a pension according to their degree of impairment, with additional allowances for the upkeep of their dependants. Although the scheme purported to provide a 'family wage', the rate at which it was paid was often inadequate to support a household. In 1920, the Royal Commission on the Basic Wage recommended that a family of four required £5/16/0 to live in a 'reasonable standard of comfort'.[12] In the same year, the *Australian Soldiers' Repatriation Act* set the 100 per cent war disability pension rate at £4/2/6 per week for a comparable household.[13] This amount effectively consigned disabled soldier families to the ranks of the working poor. War disabilities, however, were worth more than the impairments of civilian life. The federal invalid pension for disabled civilians was a mere 15 shillings per week with no allowance for dependants.[14]

The 100 per cent pension provided a modest income, yet the majority of Australia's war disability pensioners were granted much less. In 1924, there were 72 760 war disability pensioners, and well over two-thirds received a partial payment of below 50 per cent. The predominance of partial pensions reflected the typical nature of war disabilities: most men were 'shattered', rather than totally incapacitated. Disabled soldiers typically experienced respiratory, circulatory and nervous system ailments, and a myriad of other internal problems, all at continued risk of deterioration. Their symptoms included 'loss of power' in limbs, the 'dragging pain' of gunshot injury, and 'periodical attacks in the chest caused from the effects of gas'. Some severely disabled men received the 'special rate' (about double the 100 per cent rate) which acknowledged their complete incapacity. Many of these veterans, however, resided in Repatriation Department hostels, and did not receive the full amount because the Department deducted about 45 per cent to cover the cost of their maintenance.

Within the pensions system, men with 'intangible' impairments were most at risk of underassessment because their level of disability was not easily reduced into administratively manageable categories.[16] Internal damage, fits, psychological disturbance and 'invisible' symptoms such as pain or 'feelings of malaise' were difficult to quantify. Yet these types of internal disabilities, more conspicuous by their invisibility than by their observability, were the norm. Moreover, disabled soldiers on partial pensions were subject to monthly medical reviews, and their payment could be reduced, to the consternation of some men. When Samuel Mattingley's pension was reduced from 75 per cent to 50 per cent in 1920, he wrote angrily to the Department of Repatriation: 'I had two pieces of metal penetrate my lung and am

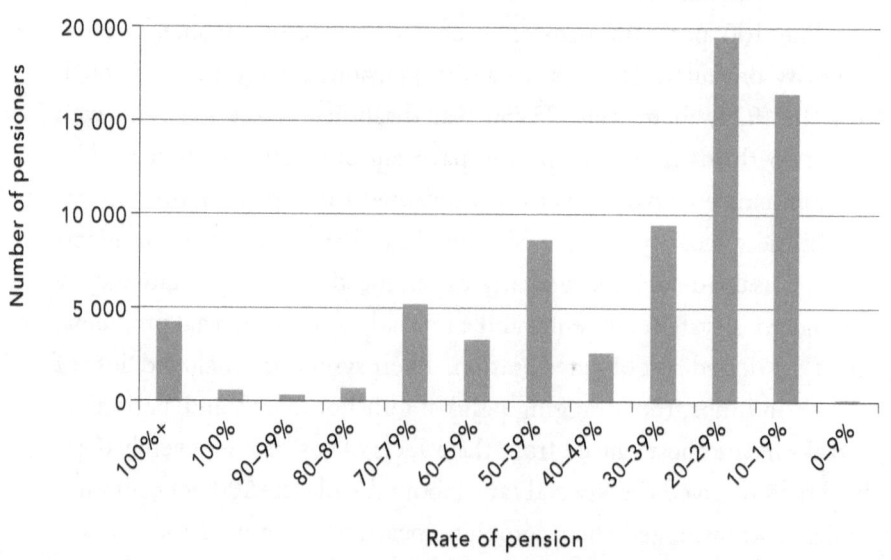

Table 3.1 The majority of disabled ex-servicemen received partial pensions, as this official data from 1924 illustrates.[15]

always liable to become worse while lads with limbs off have their trouble over'.[17] Indeed, while Australia's limbless soldiers – numbering less than 3300 – were assured of ongoing and relatively generous payment for their losses, the majority of returned men with a lack of 'obvious disablement' struggled with partial pensions that were continually subject to reassessment. Fluctuating partial pension payments did little to place men in a secure position of breadwinning: if anything, they contributed to the instability of the household economy.

Although the government lauded the generosity of the war pensions system, disabled soldiers sometimes experienced the assessment process as unjust. The role of repatriation doctors was to quantify scientifically the somatic link between a man's impairments and his war service, and provide a percentage rating. Medical boards based their decisions on clinical evidence from veterans' service records, and discounted 'constitutional' health problems or those resulting from civilian life. Yet, the attribution of impairment and the determination of the level of incapacity were not always straightforward. For example, disagreements between medical officers resulted in inconsistencies and there was considerable variation in the acceptance of shell shock (see chapter 5).[18] Furthermore, the unintentional destruction of the clinical records of the AIF in 1919 meant that official documentary medical evidence was not always available.[19] Some veterans attempted to turn the subjective nature of the system to their advantage by exaggerating their wounds to gain a higher pension.[20] Medical boards, however, were vigilant against fraud. Although the Department publicly maintained that soldiers received 'the benefit of the doubt' and many Repat staff were returned men themselves, generosity was not a feature of the system. The repatriation bureaucracy looked disapprovingly upon claims which appeared to be fraudulent, fearing that they would increase the national repatriation bill and that 'the cloud of pension' would lead veterans towards a life of idleness.[21]

PENSIONS: A FAMILY ISSUE

Although pensions were granted on the basis of wounds to a soldier's body, they constituted the means of survival for entire households – pensions were a family issue. When the Repatriation Department rejected or under-assessed a soldier's disability, it not only disavowed responsibility for an impaired body part, but effectively condemned the veteran and his kin to a future of financial hardship. During the 1920s, Mavis Floyd's family faced significant material privation as the result of an inadequate war pension. Upon enlistment, Mavis' father, Gordon, had been employed as a cleaner, but afterwards could no longer work because of physical debility. He had been reluctant to enlist because of ill health resulting from childhood rheumatic fever, but he joined up in 1916 after receiving a white feather. At the front, he suffered continual ill health, and was wounded in the knee. In 1919 he was discharged with a small partial pension for myalgia of the leg, arthritis and heart troubles. Gordon repeatedly applied for a larger pension, but was rejected on the grounds that his disabilities were caused by 'pre-existing' health problems. As evidence, the Department used a letter written in 1916 by his well-meaning brother to stop his enlistment. The family was outraged.[22] From their perspective, Gordon had been pressured to enlist and his poor health was further damaged by war. In their eyes, the Department reduced his complex history to one of mechanical physical causality. The household was never again able to reach the level of financial wellbeing that it had experienced before the war, and the continual rejection of Gordon's claim for a pension increase was an ongoing source of bitterness within the family.

Within some households, the battle for a better pension became a family obsession. Letter writing, medical assessments and visits to the Department became regular activities in the household calendar. According to Keith Falconer, his father Frank 'spent most of his spare time trying to get his pension improved'.[23] Frank Falconer sustained a severe head injury in 1916, and 'had a big steel plate in his head where they pushed his brains back in', but his chronic pain and migraine headaches were not fully recognised by the Department. Frank's wife provided emotional support to her husband as he attempted to secure pension justice. In other cases, wives personally took up the fight for a better pension, and wrote to or visited the Department to demonstrate the plight of their families. Parents of disabled soldiers also drew attention to the injustices of pensions system. Through organisations such as the Sailors' and Soldiers' Fathers Association, they rallied together and lobbied for more generous provisions.[24] Family members' interventions, however, were usually not sufficient to reverse a decision. The Department's primary relationship was with the former members of the AIF, not their relatives. It regarded soldier breadwinners as the income conduit into the family, and took no responsibility for the wellbeing of families whose pension did not stretch far enough.

Disabled soldiers and their kin despaired at the financial consequences of an ungenerous assessment. Under-pensioning not only led to financial hardship but generated anxiety within the home. Dealing with the 'Repat' was stressful because of the adversarial nature of the process.[25] For Frank Falconer's family, ongoing battles with the Department and continual financial troubles created unbearable tension within the home. Keith Falconer recalled that his parents had a loving relationship, but remembers 'dreadful arguments' about money: 'I think Mum nearly walked out at one stage … because there was no money, and he'd gone broke on the farm, and he wasn't on the right pension, on a *proper* pension'.[26] Many families were dispirited at the pension assessment process and felt betrayed by the government. The Repatriation Department employed narrow definitions of incapacity, ignored veterans' socio-economic context, and discounted factors which led to unemployment, such as discrimination against disabled workers. By assessing the body of the soldier alone, the broader moral obligation of the state to the domestic world of men and their families was all but removed from the assessment process. In 1919, one 'rejected' disabled soldier darkly observed that his family would have been better off had he died on the battlefield.[27] Indeed, the fixed pensions provided to dependants of the war dead provided greater financial security than the partial pensions subject to reassessment paid to the disabled.

EMPLOYMENT TROUBLES

Most disabled soldiers supplemented their pensions by paid employment. But veterans often struggled to find work suitable for their physical and mental limitations. In the immediate postwar years, the high unemployment rate also increased their difficulties. Between 1920 and 1921 the unemployment rate jumped from 6.5 per cent to just over 11 per cent, partly as a result of thousands of returned men looking for jobs.[28] Throughout the 1920s, unemployment fluctuated between 7 and 11 per cent, and disabled soldiers were often pushed to the fringes of the labour market.[29] War disabilities affected each man's employability differently. One-eyed soldiers were unable to undertake work that required them to judge distances. Deafness was a drawback for men trained as shop assistants. Some facially wounded men found that their disfigurements barred them from jobs that brought them into contact with the public, yet others successfully pursued careers in teaching.[30] Skilled tradesmen sometimes lost their trade due to their impaired dexterity. As one carpenter observed, the gunshot wound to his right thumb was 'a great hindrance' in his calling.[31] The problem for most disabled soldiers was not that they could not work, but that many could only undertake certain classes of work.

The government, however, did not legislate for the mandatory employment of disabled soldiers.[32] Instead, it espoused a policy of 'preference' and encouraged employers to hire returned men over civilians. Yet, 'preference' applied equally to all classes of returned soldier. Employers were not instructed to show greater favour to

This cartoon highlights the plight of disabled soldiers, who were not always welcomed back by former employers. *Remnants from Randwick*, no. 2, 1919. Image courtesy of Special Collections, Baillieu Library, University of Melbourne.

disabled soldiers, and many preferred not to hire 'sub-efficients'. Businesses could legitimately refuse to appoint disabled soldiers on the grounds that they were medically unfit to do the work required. In an age preoccupied with industrial efficiency, employers feared that productivity would be undermined by workers with 'headaches, nerves and chest troubles' and limb joints that were 'apt to slip out at times'.[33] While some employers were accommodating towards disabled soldiers, the lack of legislation to compel employers to hire them meant that they were a vulnerable population of workers. By the early 1920s, it was clear that the disabilities of returned soldiers were less a badge of honour than a sign that they were unfit for employment.

At greatest risk of unemployment were partially disabled soldiers only able to do 'light' labour. Partial disabilities were particularly devastating for working-class men and labourers who depended on strong functioning bodies for their livelihoods. Such men constituted the majority of disabled soldiers, as over 80 per cent of the AIF were tradesmen, labourers, or had a 'country calling' prior to enlistment.[34] 'Mild' conditions, such as lung damage, meant that although not severely impaired, such men were often unable to complete a day's work. Larger employers, such as city councils, sometimes reserved 'light work' positions for disabled soldiers. The lack of such positions, however, remained one of the biggest problems facing disabled men. Some retrained for 'light' desk jobs but were not always successfully employed because a number did not have the educational background or aptitude for administrative work.

Many disabled soldiers found employment in insecure, low status jobs or outside the formal economy. Some accepted inferior conditions and worked for employers who illegally deducted an amount equal to their pension payment from their wages.[35] Sadly, Australian trade unions provided little support for disabled soldiers, for despite their rhetoric of solidarity, they showed a reluctance to employ disabled men, including their own members.[36] Lift attending was one of the main avenues of employment for disabled soldiers without a trade or education. Some disabled soldiers worked as kiosk vendors and street musicians, and some begged. Blind soldiers sold their poetry printed on cards to passers-by.[37] Severely disabled soldiers worked in sheltered industries established by the Red Cross, such as the Disabled Soldiers' Weaving Industry, Disabled Soldiers' Pottery Factory and Furniture Factory.[38] Other men established their own small businesses in traditional trades, such as boot-repairing, which meant they could work at their own pace. Such artisan-workers, however, often found it difficult to compete against mechanised businesses. For example, by 1929 blind soldiers trained to repair boots by the traditional hand-stitching method found it hard to gain employment, as practically all cobbling work had become machine-based.[39]

ECONOMIC SURVIVAL STRATEGIES

For many disabled soldiers, becoming a family breadwinner was an unachievable goal, and they struggled to support their households. Families, however, were not passive witnesses to their financial demise; they pulled together and adapted to their circumstances as best they could. Some sympathetic relatives employed disabled soldiers in family businesses on the understanding that they could take plenty of time off for ill health.[40] Other families received ongoing financial assistance from relatives, or moved in with extended family.[41] In some households, wives and older children undertook part-time work, and the household economy was based on multiple incomes. Within the home, wives also cut costs by making clothes, and accepting 'seconds' or 'off-cuts' from family members who worked in food or clothing industries. Such strategies for managing financial hardship were not unique to disabled soldiers. Co-operative family models of economic survival were evident in the households of non-disabled and disabled civilian men. For veterans who had been promised economic security after their return, however, financial dependence upon family members represented a loss of independence, an ideal so stridently promoted by the Repatriation Department.

Within repatriation rhetoric, wives were officially classified as 'dependants'. In reality, women's labours could make the difference between subsistence and destitution for the family even if this was not always publicly apparent.[42] During the 1920s, disabled soldiers' wives were often the economic lynchpins of their households. They were domestic managers, financial planners, wage earners and, in some cases, breadwinners. In the immediate postwar period, wives of disabled soldiers managed their household economies in a difficult macro-economic context. During the war, the cost of living increased dramatically, and some official sources estimated it had risen by up to 60 or 70 per cent.[43] The retail price of food and groceries rose sharply in metropolitan centres, and wages fell behind the cost of living.[44] These structural economic difficulties increased the financial challenges of families whose disabled soldier was under-pensioned or inadequately employed.

Women's role as financial managers varied greatly according to the varying incomes and spending patterns of their households. Pensions were paid fortnightly, and wives had to make judicious decisions about the expenditure of money, plan for uncertain work patterns, and manage unanticipated expenses. They budgeted around periods of lost employment income due to their husbands' ill health and responded to the sudden loss of income if soldiers' pensions were reduced or terminated. Wives of disabled soldiers faced a tremendous amount of pressure to make ends meet financially from day to day. The economic importance of disabled soldiers' wives, however, was seldom acknowledged in official and public commentary. In its publications, the Repatriation Department depicted disabled soldiers as men on a journey towards becoming independent breadwinners. When the financial contribution of their wives to their households was mentioned, it was often described as mere 'assistance'.

The first measure taken by wives was reducing expenditure within the household. In 1926, the Mead family lived on a pension of £4/5/6, but in late 1927 the amount was reduced to £2/2/0 when Richard Mead entered a repatriation sanatorium. In this instance, his pension was reduced by the Repatriation Department because of its policy of withholding a portion of the payment while a soldier was resident in a repatriation facility. The drop in Richard's pension exacerbated the financial pressure on his wife, who was left to pay for expenses, many of which (rent, rates, schooling costs) remained the same regardless of his absence. Mrs Mead described her circumstances to the Tubercular Soldiers' Aid Society:

> ... we are not having proper food – I have dispensed with the weekend joint for weeks now, trying in all ways to lessen expenses – but it is all too big an undertaking to try & pull up back rent & pay rates which have now started – The children are needing warmer clothes ... our position is more serious than it has ever been & I have been in very poor health myself lately.[45]

Iris Mead saw it as her responsibility to 'lessen expenses' and skilfully stretch the pension as far as it would go. Her first austerity measure was to reduce the amount and quality of food she prepared, a step that compromised the health of her children. The family was in arrears with the rent, money which Iris perhaps spent on more pressing household essentials. We do not know if she took other measures to supplement the family's pension income. She may have pawned items of value such as war medals and wedding rings, gone into debt with shop keepers, or grown vegetables for sale.[46] The Mead family had been scraping by financially for almost two years, but despite Iris' best efforts they could not pay their way. We do know, however, that the family was in debt to the State Bank of South Australia for £9/15/8 and was being threatened with legal proceedings.[47]

As well as managing the domestic finances, wives of disabled soldiers also operated home-based businesses with their husbands. Indeed, the Repatriation Department often factored in the value of wives' labour when it assessed applications for business loans. In 1918, Bertram Partridge applied to the Repatriation Department for assistance to establish a small poultry business. Bertram was a totally blind soldier on a 100 per cent pension, and his application was viewed favourably because of the prospect of his wife's support. The departmental officer noted that Mrs Partridge was a 'very capable woman' who was already assisting her husband to keep a small number of fowls, and granted the generous sum of £130/4/2.[48] The establishment of cottage industries was attractive to disabled soldiers because they could determine the nature of the work and structure their daily schedule around their physical limitations. We shall never know the extent to which Mrs Partridge assisted her husband, or whether she had responsibility for certain aspects of the business, such as bookkeeping. Nonetheless, such home-based businesses allowed disabled

Digger M. Tremain

† WHO WAS BLINDED IN THE WAR,

is now open to receive your razors and scissors. Razors ground and set, 1/6; scissors, 6d. Country orders promptly attended to. Orders may be left at Messrs. Lawrence & Levy, King William street, or at 22 Ballville street, Prospect. A trial solicited.

In some instances, disabled soldiers became self-employed so they could work at home with the assistance of family members. *Diggers' Gazette*, 7 July 1922. Image courtesy of the State Library of South Australia.

soldiers to engage the unpaid labour of their wives, and still be seen as independent breadwinners in the eyes of others. Publicly, disabled soldiers' wives usually concealed the extent of their own contribution to the enterprise. In the early twentieth century it was more respectable for women to be dependent on a breadwinner than engaged in wage earning activities. Some disabled soldiers, however, could not have achieved 'independence' without their wives. From the outside, such family units appeared to comprise a breadwinner and dependants, while a complex dynamic of economic interdependence was actually at play.

Some female 'dependants' of disabled soldiers did enter the external workforce as breadwinners, but little evidence remains of their working lives. We do know that they received significantly lower wages than male workers on the 'family wage'. The Harvester Judgement recommended that women's wages were set at about 54 per cent of the male wage in most industries, even if a woman was the primary breadwinner. This meant that the female relatives of disabled soldiers could not realistically hope to sustain their households financially through employment. During the 1920s, Archie Duggan, a bachelor, lived in Adelaide with his two sisters and his invalid mother. His tuberculosis prevented him from working, and he had been rejected for a war pension. The family relied heavily on the income that his two sisters generated outside the home, but this was insufficient, and in the late 1920s, Archie turned to the Tubercular Soldiers' Aid Society for assistance:

> At present there are four of us at home, and our total income is £4 per week – 30/- from me [from a private superannuation fund], 30/- from my sister Audrey, and £1 from Betty who is teaching at Moonta. 30/- of this goes for rent, so that £2/10 has to keep four people in food, besides firing, electric-light, gas, water and district council rates, and land tax.[49]

Archie and his mother were both dependent on his sisters' wages. Audrey and Betty were clearly carrying the burden of breadwinning, yet because they were classed as 'dependants' within the wage system their earnings were inadequate to support the household. Had Archie's siblings been male rather than female, the family's collective income may have been substantially higher.

SOLDIER SETTLER FAMILIES

Economic interdependence characterised the household economies of disabled soldier families in towns and cities, as well as in rural Australia. In country areas, soldier settler households were particularly dependent on a collective family approach to income generation. During the war, state and federal governments established the Soldier Settlement Scheme to reward returned soldiers with the opportunity to attain 'landed independence'.[50] Under the scheme, nearly 40 000 returned men were granted blocks of land on the basis of an attractive long-term loan agreement. There was great public support for the scheme, and many believed that 'every soldier should get a chance if he desired to go on the land, especially if he was suffering from war injuries, it being supposed that his health would benefit by living in the country'.[51] The prospect of becoming a self-employed farmer was appealing to disabled soldiers who struggled to earn a living within the mainstream labour market, and they applied in significant numbers. Only a small number of applicants were rejected on the grounds of impairment, and the archives are replete with qualification certificates issued to gassed, shell-shocked, and physically impaired veterans. The experiences of settler families varied from state to state, but Victoria provides a useful case study. In that state, the files of the Closer Settlement Board indicate that as many as 40 per cent of all settlers were disabled.[52]

In 1924, the *Limbless Soldier* magazine declared that a 'capable and hard-working wife' was the 'most valuable asset' a disabled man could have on a farm.[53] At the heart of the soldier settlement scheme was the 'family production unit'.[54] Soldier settlers, both able-bodied and disabled, relied heavily upon the labour of their wives and children as they tried to make a success of their holdings. Wives not only managed the domestic sphere, and bore and raised children, but undertook a range of labouring, agricultural and business tasks. The Closer Settlement Board valued women's capacity to compensate for their husband's ill health, something which referees emphasised: '[The applicant] served 4 years at the war during which he developed trench fever, which interferes with his working at regular wages … His wife, who is personally well known to me … was brought up on a farm and is a very capable woman, and I have no doubt that between them they can easily manage a small dairy farm'.[55] Despite the assistance of a wife, soldiers' disabilities and ill health could ultimately lead to the failure of their farms. For families, this could be disastrous because they could not leave easily without paying their debts, and 'light' jobs were scarce in rural areas. In such cases, wives shared the mental torture of debt and an uncertain future as their husbands' health deteriorated to the point where they could no longer work.

The Watson family's struggles during the early 1920s offer an insight into the challenges faced by soldier settler households headed by disabled veterans. In 1919, John Watson applied to the Closer Settlement Board for land, optimistically reporting that his own health was 'fair'.[56] He had been discharged from the army on the grounds of 'medical unfitness' and was receiving a small war disability pension. Despite John's ill health, the Board was impressed with reports that he had previously been a dairy farmer and was 'a conscientious and reliable & a thoroughly good hand with horses and machinery'.[57] He was declared 'fit for land' and granted 55 acres (22 ha) in Dandenong. As in so many cases, character references formed the basis of the decision, rather than a realistic assessment of a soldier's physical capacity to become a farmer. By 1922 Watson's health had declined and he was admitted to repatriation hospitals in Melbourne and Bendigo. His wife, Mary, took over running the block, and her manual labour and agricultural management skills became crucial to the maintenance of the farm. Her efforts were praised by the Inspector, and their eight children, ranging in age between five and eighteen, probably assisted her with milking and market gardening tasks.[58] Sadly, John Watson died during his hospitalisation. After his death Mary reported that she was 'unable to carry on the block' alone, but departure meant that she stood to inherit a debt of over £550. She angrily wrote to the Board describing how John had 'bravely & untiringly with such a sick body … struggled to meet every responsibility' but failed 'through the "Pleuro" and illness'.[59] Mrs Watson was relieved of her debt to the Board, but the family left the property with nothing.

The Watsons' particularly heartbreaking story illustrates the ways in which war disability affected some families' capacity to make a success of their blocks. We must remember that the Soldier Settlement Scheme often proved disastrous for able-bodied veterans for a combination of reasons, including small blocks, the inexperience of settlers, lack of capital investment and falling produce prices.[60] For disabled soldiers, however, the difficulties were amplified, because many were simply physically and mentally unfit for heavy farm work. Progress with basic land clearing and farm work was slowed because men were unable to undertake strenuous labour. Periods spent in hospital caused settlers to fall into arrears with their payments. Some disabled soldiers had to carry the additional expense of employing men to assist with heavy work, and many eventually requested to be relieved of the block due to health problems. In 1921, James Inman applied to give up his land because the repetitive action of using a plough was further damaging his 'burnt hands caused by an explosion' during the war.[61] In 1925, the Report of the Royal Commission on Soldier Settlement in Victoria identified war disability as significant among the causes of the scheme's failure.[62]

STORIES OF PROSPERITY

In urban labour markets and on soldier settlement farms, many disabled soldier families faced bleak financial prospects – but not all. A significant proportion of disabled soldiers were able to earn a family wage and support their households, despite their impairments. Disabled soldiers with professional or clerical skills often became good providers. Indeed, in 1925, the Repatriation Department noted that disabled soldiers who were able to pursue sedentary or intellectual occupations did not feel 'the handicap of their disability' as greatly as the unskilled worker, artisan, or those on the land.[63] Despite the loss of an arm, EJ Holloway managed to become a catering manager for the Melbourne-based Coles department store, and by 1931 was reported to be in a job that paid £1000 a year.[64] Disabled soldiers with specialist skills also fared well. In 1917, Henry Stone returned to work as a sugar cane inspector at the Colonial Sugar Refining Company (CSR) in Queensland, and was given a new position better suited to his poor health.[65] Despite his ongoing health problems, CSR was keen to retain Henry because there was a shortage of skilled sugar workers. Men sometimes benefited from both employment and pension income, as pension payments were not reduced according to men's earnings. Employment, however, usually prompted the Department to reassess veterans' level of 'incapacity'.

About half the fathers of my interview informants were engaged in professional employment or business, and experienced little difficulty in supporting their families during the 1920s.[66] Margaret Cramond's family did not suffer great financial deprivation as a result of her father's war disability. Alfred Plane lost one leg below the knee at Pozières, but successfully resumed work as an insurance agent on his return. His physical loss made relatively little difference to his employment prospects, as he had a strong prewar track record in that industry. Indeed, as Margaret told me, not many people would have known he had a missing limb, as the loss of the leg below the knee was reasonably easy to conceal with a prosthesis.[67] Alfred's steady work with a large insurance firm meant that the family was quite comfortable. In rural Australia, a number of disabled soldier settlers were also financially successful, especially those who entered into the scheme with a non-disabled family member. Harold Wallace was granted a property near Traralgon in Victoria in 1920, despite being on a pension for shortness of breath and pains in the chest due to gassing.[68] His file does not record the demise of the farming business, perhaps because he jointly took up the block with his brother, an experienced farmer, who was not a returned soldier.

Some disabled soldier families had a bright economic outlook. This was, however, occasionally due to the assistance of relatives, rather than the soldier's own capacity to generate an income. Ongoing material aid provided by a wealthier branch of the family could prevent a family's descent into destitution. In the late 1920s, Betsy Burchett's father, John Godber Brown, developed a war neurosis and was unable to work. He became a permanent resident of the Bundoora Rest Home. Betsy explained to me that after her father's hospitalisation, she and her mother went to live with her maternal grandparents in Box Hill, and were financially supported by a bachelor uncle who had a well-paid position as a sales representative at a butter company. Her father's brother, who was the general manager of the Myer department store in Bendigo, also provided monetary assistance. Betsy recalled a middle-class childhood in which she wanted for nothing. She was given horse riding lessons, tennis lessons and was lavished with attention from both sides of the family in her father's absence – 'I was absolutely spoiled by everybody!'[69] Betsy and her mother became 'dependants' of the Brown family, an arrangement made possible by the extended family's wealth and goodwill.

DEPENDENCE ON CHARITY

While some families received material assistance from relatives, others were unable to call upon the resources of kin, and turned to charitable organisations. For disabled soldiers and their families locked in a cycle of ill health and intermittent income, charity was an important second tier of welfare. Men and their dependants could approach a range of organisations including the Red Cross, the Centre for Soldiers' Wives and Mothers, veterans' groups, and patriotic funds. Those soldiers who could turn to disability-specific organisations were at a distinct financial advantage over those limited to applying to generic charities. Organisations such as the Limbless Soldiers' Association (LSA) were well organised and able to raise funds which they channelled to 'amelioration cases'. Some families received weekly payments which supplemented their pensions indefinitely.

Requesting assistance, however, was a shameful experience for some men, as it indicated that they had failed to become self-reliant. When George Goodwin applied to the Tubercular Soldiers' Aid Society for assistance in 1926, he declared his abhorrence of handouts – 'God how the word charity stinks in my nostrels'.[70] For Goodwin it was humiliating to apply for assistance because it meant admitting defeat. The stigma of charity saw disabled soldiers' wives commonly take the leading role in asking for help. The dependence of women on welfare was more naturally a 'feminised' state, and they could approach a charity without the shame of being considered a failed breadwinner. The dishonour of male charity was such that the Red Cross in Sydney designated the wives of disabled soldiers the primary recipients of assistance. Its After-Care Department was located adjacent to the Rose Hall convalescent home and provided clothing, food parcels and medicines to the wives and children of disabled soldiers.[71] It dealt exclusively with dependants of disabled soldiers as the gateway into the household. Through this structure, the Red Cross removed the burden of accepting charity from disabled soldiers, and made it the responsibility of their dependants. It was a solution that allowed financial assistance to flow respectably into the whole family unit, and allowed a façade of manly independence to be preserved, even if the reality was otherwise.

Charitable organisations, such as the Red Cross, and disabled soldier associations, acknowledged and responded to the collective plight of entire families. By contrast, the Repatriation Department showed little interest in the welfare of veterans' family members, apart from the fortnightly payment of dependants' pensions. The Department's role was to respond to individual veterans within the provisions of the *Australian Soldiers' Repatriation Act*. It deemed that the appropriate level of pensions and benefits for each man could be mathematically calculated upon the extent of the damage to his body, regardless of his family context. Charities did not assess applications with reference to such narrow grounds, but considered the broader social circumstances of the veteran and his kin. The Red Cross explicitly welcomed officially 'unaccepted' men, and was prepared to give them the benefit of the doubt as to whether their illness was caused by the war. Charitable organisations responded to families who fell through the cracks of the official war pension system. In 1922, the Red Cross After-Care Department in Sydney saw an average of 150 families each week, many of whom had 'heart-breaking stories'.[72] The wives of disabled soldiers were described as 'old-young women', aged by worry and financial strain.[73]

Some disabled soldier families could not afford basic household expenses. A partial pension did not stretch very far, and charities such as the Red Cross provided 'temporary relief grants' as well as milk, food and warm clothing, which the families of disabled soldiers were simply unable to provide.[74] Large families headed by middle-aged men who married before the war were particularly vulnerable as they struggled to pay for the basic needs of seven, eight or nine growing children. Expensive but essential purchases placed a strain on the household purse. At the beginning of the year, families applied for assistance to purchase children's school books. Between April and July, they lodged applications for winter clothing, new shoes, undergarments and blankets.[75] In 1924, a good quality man's overcoat could cost up to £4/4/0, a sum equivalent to some household's weekly pension payment. Christmas time brought with it the burden of children's expectations: 'I have not any money to get them any toys or clothes' wrote Mrs Edwina Gleadle to the Tubercular Soldiers' Aid Society.[76]

Disabled soldiers often applied to charities while they waited for a decision about a war pension. Men often had to wait for weeks or months for a judgment. Some families turned to charity after an official decision to reduce the breadwinner's pension. In 1926 Thomas Reid and his family were just surviving on a 100 per cent pension of £3/10 but the following year his pension was reduced to 75 per cent, and he despaired that the family was 'unable to manage on that amount' at all.[77] Some families looked to charities to assist with the payment of debt. Rent, rate and tax bills that came all at once quickly became debts that could not be repaid on a small and unstable income. In 1926, John McMaster, an unpensioned disabled soldier, owed his sister £15, the grocery store £4/19/7 and an unknown creditor £10.[78] Applicants in arrears to their landlords turned to charities for the 'payment of rent for a period'.[79] 'Rejected' veterans asked for help with private physicians' bills, because the Repatriation Department was not obliged to pay for their medical treatment. Sometimes charitable agencies provided monetary assistance in the form of a loan rather than a gift, which then itself became a debt for which the veteran sought further charitable assistance.[80]

In the early 1920s, many disabled soldiers were young men marrying and starting families. For these couples, a war disability pension did not adequately cover the costs associated with pregnancy, the arrival of children or raising a young family. In 1920, Mrs Violet Fraser was six months pregnant when she applied to the Centre for Soldiers' Wives and Mothers. Her husband, Ernest, had been wounded in the eyes and ears, and was not working constantly as he was 'not strong'.[81] As the birth drew nearer, it appears that Ernest's sporadic income and small pension would not meet the costs of setting up the home for a new child, and expenses such as a cot and baby clothes. While the details of Violet's own family are only sketched in her file, it is possible that her parents' ability to offer financial support was limited because both her brothers had been killed at the war, possibly leaving widowed sisters-in-law also in need of assistance. As children like the Fraser offspring grew, they could become a drain upon the already stretched resources of disabled soldier families. During the 1920s, childhood conditions such as infantile paralysis and scarlet fever were common, and the cost of treating a child's illness could easily place a low-income family in debt. The Red Cross After-Care Department observed that it often assisted larger families of disabled soldiers, particularly when one or more children were affected by illnesses.[82]

It is significant that although the Repatriation Department was aware of the extent of charity received by disabled soldier families, it steadfastly refused to provide material aid to ex-servicemen's family units on the basis of need. Despite the Department's insistence that 'there is no end to the profitable things a disabled man can do', it was happy to let the charitable sector provide thousands of pounds of relief to families who could not manage financially.[83] Charities were not part of the formal repatriation system, yet the government relied heavily upon them to provide welfare and support to ex-servicemen and their families. Ironically, the Department's tough measures to encourage financial self-sufficiency meant that a number of veterans found themselves dependent on charity and became subject to the social stigma associated with 'hand outs', which the Department's own rhetoric about 'manly independence' had only served to reinforce.

Receiving charity brought with it certain obligations. For disabled soldiers and their families, a good reputation and favourable relationships with charitable agencies were paramount – it ensured their means of financial survival. Patriotic funds, charities and disabled soldier organisations alike were keen that recipients did not take advantage of the assistance provided to them, and often sent official visitors to the homes of applicants. The care with which charities and patriotic funds investigated the genuineness of applicants also reassured donors that their contributions were being prudently distributed. The Red Cross investigated each case thoroughly to ensure there was 'no danger of overlapping' with the aid provided by other organisations.[84] The Centre for Soldiers' Wives and Mothers sought to establish the respectability of applicants and the way they managed the household – 'found the place neat & tidy'; 'children well behaved'.[85] Wives were under some pressure to demonstrate that they were good housekeepers to maximise the likelihood of benevolence. Disabled soldiers and their wives wrote letters of appreciation to charitable organisations to shore up their reputation in case of future need. These letters were often obeisant in tone, and reflected the indebtedness of the recipient: 'I cannot express just how grateful I am for your kind consideration'; 'I trust you will not think I am asking for too much'.[86] Even when the claim was rejected, applicants extended their thanks for being considered and for 'past kindnesses'.[87] Within the rights-based pensions system, expressions of personal gratitude had little significance, but within the world of philanthropy they were important signifiers of respectability and deservedness.

FAILED BREADWINNERS

Reliance on charity was experienced as a sign of personal failure by many disabled soldiers. It indicated that they had been unable to live up to the ideal of 'manly independence'. For some, the pressure to achieve economic self-reliance and the weight of their own perceived failure was so great that it led to the undoing of their will. In June 1920, a returned officer, Eli Bugby, was found hanging from the rafters of his home in the wealthy Sydney suburb of Double Bay. At the coroner's inquest, Bugby's wife reported that her husband 'was gassed, and sustained shell shock at the war, and had been distressed because his employers would not reinstate him'.[88] Bugby was on a pension of £2/17/6 per week (a rate of about 50 per cent) to support his wife and child, and had apparently been waiting to hear the outcome of his soldier settlement application.[89] For a middle-class officer with a young family, the prospect of economic and social failure was perhaps too great an indignity to bear. In Bugby's delicate mental state, the idea that disabled soldiers simply needed to work harder to recover their 'industrial productivity' was less an inspiring promise than a demoralising confirmation that he had failed to become a self-supporting citizen. Bugby's troubles in gaining employment and securing an adequate pension had a shared effect on the economic and emotional life of the household. The family slid into economic difficulty together, and jointly experienced the humiliating decline in their standard of living. Even after death, the legacy of Eli Bugby's financial woes remained with the family. Mrs Bugby was left to raise her child without the assistance of a war pension, as her husband's suicide was not officially attributed to his war service.

In 1927, the Repatriation Department reflected that Australia's 'generous repatriation provisions' had ensured that most disabled soldiers had achieved an 'economic position to assume the responsibility of matrimony'.[90] While some disabled soldiers were able to provide well for their families, many others struggled to become breadwinners and their families lived in an economic twilight. Financial self-reliance was promoted as the goal of rehabilitation, but the inadequacies of the war pensions system and the resistance of the labour market to impaired workers made it difficult for a substantial number of disabled soldiers to generate sufficient income to independently support a household. Disabled soldier families were caught in a public policy paradox. Their wellbeing was purportedly assured by the capacity of their breadwinner to achieve 'manly independence'. Yet, if a veteran could not generate a sufficient income, the Department would not supplement his family's earnings and his kin suffered because they had no status other than 'dependants' under the legislation. Families who were unable to survive on their disabled breadwinner's earnings took measures within their own household economies to manage their financial burdens collectively. Their economic arrangements revolved around a model of interdependence, rather than the breadwinner/dependant model that was central to the repatriation system and formal wage labour structures. Within disabled soldier households, the financial burdens of war disability were typically shared and managed collectively, even if to the outside world it appeared that the disabled soldier was on a journey towards 'independence'.

CHAPTER 4

family relationships

> The women of Australia gave their men to help our country, and us all, they paid the price then in months of anxiety and often in distress, and are still paying the price in suffering from the effects of war ...
>
> Australian Red Cross Society, NSW, 1926.[1]

In March 1929, Miss Edwina Leonard wrote to the Repatriation Department describing the burden of care that had fallen to her family as of result of her brother's war disabilities. Jim Leonard had enlisted in September 1915 and was invalided home in 1917 with shell shock, severe trench foot and gassed lungs. Upon his return, he was 'very thin & nervy', coughing 'very badly' and a few weeks after his arrival he had a 'general breakdown'.[2] Over the following years, Jim experienced recurring physical and mental difficulties and struggled to recover his health. For much of the time, Jim lived in th family home, being cared for by his parents and sister, although during severe 'attacks' he was admitted to repatriation facilities for treatment. Edwina explained to the Department that her mother was Jim's primary caregiver and had 'treated him constantly from the time of his discharge'. Mrs Leonard developed a regimen of home therapies for Jim, including 'mustard feet baths & eucalyptus massage', and prepared 'the most nourishing & fattening foods' to build up his strength. Jim was not always an easy patient, and 'walked about at night in all seasons' which only exacerbated his chest condition. Sometimes they woke to find him 'out in the yard in his pyjamas', and brought him in to bed. The demands of home care were significant and ongoing, and Mrs Leonard had 'done little else but treat him' in the twelve years since his discharge.

Edwina Leonard's letter tells us about the lives of family carers who ministered to disabled soldiers on a daily basis. It candidly describes the personal responses and emotional adjustment of family members, and outlines the practical rituals of care that underpinned the life of these households. Importantly, it draws our attention to the interdependent family relationships within which disabled soldiers lived, and offers insight into the ways in which war disability could alter kin relations. The practical and emotional labour of such family members was largely absent in official discussions of war disability, and not widely reported in the public domain. While the Department proudly celebrated the sacrifices of disabled soldiers, it rarely recognised the sacrifices of those who took on the responsibility of their care in the home. The effects of war disability on family life and the provision of care by kin were often invisible to the outside world. Indeed, as one commentator noted, this was 'the part we do not see'.[3] Although repatriation authorities provided pensions, medical treatment and hospitals for disabled soldiers, in reality much of the practical and emotional burden of care fell to family members within the domestic sphere, particularly wives, mothers and sisters.

This chapter considers the effects of war disability on family relationships, and explores how it shaped the emotional lives of disabled soldiers and their kin within the home. Disablement placed caregiving demands upon kin, transformed family members' roles, and altered families' collective emotional worlds. As psychologists have observed, war disability has the capacity to shape and disrupt 'normal family relations'.[4] Many disabled soldiers looked to their families to provide vital practical, social and emotional support, and in some instances were profoundly reliant upon relatives within the private haven of the home. As the years passed, the demands of caregiving had a significant impact on disabled soldiers' family relationships, and often had a personal cost for family members. Yet families' experiences went largely unrecognised in official and public forums. Although family members' unpaid work was vital to the wellbeing of disabled soldiers, the Repatriation Department had no obligation to acknowledge or support kin carers. Moreover, ex-servicemen's dependence upon their families was at odds with the ideal of 'manly independence' espoused by the Department.

During and after the war, the Department did little to validate the family home as a site of repatriation for disabled soldiers. Indeed, in wider public discourse, it was Red Cross Voluntary Aids (VAs) – not the wives or mothers of disabled soldiers – who became the face of feminine caregiving for Australia's veterans.[5] Yet there were thousands of un-uniformed wives and mothers who laboured as unpaid caregivers within the home, and whose healing work with their disabled loved ones had no recognisable public face. Like VAs, many female family carers were selfless and dutiful, and embodied ideals of nurturing womanhood. Unlike their institution-based sisters, however, they were motivated less by 'patriotic duty' than familial obligation, affection and necessity. Importantly, their daily work had no clear beginning or end and they received no official support or acknowledgment for their labours. Home-based caregiving allowed families to live together and offered them the chance to develop and sustain their emotional ties. But in some instances, the strain of caregiving over many years ultimately took a toll on carers' own emotional and physical health. For kin were not just carers: they were also witnesses to the impact of war upon their loved one's body over time, and participants in a collective struggle to secure the interdependent wellbeing of every family member.

HOME AS A LOCUS OF CARE

Most disabled soldiers valued the personal support provided by their families within their homes. If given a choice, they preferred to remain with their wife and family rather than reside in repatriation homes or hospitals. Institutional life separated men from their loved ones, and prevented them from participating in the rituals, routines and exchanges of daily household life. Absence meant that men were not immediately involved in the daily affairs of their household, and could not take up their role as its head. In hospitals and hostels, disabled soldiers found themselves in all-male environments, surrounded by ex-servicemen whose spirits were dampened by illness, or who were close to death. Patients and visitors observed that the Graythwaite home for severely disabled ex-servicemen in Sydney had a 'demoralising effect' on its residents because 'head cases', the bedridden, and men with 'alcoholic failings' were all housed together.[6] There was little privacy in shared rooms, and veterans passed the day in the company of men whose behaviour or outlook may have been disturbing. At home, disabled soldiers were part of the family, not patients, and could observe and engage in the daily goings-on from their beds or the settee. In institutions, disabled soldiers were removed from the heartbeat of the home, and could not participate actively in the life of their families. Men missed dinnertime conversations, the visits of friends, and watching their children playing in the back yard.

Disabled soldiers who required specialist medical care and were unable to live at home maintained their family relationships during visiting hours. In the ward, 'home' came to the soldier as relatives shared family and community news, and kept men informed about the welfare of the household and involved in the decision-making. If the hospital was not close to the family home, wives and children were faced with long journeys. In the 1920s, most families did not own a car and public transport routes to convalescent facilities were not always direct. In 1920, Lady Munro-Ferguson, the patroness of the Red Cross, personally intervened in the case of an English war bride

Some severely disabled soldiers were unable to live with their families and resided in 'Anzac Hostels'. This photograph shows two patients in the grounds of the Glenelg Anzac Hostel, Adelaide, with nurses and visitors, c. 1925. Australian War Memorial negative number P03845.007.

whose husband was required to 'lie up for two years' with a 'T.B. spine' at Melbourne's Austin hospital in the northern suburb of Heidelberg.[7] Mrs Dickenson lived across town in Caulfield and faced over an hour's journey to visit him, or the prospect of breaking up the home and moving closer to Heidelberg. Lady Munro-Ferguson arranged for Mr Dickenson to remain at the Caulfield Hospital in the vicinity of their home, rather than being transferred, noting that 'he will be much happier and much nearer his wife'.[8]

The proximity of family was very important to 'cot cases' permanently confined to Anzac Hostels. Phillip Isaacs, a resident at the Glenelg hostel in Adelaide, was anxious to have 'the comfort of his family living near him' and initiated the purchase of a new home close by.[9] Isaacs was bedridden as a result of a gunshot wound to the spine and had originally been treated at the Keswick military hospital. While at Keswick, Isaacs had purchased a home in the suburb of Norwood. From there it was easy for his wife and children to make regular visits, and Isaacs was occasionally transported the short distance home by ambulance. Once he was transferred to Glenelg, however, Isaacs' wife and children faced a much longer journey from east to west Adelaide. Isaacs craved to reside nearer his family. For a paralysed man, the increased geographic gulf that separated him from his family must surely have compounded his sense of powerlessness. Sadly, the bank would not assist him to purchase a new property closer to Glenelg.

FAMILIES' CAREGIVING LABOURS

While some disabled soldiers resided temporarily or permanently in repatriation hostels, most disabled soldiers lived at home. Veterans lived in diversely configured family settings and their care was often a collective effort that involved the practical and 'emotional labour' of a range of family members.[10] After years of absence at the war, disabled soldiers were sometimes a constant presence in the home as a result of injury, invalidism or disability-related unemployment. Men often depended upon family members for nursing care and physical assistance. Yet the domestic labours of kin were rendered invisible within official repatriation rhetoric, which insisted that the role of families was to stand behind the disabled soldier and stimulate 'self-dependence' in the home environment. Repatriation literature insisted that families encourage veterans on their journey towards manly independence, and not undermine their ambition by smothering them with pity. In 1919, the Repatriation Department declared that families of the incapacitated 'must be sensible and urge the man to get back on the job'.[11] Some rehabilitation experts even argued that 'sympathising relatives and friends' actually lessened men's success in civilian life.[12] In reality, however, those closest to disabled soldiers knew all too well that it was often the sympathetic labours of family members that assured a decent quality of life for veterans.

Within the home, family members' provision of support was divided up according to the expected social roles of men and women. Wives and mothers most commonly became the primary givers of practical and emotional care. In the early twentieth century, women were the 'key to the house': they were responsible for practical management of the household as well as its emotional sustenance.[13] Yet their caregiving relationship with their male kin was inherently contradictory. Women were expected to facilitate men's dependence on them, but at the same time instil 'natural' male self-reliance into their sons and husbands.[14] This dual role meant that they had the responsibility of spurring invalid veterans on to a more independent outlook, as well as ministering to their needs. To this end, the feminine qualities so celebrated in nurses during the war, such as selflessness and optimism, provided a model for the mothers, wives and sisters of disabled soldiers. Returned soldier organisations well understood the therapeutic importance of a supportive wife. They were somewhat more willing than the Repatriation Department to affirm and praise publicly women's labours in the service of disabled soldiers. The

RSSILA (Returned Sailors' and Soldiers' Imperial League of Australia) reflected that a loyal wife was crucial to veterans' success in civilian life, 'especially if the man is struggling against ill-health ... an affectionate and energetic companion will carry him all the way'.[15]

Within the home, soldiers with debilitating injuries often relied heavily upon their wives and mothers. These women became what we now term 'family carers', whose support extended beyond what was normally expected of their kinship role because of their close emotional bond with the care-recipient. Home-based caregiving allowed families to stay together, but it came with its own stresses. In July 1917, Timothy Henley returned to Australia after receiving a gunshot wound to the head that resulted in near-blindness and mental troubles. After he was discharged from hospital, he went to live at home with his wife, Molly, who became his primary carer. His condition necessitated that she was 'continually with him' and she provided constant nursing care at their home in Devonport, Tasmania.[16] Molly was probably unused to the unrelenting demands of caring for a seriously injured person in the home. While she undoubtedly felt a strong desire to care for her husband, there is evidence that she was frustrated by the demands placed upon her, as the State War Council used her plight to argue for the establishment of an Anzac Hostel in Tasmania. As Mrs Henley's circumstances illustrate, the independence and individual freedom of family carers was restricted by their ongoing responsibilities to their disabled soldiers. Some disabled soldiers felt this keenly and expressed a desire not to be a burden on their families. The Department, however, was reluctant to pay a full-time nurse's wage of £3/3 per week to lift the responsibility of care from wives and mothers in the home.[17] This was arguably on the grounds of cost as well as the assumption that such caring work was the 'natural' duty of wives and mothers. Some women from wealthier families were able to complement their feminine duties by employing private nurses, while less wealthy women had to turn to extended family for respite and support.

CAREGIVING ROLES

Wives and mothers typically took a leading role in the home treatment of disabled soldiers. Feeding the bedridden, dispensing medication and maintaining surgical aids became part of the daily routine. Pensioned soldiers were required to attend repatriation clinics each month, and were supplied with pills and tonics to last the weeks ahead. Female carers ensured that medicines were correctly administered, particularly if a wound was 'flaring up' or the soldier was in pain. Some soldiers preferred to avoid repatriation clinics, and treated their maladies at home with patent remedies dispensed by the local pharmacist. Others found relief from herbal preparations, and looked to wives and mothers to apply healing compresses and massage revitalising liniments into aching wounds. As the chief cooks in the household, women also devoted their time to preparing special remedies to relieve their loved one's ills, and health-giving foods to fortify their constitution. Over the years, women developed the knowledge and expertise to attend skilfully to their soldier's ailments and accommodate his needs within the family's daily domestic routine.

Women also had an important role outside the home in their local communities as the conduit of information about their husband's impairments. Veterans typically never spoke about the war or about their injuries in great detail, and wives often explained appropriately their husband's condition to friends and family. Neighbours would often ask Mary Ann Falconer about the health of her husband, and make encouraging comments about his head injury. Yet when people said, 'Oh, Frank's looking well, isn't he?', Mary Ann felt frustrated because although his injury was not externally visible, he endured chronic headaches.[18] She would reply, 'Yes, but he's not, he's not as well as he looks', to quietly engender a better understanding of her husband's pain. Women were also often the ones who informed children about the nature of their father's war disability. Margaret Cramond's mother explained that her father's missing limb was something he could never 'get over', conveying to her that the lost leg carried some traumatic memories for him.[19] Mary Reddrop's mother would warn her if her father's leg was 'playing up'. She would say 'His leg's hurting him today' to ensure that the children behaved well, and did not add to his stress by running up to him for attention.[20]

To lighten their domestic burdens of care, wives and mothers commonly turned to other female relatives within the extended family for assistance. Women, like disabled soldiers, were also embraced by familial relationships of support. Sisters, aunts and resident grandmothers all undertook various domestic responsibilities to release primary carers to attend to veterans. The assistance of extended kin was particularly important if a soldier's wife or mother died, or was an invalid herself. John Oscar, a permanent invalid at the Brighton Anzac Hostel in Melbourne, was fortunate that his sister agreed to take on the care of his child after the death of his wife.[21] Large families were able to distribute the burden of care across a greater number of kin, which assisted them to manage better. Families were networks of survival for disabled soldiers, and the willingness of a greater number of family members to help was an advantage. Conversely, disabled soldiers with smaller families or strained relationships had fewer opportunities to share the load. In some instances, the absence of family carers meant that the responsibilities of care fell to friends, rather than kin. In 1919, after the death of his mother, Charles Berg, a paralysed soldier from Sydney, was taken in by close friends of the family, Mr and Mrs Semple, who subsequently showed him seventeen years of 'unremitting kindness'.[22]

While direct care responsibilities fell to women, there were some activities with which a range of family members, both male and female, assisted ex-soldiers. Vision impaired veterans looked to family members to read the newspaper aloud, while men with impaired mobility sought the help of kin to venture into the outside world on excursions. Some men experienced a shrinking of their social world as a result of their disabilities, and came to rely heavily upon their extended families for social interaction. Invalid men who had little to occupy their time could spend long days in the company of their families, dependent upon them for activities and entertainment. The lack of a job exacerbated social isolation, and some families 'pray[ed] for the time when these men will have employment' because it allowed men to develop friendships and external social networks.[23] As well as generating household income, an appropriate job increased men's self-esteem and offered an alternative social focus, thereby reducing their emotional reliance on kin.

Within the domestic sphere, ex-servicemen's fathers and children adopted roles of support that were gender and age appropriate. Fathers were not expected to become primary caregivers to their sons. For them, nursing was a feminine role that demanded a level of emotional engagement at odds with the self-restraint expected of Victorian gentlemen who were born in the 1860s and 1870s.[24] Fathers, however, provided practical assistance, such as helping their sons to find employment, providing transport to hospital or dealing with the repatriation bureaucracy. Children assisted their mothers with household tasks, and the eldest daughter often became 'mother's right hand'.[25] Older daughters raised younger siblings, managed the care of their disabled fathers and took on household chores, which made it possible for their mothers to work outside the home. The practice of older children carrying a domestic load was common in larger Australian families during the 1920s. The ongoing nursing of an invalid father, however, significantly increased the emotional and practical burdens shouldered by the eldest daughter. Older daughters were one of the most common groups who attended the Red Cross Ramsgate respite care home in the south of Sydney for the children of returned soldiers, and were said to be grateful for their opportunity for a holiday.[26]

While the domestic labours of some families were significant, in other households the presence of an invalid had definite benefits. Mavis Floyd grew up with her father, Gordon Mackay, at home each day, and does not ever remember him working. He was not bedridden, but suffered war-related health problems which made it impossible to hold down a job. The family suffered grinding poverty as a result of a partial pension and scant additional income. Yet, Mavis remembers the presence of her father in the home positively:

> He was very helpful with us kids. I mean with a big family like that, and the thing is, well there wasn't that much money, but potatoes and everything were cheap… but he always peeled the potatoes, and when we were little he used to wash us kids, you know, so we'd used to sit up on the kitchen table, because the bathrooms weren't what they are today, and wash us, stand us in the dish of water, and wash our feet, and always shine our shoes and everything like that.[27]

Although Gordon's impairments prevented him from becoming a breadwinner outside the home, he was able to make a productive contribution to the household. He became a stay-at-home father and undertook some typically female domestic responsibilities. His role challenged the traditional male/female division of labour within families, which was usually structured around the daily absence of the breadwinner. While the family's low income was a constant concern, Gordon's wife no doubt appreciated the assistance of her husband in raising ten children. Mavis believes that her father's constant presence in the home may even have contributed to the very close parental and sibling ties that continue to exist within the family. Gordon's health problems were a source of worry for the family, and saw him spend many days confined to bed. Nonetheless, he drew support from his family as well as making a contribution to its wellbeing in a manner appropriate to his disabilities.

FAMILIAL LANDSCAPES OF DISABILITY

Having married only after they returned from war, most disabled soldiers started families in the early to mid-1920s. Their children grew up knowing their fathers were returned 'diggers' and became witnesses to their impairments. The men and women I interviewed for this book provided an intimate perspective on their homes as landscapes of disability. The sounds, sights and smells of medical treatment often formed the basis of their early memories of their fathers. Beverley Broadbent recalls that her house was often filled with the 'awful' odour of her father's asthma powder.[28] Service in the dusty conditions of the Middle East had exacerbated an existing respiratory problem, and he regularly inhaled the fumes of the burning powder to relieve his lungs. Margaret Cramond recalls the sight of her father's white stump socks 'always hanging around drying'.[29] These special socks were made of thick knitted wool to prevent the chafing of the stump against his prosthetic leg. Margaret's mother was in charge of washing them, and in an era before tumble dryers, they were especially hard to dry in winter. 'I can always remember the trouble Mum had getting his woollen socks dry', Margaret recalled. During the postwar years, stump socks, surgical boots and walking sticks became part of the domestic landscape for many Australian families.

As they grew up, the children of disabled soldiers also watched their fathers manage a range of symptoms including coughing, pain, fatigue and 'nervy' behaviour. My informants commonly expressed a heightened awareness of their fathers' physical or mental vulnerability during their childhoods. Mary Reddrop recalls that her father would come in from working in the paddocks and carry himself in a 'heavy way' when his leg was aching badly. She knew he was in pain because 'his face would show it'.[30] Mavis Floyd's father would not allow his children to set off fireworks on Guy Fawkes Night because the noise 'brought the war back closer to him'.[31] Diane Nicholas' father returned from war 'not terribly seriously disabled' but he did have 'a large hunk of shrapnel in his lungs'. Diane saw her father's scar only once when he took his shirt off because of the hot weather. She remembers that she was horrified: 'it must have been about a foot long and it must have been about an inch or so deep, you know, this great sort of valley in his side, it was really horrible'.[32] Diane's father never openly talked about his war disabilities with her, which only compounded the mystery and fear surrounding them.

The children of shell-shocked soldiers were often aware of their fathers' increased emotional sensitivity. One of Joan Wishart's early memories is of taking a walk with her father. The two were suddenly confronted by a large German shepherd dog which had leapt over the fence in front of them. Her father stopped and clutched at his chest, and remained motionless for quite some time. When the owner of the dog came out and apologised, Joan's father told him, 'Oh, I'm an old soldier and the dog gave me a shock'. This was an important memory for Joan, because it was the only time her father ever openly talked about his shell shock. The episode also revealed the nature of his mental impairment to her, and changed the way she regarded him as a father figure. Joan said that this memory stayed with her because:

> it was the first time that I saw my father not as the strong protector, but that he was somebody who had I suppose mortal weaknesses, and probably made me, as a young child, insecure, and also the fact that he [never] said anything that indicated any form of self-pity, or, not self-pity, but I suppose demonstrated that he wasn't a super-hero to me.[33]

Such nervous 'turns' could awaken deep fears within children about the mortality of their fathers. When Gwen Summers was a child, her father had a nervous fit when the family's six-year-old, Douglas, wandered off at an outdoor festival and was temporarily lost. Her father broke down mentally and emotionally on the way home:

> I was really sorry for Dad, I was really scared stiff, I couldn't make out what was wrong with Dad. When you're about eight or nine you think your Dad might die, and that was what was really frightening to me, was that Dad was going to die. He was so upset, and I thought he might have been going to die, you see, and I was scared stiff. I was really frightened. We had to sort of help him home, and mum got him home into bed.[34]

In this instance, Gwen saw her father in a mentally vulnerable state, which distressed her. While the disappearance of a son was an understandable stressor, Gwen's recent discovery that her father had been diagnosed with shell shock compounded her anxiety that this incident could be the trigger to a complete mental collapse. The psychological breakdown of returned soldiers was often reported in newspapers, and no doubt informed her concern that her father might die prematurely as a result of his nervous troubles.

Children's memories of their fathers' war disabilities are not always traumatic. Sometimes, families generated positive and affectionate meanings for physical disabilities. Alfred Plane developed a light-hearted game for his children using his missing leg, which they played together in the morning upon waking. As Margaret, his daughter, fondly recalled: 'as quite tiny children we used to love hopping into bed with him, and he'd put his good leg around us and we'd sit in the middle there, and we'd call that "the pool"'.[35] For Margaret, 'the pool' was an opportunity for the family to bond in a way that incorporated the absent limb in a playful way. Within the family, Alfred's impairment was not a source of upset, but a part of the everyday physicality and intimacy of the relationships in that family. While some historians have referred to limbless soldiers as men 'distorted in shape' who assumed a 'grotesque presence' in the public domain, Margaret's experience reveals that a lost limb could have a range of affirming meanings within the private family realm.[36]

Alfred Plane (right) with his family on a beach holiday in about 1931. Left to right, Alison, Jean and Margaret. Alfred lost his right leg at Pozières, but his disability was not always apparent in public settings because he wore a prosthetic limb outside the home. Photograph courtesy of Margaret Cramond.

INTIMATE LEGACIES

Some war-related conditions particularly affected the wives of disabled soldiers, and only became apparent within the intimacy of the marriage relationship. In some cases, wounds affected men's sexual functioning. Soldiers feared genital dismemberment on the battlefield, and while such injuries appear to have been relatively rare, they did occur. One man was shot in the penis by an explosive bullet, and another sustained 'crushed' genitals after his horse landed on top of him.[37] Spinal injuries and paralysis also resulted in the 'loss of manhood'.[38] Some men had a lucky escape. Despite being 'shot through both testicles and arm and leg' during the Gallipoli landing, one man subsequently married and was able to have children.[39] It was not only physical injury that endangered men's sexual capacity. Psychological problems also resulted in sexual dysfunction in some men. During the 1920s, Mrs Alice Judd experienced the 'loss of her husband's affection' as a consequence of his worsening war neurosis.[40] Ray Judd had returned 'a changed man[,] morose, restless, discontented, nervy' and experienced 'attacks of dizziness & trembling' as he settled back into his home life.[41] Mrs Judd despaired at his small pension and the lack of regard the family received from the Repatriation Department. In one instance, she made personal representation to the Department to vent her frustration at the cessation of sexual intimacy in her marriage, and threatened to 'consult a solicitor' in order to ascertain if she could sue for this loss.[42]

While some wives suffered a loss of sexual intimacy, others became victim to the consequences of their husbands' wartime sexual liaisons. One of the most perilous war-related ailments brought into the family realm by returned soldiers was venereal disease. During the war, the government insisted that venereally diseased soldiers would not be released into the community until they had been 'rendered non-infectious' and posed no risk to their families.[43] Many years after the war, however, it became clear that the 'intensive' treatment given to men may not have been fully effective in all cases. In 1923, one medical commentator warned that 'there must be a great many uncured syphilitics in civil life at the present time, who having had an army course of treatment, believe they are cured'.[44] Some women became aware of infection upon the return of their husband, but the asymptomatic nature of syphilis and gonorrhoea meant that it could go undetected for many years. Venereal disease was contagious and hereditary, and often manifested itself with tragic consequences. Untreated syphilis led to a range of symptoms including paralysis, insanity and ultimately death, while unchecked gonorrhoea resulted in miscarriages, sterility and child blindness. During the 1920s, some tragic cases of delayed family transmission emerged as soldiers' wives realised that their marriage bed had become a bed of infection.

In one such instance, Mrs Anne Potter was quietly informed in 1925 by the Inspector-General of the Insane 'that it would be as well if she had a blood test taken'.[45] Mrs Potter was the wife of a twenty-eight-year-old returned soldier mental patient, Gilbert Potter, who had contracted syphilis on active service. The couple married in 1922, and it appears that Anne Potter was unaware of her husband's venereal condition. Gilbert was also conceivably unaware of his own infectiousness, or in denial that *spirochaetes* were still active in his body. He may even have attributed some of his symptoms to the physical injuries he sustained in France. Gilbert's doctors concluded that he 'probably did not receive efficient treatment' for the syphilis he had contracted while in the army.[46] Mrs Potter not only faced the imminent death of her husband from general paralysis of the insane (the final stage of syphilis) but was confronted, perhaps for the first time, with his pre-marital sexual history. She also had to cope with her own potential infection and the stigma associated with the condition. Venereal disease was particularly shameful for women because of the pressures of sexual respectability, which were much greater than those that governed men's sexual behaviours.

Returned soldiers with venereal disease and their wives were, in the main, not treated generously by the Repatriation Department. Gilbert Potter was officially rejected as a repatriation case, because his syphilis could not be proved as 'war caused', despite the army actively taking responsibility for his treatment during the war.[47] Importantly, the Department provided no treatment for Mrs Potter. The Department did not recognise its moral duty to ameliorate the effects of wartime VD within soldiers' families. This is perhaps one of the most distressing aspects of the government's reluctance to recognise the interconnectedness of soldiers with their families. We know little about Mrs Potter's fate except that she found herself in impoverished circumstances owing to Gilbert's illness, and was most probably syphilitic herself after three years of sexual relations with him. She was not, however, eligible for treatment at the expense of the Department, and was referred to a private doctor. Like many women of her era, Mrs Potter faced significant anxiety about the loss of her health and social reputation as she commenced a time-consuming treatment program. Yet despite the devastating personal impact of VD upon soldiers' wives and children, as well as the significant public health implications for the community, the Department viewed 'certain diseases' as a private matter relating to the 'default' of the individual soldier, and offered families no assistance.

LIVING WITH SHELL SHOCK

While family relationships were significantly transformed by illness and physical disability, shell shock had some of the most disturbing consequences for ex-servicemen's kin. During the 1920s, the term 'shell shock' referred to a diverse range of mental and emotional symptoms that could be traced back to soldiers' war service. The family members of these men lived with veterans whose behaviours were erratic, difficult to understand and had an unsettling effect within the household. In 1917, Mrs D Brown married Albert Brown, a soldier who had been wounded in the leg at Gallipoli. In the years after the war, she noticed a decline in his mental outlook. He became subject to 'moody turns' and 'would sometimes sit for hours without speaking & if spoken to would not reply for some seconds'.[48] Albert's sister, May Brown, reported that he would sit in an armchair biting his nails and staring into space. During the early 1920s, May moved into the Brown household, to assist her sister-in-law, as Albert had become increasingly paranoid that 'someone was working against him'.[49] In 1928, Albert was admitted to the Royal Park Receiving House after having a nervous breakdown, which the Repatriation Department wholly attributed to his war service. The Brown family's experiences illustrate that mental impairment had consequences for soldiers' kin unlike those experienced by families of the physically disabled. A returned serviceman's mental state changed the atmosphere of the household, and pervasively reached into the inner emotional and psychological worlds of his family members.

Many families lived with the distressing symptoms of shell shock on a daily basis. Mental trauma was often accompanied by sleeplessness and dreams which could rouse the household. Henry Nugent was discharged with neurasthenia and slept fitfully because, as his wife reported, he 'still sees former war scenes'. She experienced disturbed rest herself because he 'keeps singing out that all the men in the army are getting killed'.[50] At times, Henry would walk about the city, generally going to the Shrine of Remembrance, but was unable to recall his wanderings.[51] In some families, the nocturnal anguish of returned soldiers was such that couples chose to sleep in separate beds. Shell-shocked soldiers sometimes turned to alcohol to ease their mental suffering. This could heighten their emotional state and lead to suicidal or violent situations requiring police intervention. Employment and financial problems could further undermine their mental health, and some men found themselves entangled in a vicious circle. The burden of caring for such men was great, and as the *RSA Magazine* advised in 1919, required an unusual degree of unselfish devotion. Wives were encouraged to be understanding of their husbands and 'help him realise that he can get well, give him incentives to recover, and keep up his courage'.[52]

Some wives, however, struggled to soothe their husbands' mental distress because a number of shell-shocked soldiers were violent towards them. Joyce Muir believes that her father's violent behaviour can be traced to the trauma he experienced at Gallipoli and on the Western Front. After his return, Gerald Muir regularly vented his rage at the family, as Joyce recalled:

> [Dad] would fly into this temper, and he destroyed so many houses, and our belongings ... he'd pull the electric light fittings out, he'd smash every piece of crockery in everything in the house, he'd destroy the house, he'd throw a pot of tea you know, that you hadn't had, the pot of tea would get thrown over the curtains and things like that.
> He went crazy, it was just a case of going crazy.[53]

Gerald created a permanent atmosphere of fear within the household by regularly assaulting his wife and 'belting the living daylights' out of his son. Although the Department did not officially class Gerald as a psychological casualty, the evidence was clear enough in the eyes of his family members. During the postwar years, many wives complained directly to the Repatriation Department of the cruelty and abuse suffered at the hands of their husbands, who had 'changed' after their return.[54] Yet, while some ex-servicemen were violent to their families, it does not follow that all abusive behaviour can be traced to a 'mental' condition, that all shell-shocked soldiers were violent, or that even being a combatant was a prerequisite for violence.

Male domestic violence against women was not limited to psychologically disturbed veterans. It was a phenomenon prevalent in Australian culture that cut across the boundaries between soldier and civilian, disabled and non-disabled. Domestic violence blighted the lives of many women and children well before the war started. For some, the enlistment of a husband brought welcome relief from the stress of abuse as the violence temporarily ceased.[55] There are also instances of soldiers who perpetrated domestic violence after the war, but never saw active service.[56] Civilian men were also violent to their kin during and after the war, whether they were mentally affected or quite sane.[57] While it is important to expose the violence experienced by the families of mentally disabled soldiers, we must not lose sight of the diversity of emotional consequences that shell shock had for Australian families.

Some shell-shocked men were not outwardly violent, but morose and gloomy in temperament. I asked Joan Wishart whether her shell-shocked father, John Hargreaves, ever exhibited angry or violent behaviour. She answered:

> No, never ... Well I wouldn't be surprised that you know, [of] men using a reaction of violence. But no, not with Dad, he wasn't that sort of person ... I think any anger or violence that he felt was sort of directed inwards and came out in depression ... Dad was not an aggressive person and didn't engage in disagreements with people ... I think possibly if he'd been more positive and aggressive ... he wouldn't have fallen into depression, but I don't think he could ... [stand up to others].[58]

Joan's dominant memory of her father's behaviour was his depression, which worsened as he aged. She told me that John spent a lot of energy trying to conceal his psychological difficulties, and recalled that he presented a 'wonderful front' to the outside world. Growing up, Joan was aware that her father was 'always emotionally dependent' upon her mother. Caroline Hargreaves was generous in her emotional support of her husband, and John 'doted on her, absolutely'. In this instance, it was not the violence of a shell-shocked man that shaped daily life, but his depression and dependence on his wife.

The emotional support provided by the wives of veterans experiencing alcoholism or depression could be crucial to the survival of households. Many wives took it upon themselves to curb or control the difficult behaviours of their husbands, such as alcohol abuse. During the 1920s, Patrick Rouhan suffered a slow decline in his health as a result of war-related tuberculosis, and took to heavy drinking as he was 'depressed always about his general health & conditions'.[59] His wife, Dora, nursed him at home, and the doctors were impressed by the manner in which she limited his alcohol intake. 'His wife has a good hold on him', wrote one physician: 'If he gets away from her influence he is liable to get under the influence of C_2H_6O [alcohol]'.[60] While shell shock and alcoholism created emotional tensions in many households, wives were not always the passive victims of their circumstances, and some women struggled to effect positive change in their husbands. The Repatriation Department, however, showed little interest in the struggles of these families. When Mrs Jean Ingram finally sought help in relation to her husband's 'physical cruelty', which she believed was a result of his war neurosis, the Department informed her that it was not responsible for 'private' matters between soldiers and their family members. 'This Department', Mrs Ingram was told, 'could not advise her in any way with regard to her domestic affairs ... [nor] interfere as far as her husband's private life was concerned'.[61]

UNDER STRAIN ON THE LAND

On Soldier Settlement farms, the strain of living with a physically or mentally 'shattered' man was often compounded by the difficulties families faced making their holdings profitable. The family relationships of disabled soldier settlers were stressed by a combination of factors including veterans' failing health, unproductive blocks, and the descent of their households into debt. The scheme offered disabled soldiers the chance to become self-sufficient, but in reality many became dependent on family members' labour for the survival of their farms (see chapter 3). While some families made a success of their blocks, the lives of many were, as historian Marilyn Lake has noted of Victorian settlers, 'shaped by a context of material poverty which generated daily stress and anxieties'.[62] The wives of disabled soldier farmers carried physical and economic burdens, undertaking arduous labour alongside their husbands, raising children and managing on a tight household income. As a consequence of their demanding 'triple shift', wives shouldered a considerable emotional load. Moreover, on top of their own worries, they also shared the psychological disappointment of their husbands who had once had great hopes for their farms, but were crushed under the weight of debt and had come to perceive themselves as failed breadwinners.

On the land, the pressure on wives could be detrimental to their own emotional health. In 1927, Mrs McMahon had a nervous breakdown after struggling to carry her domestic and farming load on her husband's block in Korumburra. Her husband, George, was discharged in 1917 with an injury to the right leg and eye. In 1921, he took up a 108 acre (44 ha) block but progress was slow: George had little farming experience, and the property was infested with rabbits. After he married, the Closer Settlement Board was pleased, as they considered he would 'do considerably better' on the farm with the practical assistance his wife could offer.[63] George's health, however, gradually deteriorated to the point where he was not able to do heavy manual labour and Mrs McMahon could not keep the farm going by herself. Her husband's invalidism, the imminent failure of the farm and the prospect of further debt all contributed to her nervous breakdown in mid-1927. In early 1928, the lease was cancelled on the grounds of George's war-related health problems and the couple moved to Melbourne to seek a less physically demanding lifestyle.

In remote rural areas, the lack of medical services compounded the hardships faced by disabled soldier settler families. Ex-servicemen in the city had relatively easy access to repatriation clinics. Soldier settlers, on the other hand, often lived a considerable distance from regional hospitals. Settlers and their wives usually took up allotments during the early years of marriage, and established their farms as they started their families. Their agricultural and domestic success depended heavily on their physical and mental health; however, many women in isolated areas such as the Mallee were not able to seek medical advice about the strain they were under, nor regularly consult a doctor during their pregnancies. Doctors were not easily summoned in cases of farming accidents, and families faced a long journey to the nearest physician if a child developed an illness, such as scarlet fever. In some instances, the lack of medical services had tragic consequences. Beverley Broadbent's uncle, John Stubbs, was a disabled soldier in the Mallee and struggled to undertake strenuous farm labour with only one leg. The daily physical demands of farming, declining profits and stress over his debt saw his health gradually wear down, and he developed an ulcer. In 1929, the ulcer burst, but because the farm was too far away from medical help, he died.[64]

Sometimes, the adversity faced by the families of disabled soldier settlers caused their marriages to break down. In 1928, Frank Ingamells revealed to the Closer Settlement Board that his wife and children had left him.[65] Ingamells, an army chaplain, was discharged in June 1918 after suffering debility and nervous troubles. After returning home, he took up a soldier settlement block with his wife at Tourello in central Victoria. His wife had been used to a more comfortable existence as a vicar's wife before the war, and the strain of farming life took its toll on their relationship as they struggled to make the allotment profitable. After she left, the extent of Frank's dependence upon her became evident. The farm started to 'go back very fast' and the inspector noted that he was 'incapable single handed, of coping with the work necessary to win through'.[66] Frank fell into a state of despondency and eventually gave up the block in 1929 because he was unable to go on alone with impaired health.

Despite the personal cost of the Soldier Settlement Scheme to disabled ex-servicemen's kin, the Closer Settlement Board showed little interest in the wellbeing of families. The Board encouraged the labours of family members as integral to the success of the scheme, but offered little practical assistance or financial relief to them once their soldier's health declined. The Board's primary role was to monitor the efficiency and profitability of holdings, dispense advice and supervise the repayment of debt. Its role was to oversee, but not support, family units. The Board responded inadequately to the physical, mental and financial struggles of disabled soldiers, and seldom acted directly to ameliorate the distress of families. The Soldier Settlement Scheme had been envisaged as a reward for returned soldiers, but it resulted in the exacerbation of men's war disabilities, made enormous demands on their family members, and created financial and emotional hardship for numerous households.

CARING FOR THE CARERS

In both rural and urban Australia, the wives who supported their disabled husbands at home often found that their own physical and emotional health was taxed by the burdens they carried. The 'special attention' that wives gave to their disabled husbands was 'extremely trying', noted one blinded soldier, who concluded that women's 'health must suffer, in consequence, under such a strain'.[67] Yet, the Repatriation Department did not formally recognise the carer role of disabled soldiers' wives, nor the stress that it created, and many women were effectively isolated in their struggle to care for their husbands. The Repatriation Department took no responsibility for the health of returned soldiers' dependants, and did not provide medical treatment or adequate respite for their family members.

In the absence of assistance from repatriation authorities, the wives and mothers of disabled soldiers turned to voluntary organisations, which were often established and operated by women. In Sydney, the medical care of the soldiers' dependants was taken up by the RSSILA, which established a Women's Clinic in 1921.[68] The clinic, directed by a sole female practitioner, Dr Katie Ardill Brice, was the only one of its kind in Australia. The Centre for Soldiers' Wives and Mothers in Sydney, and Red Cross branches across Australia also provided women with personal support. In 1919, the Red Cross established Furlough House, a holiday home at Narrabeen, a seaside suburb north of Sydney, which catered to the wives and children of disabled soldiers. In 1920, Mrs Bertha Rea applied to stay at Furlough House on the grounds that she needed a 'change' from her domestic circumstances. Bertha's husband had returned home with health problems in 1919 and required ongoing hospital treatment.[69] Mervyn's injuries prevented him from resuming his job as a tram conductor, and Bertha appears to have been struggling with her husband's chronic invalidism. The arrival of her first baby only added to the emotional demands placed upon her. Furlough House offered Bertha an opportunity to receive care from others, and provided some much needed respite from her demanding home life. We can only assume that during her absence, Mervyn was cared for by another family member, or was admitted to a convalescent home.

The relatives of disabled soldiers also created their own support organisations. During the 1920s, family members could join a range of associations, including the Sailors' and Soldiers' Mothers' Association; the Australian Imperial League of Sailors' and Soldiers' Womenfolk; the Sailors, Soldiers and Nurses Relatives' Association; and the Sailors' and Soldiers' Fathers Association. These associations catered to the kin of the 'fallen and the maimed'. They typically adopted a model of mutual assistance, and members received and provided practical and emotional support. Relatives' associations provided communities of understanding for families living with the aftermath of war, much in the same way that the Red Cross became a community of 'fictive kin' for women during the war.[70] They validated the personal sacrifices of disabled soldiers' families, affirmed the purposefulness of their emotional labours, and offered members emotional succour in an atmosphere of 'unity, fidelity and goodwill'.[71] In 1922, Ada Manning of the Friendly Union of Soldiers' Wives, Mothers and Sisters encouraged women to: 'Be to each other what we have been in the past, assured that the bond that binds us is the strongest of all cords which passes like a crimson thread throughout our lives and associations'.[72] The work of these organisations indicates that family systems of support for disabled soldiers sat within broader community systems of support.

Surviving documents only hint at the complex interpersonal world of relatives' organisations, but it is reasonable to speculate that the family members of disabled soldiers established friendships during meetings, and created personal networks that extended into local communities. At the Friendly Union, female relatives of disabled soldiers met each other and were shown understanding and sympathy. After meetings, women could continue sharing their concerns about their disabled husbands and sons, and hear the experiences of other families. Women could turn to these informal support networks in times of trouble. Conversely, when things were going well, they could offer support to those in need. The Sailors' and Soldiers' Fathers Association offered its members an environment of manly fellowship during their 'smoke evenings'. Within the social networks of the SSFA, gentlemen could gather and discuss the future of their disabled sons, and express difficult emotions in the company of other similarly affected men. Relatives' organisations offered family members a 'unity of comradeship' of a kind that disabled soldiers sought in the RSSILA and disability-specific organisations.[73] The survival of these associations well into the 1920s attests to the need of disabled soldiers' families for personal and practical support as the years passed.

FAMILIAL INTERDEPENDENCE

Behind each disabled soldier were family members whose support became crucial to veterans' journey back into civilian life. Within the domestic sphere, the care of veterans was managed collectively and involved the practical and emotional labours of a range of both nuclear and extended kin. Wives and mothers, however, commonly shouldered the bulk of the domestic burden of care. They developed the skills and knowledge to provide and sustain a necessary level of home support and devoted untold hours of unpaid nursing labour to their incapacitated sons and husbands. The cost of war disability to these women was considerable and their domestic sacrifices are incalculable. In the 1920s, many Australian women looked to take advantage of increased leisure and employment choices, and valued the greater independence that became possible in their own lives.[74] These new freedoms available to the 'modern woman', however, were not easily in reach of the women whose lives had been forever changed by war disability. Although the war saw an expansion of women's social choices, the independence of women who shouldered the burdens of caring for disabled soldiers was often lessened.

The significance of the family as a therapeutic site for disabled ex-servicemen should not be underestimated. Families offered particular forms of emotional succour, dignity and care which were not to be found at the 'Repat'. The Repatriation Department, however, assumed the family to be a 'natural' site of care, unworthy of formal recognition. It failed to acknowledge publicly the enormous amount of unpaid family labour that complemented its own programs and reduced the national repatriation bill. In doing so, it missed opportunities to form partnerships with families which may have improved soldiers' quality of life and better supported family carers. Instead, official repatriation literature espoused an ideology of 'manly independence' which disavowed the healing potential of family support. In practice, however, the shared family lives of disabled soldiers and their kin were characterised by interdependent models of care. Ex-servicemen and their family members negotiated a delicate balance of independence and interdependence within the particular circumstances of their households.

The following two chapters examine in greater detail how war disability affected the interdependent lives of families living with soldiers who suffered two of the most common war disabilities – shell shock and tuberculosis. According to official war historian, AG Butler, these conditions dominated the history of the aftermath.[75] Both conditions were 'invisible' and socially stigmatised, but had an enormous reach into returned soldiers' households. As we shall see, these impairments brought with them vastly different burdens for disabled soldiers and their families.

CHAPTER 5

families and mental hospitals

> The nerve cases are, as usual, our never-ending problem
> – a problem without solution. These men are too sane for
> an asylum, yet not sane enough to fend for themselves.
>
> Australian Red Cross Society, NSW, 1937.[1]

In August 1929, Mrs Elizabeth Moffatt wrote to Victoria's Inspector-General of the Insane about placing her father in a mental hospital. Peter Henty had served in the Boer War and the First World War, and returned from the latter conflict with head wounds and injuries down one side of his body. After his discharge, he resided with his family who had been informed that his injuries were 'not supposed to be serious'.[2] As the years passed, however, Peter's mental health deteriorated and he developed 'intemperate habits'. His worsening psychological state and alcoholism made it increasingly difficult for family members to support him. After Peter made an attempt to take his own life, the family finally contacted the mental health authorities and made arrangements for institutional treatment. He was admitted to the Royal Park Mental Hospital in a depressed and 'lost' state, and the doctors noted that it was 'very difficult to get anything intelligible from him about himself or his condition'.[3] Given Peter's inability to convey his own needs, Elizabeth took on the role of family advocate and negotiated with the Inspector-General about appropriate accommodation for her father. In her letter, she provided a history of Peter's mental troubles and conveyed the family's desire that he 'be put in a home where he will be kindly treated'. She expressed a strong preference that he be transferred to the special Mont Park Military Block for returned men, a segregated facility which accommodated 'mental soldiers' away from civilian patients.

Elizabeth Moffatt's endeavours to secure suitable treatment for her father illustrate the involvement of family members in the institutionalisation of shell-shocked soldiers. While many families provided care for mentally disabled soldiers within the home, some households were unable to manage the challenges of severe mental illness and sought hospital treatment. As the locus of care shifted from the domestic sphere to the institution, family members' burdens changed. Within the home, family members were the key providers of care, and their primary concern was the daily management of their relationship with the veteran. In the external world of the mental hospital system, family members were no longer involved in the direct provision of care, but became observers and coordinators of institutional care. They cultivated favourable relationships with hospital managers, visited and monitored conditions, acted as spokespeople for veterans, and defended their right to receive preferential treatment within military mental institutions. Unlike other groups of disabled ex-servicemen, mentally affected soldiers were reliant on their families to represent their interests outside the home, because their impairments and the stigma of mental illness often left them, as one soldier patient put it, 'voiceless'.[4]

This chapter traces the involvement of kin in the lives of returned shell-shocked soldiers who resided in mental institutions. Although ex-servicemen were admitted and confined as individuals, their family members' desire to extend their sphere of care and observation into the mental hospital meant that kin had significant influence on soldiers' journeys of institutionalisation. After the return of the first shell-shocked soldiers in 1915, families became increasingly active as negotiators and critics of their loved ones' treatment in mental hospitals. Most historians, however, have neglected to examine veterans' experiences of institutionalisation, despite a well-developed literature on families' involvement in the incarceration of civilian patients.[5] Soldiers' families' interventions were, in many respects, similar to the protective endeavours undertaken by relatives of their civilian counterparts.[6] But there was an important difference. One of the most common requests of ex-servicemen's kin was for the treatment of their loved one in a segregated repatriation institution. These were known to provide a higher standard of care than civilian facilities and prevented the mixing of soldiers with 'ordinary lunatics'.[7] Once servicemen passed from the domestic domain into institutional care, they were formally the responsibility of the state. Yet families were able to exert some influence over their confinement and treatment. Kin were vital advocates for shell-shocked men within the mental health system, and played an important role in defending their entitlement to 'preferential treatment'.

THE ROAD TO THE MENTAL HOSPITAL

Shell shock was the 'saddest heritage' of war for many soldiers and their families.[8] There are no reliable statistics to indicate the extent of mental disorder among returned soldiers, nor the rate of their institutionalisation.[9] We do know, however, that war neuroses were alarmingly prevalent. Official medical historian AG Butler, posited that ex-servicemen's mental troubles accounted for about 80 per cent of the medical aftermath of war.[10] Veterans were admitted to mental hospitals with a wide variety of disorders. As one Red Cross Nerve Home worker noted, patients' complaints were 'varied and sometimes difficult to fathom'.[11] Some men were affected by physical symptoms such as blindness and deafness, flaccid limbs, facial ticks, stammering and mutism. Others suffered depression, neurasthenia, dementia, alcoholism, 'confusional & exhaustion psychosis' and 'unrest'. Within popular parlance, 'shell shock' was used freely to describe almost every mental disturbance experienced by returned men. Rather than denoting common symptoms, it was a unifying term that indicated the sufferer was a soldier, not a civilian. During the 1920s, the term 'mental soldier' also entered common usage, which perhaps better reflected the diverse spectrum of ex-servicemen's complaints. Family members tended to draw upon such popular terminology in their dealings with mental health authorities, and typically described their loved ones as 'shell-shocked', 'nervy' or 'not normal'. They rarely used psychiatric labels such as 'neurotic' or 'neurasthenic'. Arguably, such formal diagnostic terms said little about the daily reality of their soldier's mental and emotional struggles, and may have implied a permanent pathology at odds with their hopes for his recovery.

The road to the mental hospital often began in the home. While many mentally affected veterans and their families lived relatively stable lives together, some relatives found it practically impossible to look after their loved ones. The patience of even the most devoted wives and mothers could be easily taxed by unpredictable and delusional behaviours, heightened emotionality, and tendencies towards violence or depression. The care of returned soldiers frequently alternated between the family home and mental hospitals as men's psychological state fluctuated. There was great variety in the reasons for soldiers' institutionalisation and patterns of admission. Some men were taken to a mental hospital immediately after arriving home in Australia, and only returned to live with their family in the 1930s.[12] In other cases, families were 'quite willing' to provide ongoing care, but were forced to seek institutional assistance because they could not adequately supervise suicidal men. As time passed, some men were no longer amenable to reason and families struggled to control their loved one by suggestion or force. Sometimes family members sought short-term hospitalisation, requesting that the veteran was 'put away' because he was 'going off his head' worse than usual, but welcomed him home after treatment.[13] Some men were admitted only after their family support network fell away; for example, after the death of their parents or abandonment by their wife after years of home-based care.[14] For shell-shocked soldiers in a variety of familial circumstances, mental hospitals became a second home, either on a temporary or ongoing basis.

Families' experiences of the mental health system become visible to the historian's gaze through the correspondence files of state lunacy departments and repatriation authorities. This chapter is based on previously unreleased files of the Mont Park and Royal Park hospitals for the insane in Melbourne. This material provides a rich insight into families' agency and negotiations with institutional authorities. It does not, however, necessarily reflect families' experiences in other states, as the treatment of ex-servicemen varied considerably from state to state. Nor does it offer an account of men who were treated in smaller 'nerve homes', as the operational records of such facilities appear not to have survived. That said, families' expectation of 'preferential treatment' is a common theme in extant institutional records and public domain sources across Australia. The relatives who advocated for their soldiers represented a loyal and dedicated cohort. We must not forget, however, that some kin used hospitalisation as an opportunity to abandon their soldier to the state. Shell shock had a diverse impact on families. It inspired loyalty and steadfastness among kin, as well as engendering a sense of hopelessness. The story of 'forgotten' mental soldier patients, however, can be more difficult to uncover, as detailed evidence of families' estrangement was not always clearly documented.

When a family could no longer manage their shell-shocked soldier in the home, their first task was to request his hospitalisation. Families often took ex-soldiers directly to a mental institution, such as the Royal Park Receiving House or Mont Park Hospital for the Insane. Some initially reported to general hospitals, such as the Homeopathic Hospital, conceivably because it was difficult to coax a troubled veteran to visit a 'madhouse'. As families admitted their soldiers, they no doubt experienced mixed feelings. Institutionalisation relieved relatives of the onerous burden of home care and protected them from threats of violence and the distress of self-harm. But it created new anxieties. As ex-servicemen moved from the care of their kin, they entered the world of the mental hospital, an unknown and possibly dangerous quasi-public space in which they had few existing social relationships. Family members had little control over the hospital environment, the methods of treatment, or the influence of fellow patients. Even the kin of 'difficult' veterans sometimes experienced conflicting emotions as they relinquished them into institutional care. Shortly after Patrick O'Neill was admitted to Mont Park, his mother Evelyn expressed reservations and insisted he was returned 'to her own home' yet it was clear from his history that she 'could not control him'.[15]

Family members and friends accounted for two-thirds of referrals into the mental health system in Victoria of both civilian and military cases.[16] It was at the moment of admission that families commenced a formal relationship with the mental health authorities. During the assessment process, their role was primarily as informants. They provided a history of their loved one's symptoms, stated the suspected origins of the disorder, and gave details of previous treatment and medications. Family members were uniquely positioned as informants because they were witnesses to the development and manifestation of their loved one's mental disorders at close range. Their observations became an important part of the clinical record, especially if the patient was unable to describe his own symptoms.[17] Men with an established history of shell shock were usually accepted into military mental institutions immediately. However, those with insufficient evidence to connect their disorder to war service were provided with temporary accommodation pending a full repatriation assessment. The families of 'yet to be accepted' soldiers faced an anxious wait before learning the place of treatment. Overwhelmingly, their preference was for their loved one to be sent to a military mental hospital, rather than a civilian institution, for it was widely known that patients received a considerably higher standard of treatment in such facilities.

SEGREGATION OF MILITARY PATIENTS

During the war, a two-tiered mental hospital system emerged in Australia which separated veterans from civilians wherever practicable. This segregation policy reflected the government's ideology of 'preference' which underpinned the nation's burgeoning repatriation system.[18] The Repatriation Department instituted programs to ensure the privileged treatment of 'citizen soldiers' in areas such as employment, housing and land settlement, so that they would not be disadvantaged in civilian life because of their service and sacrifice. The 'preference' principle saw the establishment of specialist repatriation mental facilities to repay the nation's debt to its 'mentally afflicted heroes'. In some states, new repatriation hospitals were built, while in other states, special wards were set aside within civilian mental institutions. In these facilities, the value of segregation was conveyed to soldier patients. One psychiatrist from Broughton Hall in Sydney, recalled that 'Continuous pressure [was] brought to bear to ensure that 1) returned soldiers [were] not branded as Insane and 2) that they should be treated as far as possible on the lines of the best type of hospital treatment – not as lunatics'.[19] Some medicos also believed that shell-shocked soldiers, particularly younger men, had 'every chance of becoming normal' if they remained separate from inveterate lunatics.[20] The RSSILA was a staunch supporter of segregation, and advocated 'special treatment' for soldiers suffering mental disability, 'whose disability is due to circumstances dissimilar to civilian inmates'.[21] Segregation also had widespread popular support and public opinion was very much against the mixing of soldier 'heroes' and civilian mental patients.

In Melbourne, the main repatriation mental institution was the Mont Park Military Mental Hospital, located in dedicated buildings at the Mont Park Hospital for the Insane. Here, soldier patients received a much higher quality of care than their civilian counterparts. Of an unknown number of soldier patients treated between 1915 and 1920, 412 were held involuntarily.[22] Notably, these men were 'detained' not 'certified', a distinction made under the *Mental Treatment Act 1915*, which protected them from the humiliation of being formally labelled 'insane'.[23] They were provided with better food, and attended to by 'specially selected' staff who were paid more highly than attendants on the civilian wards.[24] Red Cross and Legacy volunteers regularly arranged musical entertainments for soldiers and took them on day trips and outings to the theatre.[25] Such treatment was designed to remind soldiers of their special status as soldiers so that they did not think of themselves as 'insane'.[26] In 1925, the Bundoora Convalescent Home for 'quiet' nerve cases opened, up the road from Mont Park. It was an impressive mansion, which had no history as a mental institution, situated on a hill in a lush garden setting. Its residents received similarly privileged treatment. One resident of Bundoora reflected that he found it to be 'a much more congenial home' than the civilian mental hospitals he had experienced.[27] During the 1920s, there was consistent demand among returned soldiers for the 130 repatriation beds available at Mont Park and Bundoora.

To the families of shell-shocked soldiers, the Mont Park Military Block and the Bundoora Home represented the most appealing types of institutions. Family members often directly petitioned the mental health and repatriation authorities to secure the treatment of their loved one in these facilities. In June 1928, Henry Walton personally visited the Inspector-General after his son, Victor, was admitted to Royal Park in an 'unbalanced' and 'delusional' state. Henry was desirous that Victor 'should not be sent to Kew [Hospital for the Insane], but would prefer his transfer to Mont Park'.[28] Henry's eagerness to secure a repatriation placement saw him visit the Inspector-General a second time to plead his son's case. Family members, such as Henry, actively intervened in this manner to ensure that their loved one received the best possible medical care. Their efforts, however, were also inspired by a deeper awareness of the cultural meaning of mental institutions. For families, the segregation of veterans in a military hospital deflected some of the social stigma associated with mental illness by separating their loved one from the 'ordinary insane'. The negotiations of family members represented an attempt to secure not only a bed, but a position of superiority above civilian 'lunatics' within this hierarchy of stigma.

THE STIGMA OF MENTAL ILLNESS

In the early twentieth century, mental illness carried an enormous social stigma for families. Although shell shock was a war disability, veterans were not immune from the shame of madness. To many observers, there were few outward signs that distinguished mentally affected men from 'insane' civilians. While physical war disabilities were popularly regarded as symbols of veterans' heroic sacrifices, mentally affected soldiers and their families often experienced shell shock as embarrassing and dishonourable. This was one of the strongest sentiments to emerge from my interviews. As Beverley Broadbent reflected, 'shell shock was one of the worst disabilities actually, because the stress and strain you'd been through, before you'd got like that, and the shame, shame, not sympathy but the shame of shell shock'.[29]

Within the community, 'mental soldiers' were often perceived as peculiar, weak in character, morally unreliable, troublesome or even dangerous. In 1928, a local residents' group complained to the Mont Park Hospital about soldier patients 'walking aimlessly' about the suburb, whom they believed posed a threat to the 'safety of our children'.[30] Some families were socially marginalised because of their ex-serviceman's mental problems. As a child, Betsy Burchett was teased at school because her father, a resident at Bundoora, was known to be 'mad'.[31] Some soldiers attempted to conceal their mental conditions in the company of others, particularly in the workplace, for fear of being discriminated against. The shame of mental disorder

The Bundoora Repatriation Convalescent Home for shell-shocked men in Melbourne opened in 1925 to accommodate 'quiet' and chronic cases. Australian War Memorial negative number H19366.

even extended into the home. Veterans sometimes felt embarrassed if their own kin witnessed a 'turn'. In some families there was absolute silence on the subject, as Gwen Summers recalled, 'you didn't talk about your war neuroses, it was something that was considered a bit shameful'.[32]

The public statements of the Repatriation Department did little to reduce the stigma associated with shell shock, or to clarify whether soldiers were 'wounded' or 'insane'. During and after the war, there was varied opinion about the extent to which war neuroses were the result of a 'genuine' injury or an underlying hereditary weakness. Unfortunately, the diverse array of contemporary theories about mental disorders, including eugenic explanations – both hereditary and environmental – the latest psychiatric hypotheses, and older community understandings, provided few clear answers to this question.[33] The government, however, tended to err on the side of hereditary determinism. Although it provided 'mental soldiers' with preferential treatment, official repatriation medical opinion held that the large majority of veterans were 'really cases of nervous break-down under the stress of war in patients so predisposed by mental instability'.[34] Indeed, identifying a 'faulty family history' was one of the repatriation physician's first diagnostic tasks. These etiological misgivings called into question the nervous and moral constitution of individual veterans. Although returned soldiers and their supporters argued strongly that shell shock had clear battlefield origins, the stigma of insanity was difficult to eradicate.

Shell-shocked soldiers were not only burdened with the stigma of mental illness, but the humiliation that they were failed Anzacs. Within the Anzac legend, mental toughness and personal resilience were celebrated as central characteristics of Australian soldiers. In the eyes of many, the Anzacs had proved themselves a 'shock proof crowd' through their heroic deeds. Shell-shocked soldiers did not measure up to this ideal. They had either been unable to stand the heat of battle, or were cowards who lacked the moral fibre to stay in the trenches and face the enemy. Such men represented the antithesis of Anzac masculinity because their 'mettle' had buckled under pressure, and they had lost their 'captaincy of the soul'.[35] In the early twentieth century, self-control was central to dominant codes of Edwardian and military manhood, and the loss of personal agency was tantamount to the loss of masculinity. This meant that the failure to recover from the 'shock' of battle was not just a medical matter; it was something that potentially diminished a soldier's identity as a man. Shell-shocked veterans not only suffered the stigma of mental illness, but their dignity as men and soldiers was often negatively affected.

These considerations undoubtedly weighed on the minds of family members as they negotiated the treatment of veterans. For men and their kin, institutionalisation was the moment at which the stigma of mental illness was at its greatest. Incarceration publicly confirmed the mental weakness of the soldier, his failure as an Anzac, and his inability to take up his masculine duty as a family breadwinner. It indicated that he had lost the last vestiges of his capacity for self-control and independence, and had become dependent on the state for his daily needs. Confinement within any class of mental hospital was shameful enough, but the prospect of treatment within a civilian asylum represented the ultimate ignominy. It was a humiliating public declaration that the veteran was 'insane', and not a military case. The dishonour associated with civilian asylums was so great that a veteran's confinement sometimes became a generational secret within families.[36] Given the strong belief in the hereditary origins of madness, the rejection of 'war causes' not only cast a slur over the eugenic fitness of the soldier, but also raised questions about the mental soundness of his entire family. As one advocate declared, if a patient in a mental hospital was no longer identifiable as a war case, 'a blot' might be placed upon his family.[37]

For the families of shell-shocked veterans, the spatial segregation of their loved ones in military mental institutions was of the utmost importance. Officially accepted ex-servicemen were afforded high quality medical care and became eligible for a war pension. Classification as a 'war case' mitigated, although it did not completely eradicate, the stigma of mental illness. It also allowed veterans to retain some of the dignity of being a soldier, even if they did not meet the Anzac ideal. Importantly, it protected kin from the suggestion of a hereditary mental weakness within the family and the public disgrace associated with such a eugenic defect. Segregation was also important to families because they did not want their loved one to 'be lost sight of' in the state mental health system. Civilian asylums were popularly imagined as dehumanising environments in which the 'most awful specimens of humanity' were crowded together with no hope of redemption.[38] They were thought of as places of punishment, much like prisons, designed for the containment of sub-human and amoral inmates, in which 'one mental case preys on the other'.[39] To families, treatment in a military mental institution represented the most humane form of care available. In repatriation facilities, veterans joined a select soldier population whose status as both 'humans' and 'heroes' was recognised. In contrast, veterans who were treated in civilian institutions joined the ranks of a large undifferentiated mass of 'lunatics' reviled by the community. They also became subject to the comparatively strict civilian mental health legislation which, for example, allowed civilian patients to be moved between institutions without the consent of their family members.

FAMILIES' INTERVENTIONS

In order to be eligible for admission to a military mental institution, ex-servicemen first had to be 'accepted' by the Department of Repatriation. This required the establishment of a causal link between a man's war service and his mental disturbance, a process that was highly subjective. For repatriation doctors, identifying the cause of mental impairment was a complex endeavour in comparison with the assessment of most physical wounds and disabilities. Indeed, the extent to which shell shock was deemed 'war caused' varied from doctor to doctor, and even state to state. In 1927, for example, there were 1286 cases of war neurosis accepted in Victoria but only 391 in New South Wales.[40] This means that Victorian families were more than three times as likely, in that year and others, to have their loved one admitted to a military mental institution than their northern counterparts. This discrepancy suggests that there were significant inconsistencies in the medical construction of war neuroses, and may even indicate that practical considerations, such as the availability of hospital beds, were taken into account. In this diagnostic no-man's land, shell-shocked soldiers and their families were vulnerable to underassessment and rejection. These uncertainties, however, could sometimes work in their favour. Many family members used the assessment period as a time to persuade the authorities, formally and informally, to accept their soldier's case. It was during this stage of institutionalisation that the role of family members shifted from being one of information providers, to negotiators and advocates.

During the assessment period, family members were invited to attend personal interviews with repatriation and lunacy officials, to establish the cause of the veteran's disorder. They were also required to complete a formal record of evidence which, along with more clinical medical data, became part of the soldier's case for treatment within the repatriation system. Family members were well aware that their testimony could hold the key to the type of institutional care their loved one would receive. In their interviews, written evidence and correspondence, they carefully constructed an etiological pathway between the war and their soldier's mental decline, to ensure official acceptance. After Jim Barnett was admitted to Royal Park suffering from delusions in 1929, his father, Charles, wrote to the Repatriation Department declaring that he had noted a 'marked change' in his son's personality since 1919.[41] This statement was supported by Jim's wife who described his 'odd behaviour' and eventual 'breakdown' after his return from the war.[42] Charles openly dispelled any suggestion of hereditary insanity, declaring, 'There is no mental trouble in his Mother's or my side of the family'.[43]

After linking their veteran's mental state to war strain, family advocates often directly requested his treatment within a repatriation institution. In 1930, Mrs Dora Beale wrote to the Repatriation Department after her son Michael had a nervous breakdown. She described how he had returned home 'a complete wreck' after five years' war service.[44] His wife, Mary, also wrote a supporting letter, in which she stated that Michael had 'not felt fit' since the war, a claim which, she noted, he often made himself during his saner moments.[45] Despite his physical and mental troubles, Michael had never sought official medical assistance nor applied for a pension, because 'if possible he always preferred not to bother the department'.[46] After his breakdown, Mary and Dora became the initiators of institutional care. As they argued his case, they openly expressed anxiety about civilian mental hospitals: Dora wrote, 'I earnestly hope that he will be looked after as a returned soldier until he recovers his health and strength of mind & not be sent to Kew [Hospital for the Insane]'.[47] Mary expressed a preference for the Bundoora Convalescent Home. 'Could he be put on the waiting list for Bundoora could that be managed for him?' she pleaded.[48] Dora and Mary became strong and articulate advocates for Michael, and his 'confusional psychosis' was eventually accepted as war-related.

Family members negotiated with the authorities knowing that the latter wielded enormous power over the institutional treatment of their soldier. Just over half the family letter writers to the Victorian repatriation mental health authorities were women. Their role as correspondents may have been an extension of their duties as carers in the home, or reflected families' desire to inspire sympathy with an epistolary voice that was female. Conversely, the significant number of letters written by fathers was perhaps the result of families' decisions to lend the full weight of male authority to their sons' cases. The correspondence of both female and male writers is commonly characterised by a polite tone. In the early stages of the institutional relationship at least, family members' letters are imbued with a sense of humility and indebtedness, which at times is more pronounced in women's letters. Kin usually requested an institutional placement, rather than insisting upon it, to carefully lay the foundations for a positive relationship in the future. The letters of kin are typically different in tone to those written by irate disabled veterans or organisations, such as the RSSILA, who adopted a language of rights as they demanded better treatment. When Elizabeth Moffatt penned her letter to the Inspector-General regarding the institutionalisation of her father, she gently asked, 'Do you know he is a returned soldier?'[49] She adopted a submissive tone and deferred to his superior medical wisdom as a means of showing respect. 'We shall be pleased to have your advice on the matter' she wrote, asking for her father to be placed in the 'home for Ret. Men'. Perhaps fearing that the directness of her request might antagonise the Inspector-General, or result in a placement in a civilian asylum, Elizabeth added a supplicatory postscript, 'I would remind you again that we are not agitating for my fathers removal from Royal Park & shall leave that in the hands of Dr Philpott & yourself'. Through such careful 'emotional performances' kin usually requested an institutional placement, rather than insisting upon it.[50] In doing so, they struck a balance between asserting their rights as family members and cultivating harmonious relationships with soldiers' care providers.

Family members were greatly relieved when their loved one was accepted. They felt assured of superior treatment, and unlike families of civilian mental patients they did not have to pay a weekly 'maintenance fee' of 4/4½d.[51] For some kin it also removed the need to fund ongoing private treatment. In 1927, Reginald Mackie, a resident of the middle-class suburb of Hawthorn, paid for his son to be treated in a small private mental hospital. This arrangement possibly carried less stigma than treatment in a larger institution, something which may have been important to his social standing. In December 1927, perhaps reconsidering the financial sustainability of the arrangement, Reginald contacted the Department of Lunacy to enquire about whether Peter could be accepted into a military mental facility. The Inspector-General was not optimistic, noting that Peter's private physician had suggested that he was 'really not a war case at all' but simply an alcoholic.[52] After much negotiation between Reginald and the Repatriation Department, however, Peter's mental troubles were accepted. Reginald was nothing short of elated. 'My son is now amongst the soldiers at Mont Park and I am very pleased at the splendid treatment he is receiving', he wrote to the Inspector-General.[53] Reginald ultimately had to compromise his desire for private treatment, which he may have believed provided more specialised care than a larger hospital and did less damage to the family's reputation. Peter's admittance to a military ward, however, removed the burden of financial responsibility and bolstered their reputation in a different way. Mr Mackie could now convincingly speak of his son's condition as a consequence of war, rather than as a personal or hereditary weakness, an assertion he was less able to make when Peter was in a private hospital.

For veterans' families, military mental institutions not only lessened the stigma of insanity, they could also conceal the even greater shame of syphilitic madness. In August 1928, Mrs Enid Clancy visited the Inspector-General, stating bluntly that her husband, Edward, 'should be sent to the Soldiers' Block'.[54] In 1927, Edward's mental health had started to deteriorate rapidly, and within the year he was admitted to the Mont Park civilian hospital where he was diagnosed with general paralysis of the insane. We do not know whether Edward contracted syphilis before, during or after the war, or whether Enid knew of his condition. She may have believed truly that he had a war neurosis, but it is equally possible that she was aware he had syphilis, especially if she too was infected. If Enid did know, her request for his transfer to a military ward perhaps represented an attempt to minimise not only the stigma of madness, but the indignity of venereal disease. Edward had a record of distinguished service during the war, and was mentioned in dispatches for outstanding gallantry at

Gallipoli. Understandably, in the eyes of the community, Enid would have preferred Edward to die from a war-related mental disorder in a repatriation hospital, rather than from venereal lunacy in a public asylum. If his case was not accepted, her social standing, and Edward's memory as a soldier, were in danger of being disgraced.

FAMILIES' NEGOTIATIONS WITH AUTHORITIES

For some families, the unthinkable happened. Although their loved one was officially recognised as a repatriation case, they discovered to their horror that he had been placed in a civilian asylum. Throughout the 1920s, there was a shortage of beds in military mental hospitals. To ease the pressure, hospital authorities sometimes transferred soldier patients to civilian facilities, but did not necessarily inform their families. In March 1929, Edwina Leonard visited her brother at Mont Park and was shocked to discover him in a civilian ward. Upon returning home, she wrote angrily to the medical superintendent requesting that her brother was immediately transferred to the military wing 'where he rightly belongs'.[55] Given that Edwina already had an existing relationship with the institution, and Jim had already been accepted as a war case, she perhaps felt secure enough to convey her indignation in a relatively stern manner. Edwina was concerned that an ordinary state asylum would be detrimental to Jim's recovery, and undermine the years of nursing care that she and her mother-in-law had provided in the home. Edwina's persistence paid off. After a visit to the superintendent, she was assured that 'when opportunity offers', Jim would be transferred.[56]

It is difficult to assess the extent to which the advocacy of family members made a difference to the placement of shell-shocked soldiers. The Department prided itself on the scientific basis of its decision making, and did not openly identify the pressure of family members as a factor in the acceptance of ex-servicemen. It is clear, however, that relatives with persuasive communication skills and the confidence to petition government authorities made valuable advocates. Within the Department of Lunacy archive, middle-class families are over-represented as advocates. Arguably, their educational background, professional skills and cultural capital allowed them to negotiate more confidently on behalf of their loved one, in person and in correspondence. They may also be over-represented because they often went directly to the Inspector-General, who documented their requests. By contrast, the verbal communications of family advocates with hospital administrators do not appear to have been recorded to the same extent.[57] As a consequence, the nature and efficacy of such interventions is not easily discernable. We do know, however, that some family members turned to the RSSILA to advocate on their behalf, perhaps because they felt emotionally unable or socially ill-equipped to undertake high-level negotiations about matters of such importance to them.[58]

After soldiers were admitted to military mental hospitals, their family members often remained involved in their lives. Although veterans were physically confined away from their family residences, the boundaries between home and hospital were porous. Through visits and periods of leave, soldier patients and their families sustained and managed their relationships. During visits, family members brought comforts from home, such as food parcels, and were watchful for signs of improvement in their loved one's condition, while patients sometimes used visiting hours to appeal to kin for their release.[59] The journey to Mont Park and Bundoora presented practical difficulties for some families. These institutions were awkward to reach from the south or west side of the city, as Miss Bell of Geelong found when she had to catch two trains and a bus to see her brother.[60] Rural families also faced the dilemma of distance, and often relied on written reports from hospital managers about their sons' progress. Some families who resided in suburbs close to civilian mental hospitals, such as Kew, agreed to the placement of their loved one in the local asylum so that visits would be more convenient.[61] Such relatives no doubt believed that their regular personal support played a crucial role in the recovery of their loved one. Within rural Victoria, some advocates felt that a man's removal to Melbourne's Mont Park Military Hospital would cause him greater distress than placement in a local asylum because it would separate him from his social support network.[62]

TRIAL LEAVE AND VISITING HOURS

Soldier patients were allowed home on weekend, trial or extended leave if their mental state improved. During periods of leave, ex-servicemen re-entered the domestic sphere and tested their ability to live a more independent life. The presence of the veteran in the home also allowed relatives to make a realistic assessment of their capacity to provide future support. Patients' leave also benefited mental hospitals, as it freed up much needed beds. Institutions carefully documented the leave process to ensure that an appropriate relative could supervise each patient after his departure. The nominated family member was required to sign a form guaranteeing they would provide suitable care. Many veterans successfully made the transition to permanent residence in the family home during a period of leave, and never returned to hospital. Other families, however, optimistically accepted their loved one home on leave, only to readmit him a short time later because they were unable to cope.[63]

For families whose soldier was ineligible for leave, visiting hours took on an enormous emotional significance. Betsy Burchett's early childhood was structured around weekly visits to see her father, who was admitted to the Bundoora Home in 1929. The family had a strong sense of his special status as a soldier, and valued his placement in a repatriation rather than a civilian institution. Betsy reminded me, 'we were never going out to Mont Park, we were going to *Bundoora*. We never were going to Mont Park'.[64] During the visits, Betsy and her mother spent time in the garden with John, discussing the progress of the gardens. They often lunched in the Bundoora dining room, and

John Godber Brown (left) was admitted to the Bundoora Convalescent Home in 1929. His daughter, Betsy (right), spent much of her early childhood paying weekly visits to him with her mother. Photograph courtesy of Betsy Burchett.

Betsy recalls John's concern to sit at a distance from the other veterans. 'He didn't want *me* to see all these other people', she told me, describing the family's negative feelings about the mentally ill. When she was ten, John banned Betsy from visiting Bundoora, because he feared that exposure to mental patients would 'alter' her as she grew up. Betsy's mother explained that it was for her own good, and that her father felt it was his duty to try and protect her. Her exclusion, however, remains a deeply upsetting memory to this day. Betsy did see her father occasionally, but it was 'not a regular thing'. John's institutionalisation effectively meant his permanent absence from home, and the cessation of visits only confirmed this loss.

POOR CONDITIONS AND COMPLAINTS

While visits allowed family members to maintain their relationships, they were also a means by which kin could monitor the welfare of their loved one and scrutinise the quality of care. While it appears that military institutions did offer a higher quality of care than civilian facilities, this was not always the case. The conditions in some military mental hospitals were by no means first-rate. At the end of the war, there were insufficient psychiatrists appropriately trained to treat shell shock cases, and there were problems employing suitable attendants. Mont Park was crowded and the sewerage system was 'always in fault, either being choked up or flooded out'.[65] Basic items such as socks, shirts and soap were supplied irregularly. Theft among patients was a problem, and residents lived with the fear of violence, even murder, from fellow ex-servicemen.[66] In addition to this, some hospital attendants were charged with 'ill-treatment of patients by way of physical violence'.[67] At Mont Park, one of the most significant problems was the lack of a satisfactory scheme of classification of patients to separate mild from severe cases. Not surprisingly, some patients experienced Mont Park as a stressful environment. In 1924, one patient complained that the environment was 'terribly telling' on his nerves and requested release on the grounds that his mental faculties would become 'impaired' if he remained.[68]

Curiously, there are few formal letters of complaint from family members in the Victorian Department of Lunacy archive. This could be a result of departmental culling before the files were handed over to the repository. It may, however, be a sign that families preferred to make verbal complaints to avoid any 'complaining correspondence' being used against their loved one. Mrs Albert Brown preferred to keep her complaints informal. In 1928, her husband was admitted to Mont Park as a repatriation case, but was later placed in a civilian ward due to overcrowding in the military block. In a personal interview with a Repatriation official she complained about 'the amount and quality of food he is receiving' in his new ward.[69] She explained that she visited Albert twice a week with a hamper of provisions, and was concerned that 'each time he is so hungry that he eats the lot'. Despite her concerns, however, the official noted that 'she does not wish to make any official complaint as apart from the meals as she considered the treatment her husband receives as wonderful'.[70] We can only speculate on the reasons why Mrs Brown chose to make an informal rather than an official complaint, and whether she feared that a more vigorous protest would detrimentally affect Albert's transfer back to the military wards. Her conciliatory tone is characteristic of family members' interactions with the Lunacy Department as they sought to keep the authorities on side.

Rather than share their grievances directly with mental institutions, some families preferred to express their complaints to soldier advocate organisations such as the SSFA and RSSILA. In 1923, the SSFA heard from one father whose son had 'virtually escap[ed]' from Mont Park, declaring that if he remained there he would soon become a 'hopeless lunatic'.[71] The sister of another patient informed the RSSILA that her brother 'had not even the common privileges of cleanliness, and was not allowed to keep his own towel, soap and toothbrush'.[72] Family members hoped that by complaining to these organisations and sharing their experiences, they would bring the plight of 'mental soldiers' to the attention of the government and change the way military mental institutions were managed. Indeed, during the 1920s, the SSFA, RSSILA and organisations representing the wives and mothers of veterans conducted a number of campaigns in various states to improve the institutional care of ex-servicemen.

POLITICAL ACTIVISM

In 1924, the RSSILA devoted much of its annual national conference to the question of returned soldiers' treatment in Perth's Claremont Hospital for the Insane. It heard from numerous community campaigners, such as the president of the Western Australian branch of the National Council of Women, who declared that she represented 'several thousands of women' concerned about the plight of soldier patients.[73] She called for an end to the 'old barbarous methods' of treatment in favour of more scientific approaches. Similarly, the president of the Housewives' Association chastised the government for being 'grossfully neglectful of mental soldiers' and demanded the establishment of new segregated institutions in 'attractive surroundings' close to the city to enable relatives and friends to visit easily.[74] Through their alliances with such organisations, family members' individual complaints were powerfully transformed into much larger political concerns. By working under the auspices of existing lobby groups, family members could voice their concerns, without necessarily revealing their identity. This was important for those seeking to avoid the public shame associated with their family's predicament. It was also a protective mechanism for kin who were anxious not to prejudice the mental health authorities against their loved ones.

While many family members worked for change in relative anonymity, some mobilised, in a most public fashion, to defend the rights of their loved one — they became activists. Fred Jacoby was a notable parent activist in Perth during the mid-1920s. His son, Fred junior, was a resident in the military ward of Perth's Claremont Hospital for the Insane, after returning from war with 'neurasthenia'. Jacoby senior was the leader of, and most probably established, an association called the Mental Soldiers' Parents of Western Australia. In 1924, he was the driving force behind a campaign to reverse the practice of integrating military patients into the civilian asylum population. Jacoby was an outspoken supporter of segregation, believing that the government had a moral obligation to honour its pledges to the nation's soldiers who had 'voluntarily sacrificed everything for us'.[75] He also demanded the right of parents to visit on a daily basis, the right of kin to arrange private medical assessments, the abolition of patient uniforms, and the appointment of a parent to the Board of Visitors. He sought to make the hospital environment a more friendly and egalitarian place for returned soldiers by insisting that no badges of authority or uniforms be worn by attendants. Jacoby was a prominent and highly respected hotelier and entrepreneur in Perth. The naming of a local park after him attests to the strength of local admiration. His willingness to advocate openly for his son and the soldiers at Claremont, and risk the public stigma of mental illness, can perhaps be explained by his confidence as a businessman, his relatively secure social standing, and the knowledge that he had the support of his community.

Family advocates, such as Fred Jacoby, publicly defended the interests of soldier patients with an awareness that mental ex-servicemen were often unable to look after themselves. Shell-shocked soldiers were among the least vocal and poorly organised of all returned men. The nature of their illness and the stigma associated with it undermined their confidence to articulate their concerns and engage systematically with mental health authorities. While some patients complained coherently to hospital managers and wrote to government authorities, many found it difficult to communicate effectively, particularly in public forums. Moreover, the complaints of mentally disturbed ex-soldiers were easily interpreted as the ravings of paranoid men, which prompted those who wrote to the press to use a pseudonym.[76] Unlike physically impaired veterans, who formed powerful lobby groups such as the Limbless Soldiers' Association, shell-shocked soldiers were less able to unite and represent collectively their own interests. Indeed, mental illness often isolated veterans from their social world, and compromised their ability to sustain interpersonal, much less political networks. Shell-shocked soldiers did not establish associations, but relied on the advocacy of family members and dependants' interest groups, as well as that offered by generic returned soldier organisations.

In Victoria, family advocates were at their most vocal as a political force in the early 1920s when, on several occasions, the Repatriation Department announced its intention to merge soldiers and civilian patients together in mental institutions.[77] The Department's proposals reflected its waning commitment to segregation. The dual system was proving costly to maintain, cumbersome to administer, and created pressures of space within institutions. The Department also believed that there was little clinical difference between soldier and civilian patients, and that the incidence of war neurosis was decreasing.[78] Its attempts to transfer military mental patients generated much consternation among veterans' relatives. In 1922, one father declared, 'anyone who knows how lunatics in State asylums are regarded, and the difficulties which have to be overcome before they can be released, will view with horror the proposal'.[79] The SSFA mounted fierce resistance by lobbying the Minister for Repatriation, engaging the assistance of members of parliament, and publicising their cause to win community support. Their efforts were sympathetically reported by newspapers which exposed the unjust treatment of soldier patients and praised the vigilance of 'the dads', as they kept their 'eyes on Mont Park'.[80] By the mid-1920s, the same families who had been reassured by the government's wartime promises of segregated treatment were now fighting for its preservation.

It is significant that family advocates did not call for improved conditions in civilian mental hospitals. Rather, they managed the stigma of shell shock by asserting that soldiers were superior to another stigmatised group: the civilian insane. In the SSFA campaigns of the early 1920s, members tended to use nineteenth-century terms such as 'lunacy' and 'asylum' as pejoratively to describe civilian patients, and reserved the more modern idiom of 'mental illness' for veterans. In doing so, they defended the boundary between shell shock and 'true' lunacy, portraying 'confirmed lunatics' as a less deserving group. Families were eager to preserve what remained of the heroic social status of their soldier and protect their own standing in the community. To this end, they harnessed and reinforced the existing stigma associated with insanity for their own purposes. They affirmed the 'otherness' of the civilian insane and created an identity of superiority for shell-shocked veterans. In this process, the meaning of institutional 'space' was a crucial marker. Shell-shocked soldiers' symptoms often differed so little from those of mentally ill civilians that the place of treatment became one of the key signifiers of veterans' superior public identity. Unfortunately, declaring the superiority of soldiers to the civilian insane was one of the few forms of control families could assert to lessen the shame of mental illness and protect their loved one.

While many soldiers in mental institutions were actively supported by family members, others received little or no assistance from kin. During the 1920s, Robert Mundey's anti-social behaviour was so extreme that he alienated his family and friends.[81] Robert enlisted at the age of sixteen, and was discharged with gunshot wounds, gassing, and shell shock. After his discharge, he became subject to 'fits of an epileptic character', took to drinking and exhibited violent and erratic behaviour. Within his close-knit Victorian rural community, Robert was a tragic and frightening figure prone to public outbursts of abuse. He was admitted to local hospitals on a number of occasions, but finally banned because of his offensive behaviour towards staff and other patients. By 1926, he was camping alone in a hut, unable to secure appropriate accommodation or support from his family or community members.[82] Sometimes, he claimed entitlement to treatment 'in an Asylum or home' but after being admitted he often violently rejected assistance from hospital staff.[83] During the 1920s, Mundey's social support network broke down as a result of his mental problems. By the 1930s, he had no advocates left, either within his own family or the repatriation system.

THE WALLS OF THE ASYLUM

Shell shock had consequences for veterans and their families that were vastly different to the challenges arising from physical injury and disease. Mental impairment brought with it the burden of social stigma. Many experienced shell shock as a dishonourable condition because it was commonly regarded either as the sign of a hereditary flaw or a personal weakness. The diminished agency of 'mental soldiers' also created particular demands on family members. While some kin were passive observers of the treatment of their loved one in mental hospitals, many redirected their energies towards active engagement with the authorities and became advocates for their soldier within the mental health system. Some kin defended the interests of ex-servicemen, not only at the institutional level, but in broader political forums, and in some cases they became activists. Their work reflected a desire for the best possible treatment for their loved one and to lessen the stigma of mental illness for the veteran and his whole family. To this end, family advocates employed the language of 'preference' to ensure separation of their soldier from civilian mental patients. Soldiers' treatment in repatriation mental institutions was proof that they were 'war-damaged' rather than insane, and publicly affirmed their special status as heroes. For some families, the act of securing a Repat bed was one of the few avenues left through which they could express their loyalty and affection for their 'lost' loved one.

Family support played an important role in the lives of shell-shocked soldiers, both within the domestic realm and in the external world of the mental hospital. In the home, family members were responsible for providing nursing care as well as practical and emotional support. From the moment their loved one entered an institution, however, family members' responsibilities shifted: the burden of care was transformed into a burden of protection. While soldier patients were formally the responsibility of the Repatriation Department after admission, the unfamiliarity and perceived dangerousness of mental institutions meant that family members took on the role of protecting their loved one and monitoring his care. Parents, wives and sisters became the guardians and companions of returned soldiers in the external world of the mental hospital and journeyed with them during the institutionalisation process. Despite being physically separated, they remained connected by the bonds of kinship and familial obligation. Indeed, for soldiers and their families, the 'walls of the asylum' were not just those which separated the sane in the outside world from the insane within the institution: there were also 'walls' within the mental health system to be defended.

CHAPTER 6

tuberculosis: the 'family disease'

> In Australia there are hundreds of young men who, after
> noble service at the fighting fronts of the old world,
> returned in the clutches of a cruel malady.
>
> *Register*, Adelaide, January 1921.[1]

Not all families lived with war disabilities that were the result of artillery fire or the 'shock' of battle. One 'non-battle' disability was surprisingly prevalent among returned soldiers – tuberculosis. This infectious disease had particular consequences for Australian families after their 'TB soldier' returned home. One such family was the Rouhans of Melbourne. In 1915, Patrick Rouhan was diagnosed with pulmonary tuberculosis while on active service at Gallipoli, as a result of climate and exposure. He was invalided home in 1917 and his British war bride, Dora, and their child joined him in 1919. As they settled into civilian life together, Patrick struggled to throw off his tuberculosis, and found it difficult to earn an income sufficient to support his growing family. In 1920, his boot repairing business failed 'owing to ill health', and shortly afterwards he was granted a full pension as a 'totally incapacitated tubercular'.[2] In 1923, Rouhan wrote to the Repatriation Department lamenting his family's plight, and explained that his own children had become infected with the disease: 'I have 4 young children, the oldest is just 6 years old and all are affected. They are always under medical treatment. Infact I go short of the necessary things which I should have so that I can give my children a chance to grow out of the disease if possible, *they being affected through myself*'.[3]

Patrick despaired that his infection had transformed his house into a 'consumptive home'. Against a backdrop of poverty, the daily life of the household was organised around his care and the prevention of further infection. Patrick slept in a tent outside to maximise his exposure to fresh air and protect his family from germs. Dora nursed him by providing a nutritious diet and treated him with home remedies to build up his strength. They worried about the future of their 'consumptive children' and the 'indifferent health' that Dora experienced from time to time.[4] Their domestic lives were shaped by invalidism, unemployment, and the ongoing threat of infection. For Patrick Rouhan, and other similarly affected ex-servicemen, tuberculosis cast one of the 'longest of all the shadows of war' over family life and the health of their loved ones.[5]

In 1920, the Repatriation Department estimated that about 3000 soldiers like Patrick Rouhan had returned to Australia with war-related tuberculosis.[6] Tubercular soldiers were the bearers of an infectious disease with morbid and fatal consequences, not only for themselves, but for their families. Tuberculosis was markedly different from other physical war disabilities. It was not a static wound, but an 'invisible foe' which insidiously ate away at the body of the soldier, slowly transforming men with fit, athletic physiques into frail wasting forms.[7] As well as being a disease of war, the 'white plague' was also a socially stigmatised 'scourge' that was already rife within the civilian population. Along with the 'red plague' (venereal disease) and the 'blue plague' (alcoholism), tuberculosis was widely perceived as a threat to the health of the nation, and sufferers were regarded as a 'menace to others'.[8] While wounded soldiers' physical losses were popularly regarded as signifiers of their heroic battlefield sacrifices, tubercular soldiers were viewed as men polluted with an 'enemy poison' – a poison which could be transmitted to others.[9] The disease often revealed itself slowly among returned soldiers, after marriage or the arrival of children. Because of the delayed emergence of latent cases, the extent of the disease among ex-servicemen and their family members only became apparent well into the 1920s.

This chapter examines the consequences of war-related tuberculosis for returned soldiers' families. In 1943, historian AG Butler declared that tuberculosis had far-reaching effects on the lives of ex-servicemen and caused problems of 'extreme complexity' for both veterans and the Repatriation Department.[10] At the heart of the complexity of the disease was its communicability. As one of the few infectious diseases of war, tuberculosis presented a formidable range of medical and social problems that set tubercular men apart from their physically wounded comrades. Tuberculosis did not fit neatly under the heading of 'war disability'. While archetypal battlefield injuries, such as lost limbs and gunshot wounds, were physically restricted to the body of the soldier, tuberculosis was a living organism that could escape the body. In the home, *mycobacterium tuberculosis* from the trenches of Gallipoli or the Western Front could be conveyed by the soldier through his sputum into the lungs of his family members, crossing the corporeal boundaries that separated veterans from their civilian kin. This meant that tubercular soldiers were not just 'disabled' by their condition, they were also potential transmitters of disablement.

In some respects, the impact of tuberculosis on soldiers' families was not dissimilar to the effects of other physical war disabilities. In many instances, however, the infectious, stigmatised and progressive nature of the disease placed particular burdens on households that set their experiences apart. Yet historians have been slow to investigate the unique place of tuberculosis in the history of war disability.[11] Not confined to the body of the soldier, tuberculosis had distinctive consequences for the health and wellbeing of veterans' families. However, although these men potentially spread the 'battlefield bacilli' to their kin, the Repatriation Department accepted no responsibility for the screening, treatment or support of their family members. In the case of war-related TB, the disavowal of relatives' health was particularly surprising given that this disease, unlike most other war disabilities, transformed family members into potential spreaders of infection who could endanger the health of the community at large.

A tubercular soldier rests at the Bedford Park Sanatorium, Adelaide, after his return to Australia, c. 1919. Photograph courtesy of the State Library of South Australia, SLSA, B49003.

THE WHITE PLAGUE

In order to understand the effects of tuberculosis within returned soldiers' families, we need an appreciation of the disease, both from a current and an early twentieth-century perspective. Today, tuberculosis is known to be an infectious inflammatory disease produced by the tubercle bacillus *mycobacterium tuberculosis*. It is chronic in nature, and damages the lungs by forming 'tubercule' lesions (this is known as pulmonary tuberculosis or phthisis), but it can affect other parts of the body such as the spine and internal organs. The condition is contagious, and is transmitted person to person, most often through the inhalation of sputum droplets coughed into the air by the infected person. The infection, however, can only be spread by a person who is in the 'active' stage of the disease. Exposure to *mycobacterium tuberculosis* does not automatically lead to illness, and symptomatic people only constitute a proportion of those infected. The chances of the infection becoming active are increased by factors that compromise the body's resistance and immunity systems, such as malnutrition. The progression to active TB can happen within months after infection, or be delayed for years. The symptoms include chest pain, difficulty breathing and moving around, coughing, weight loss and fatigue. In the final stages, the lungs may become so damaged that blood is coughed up, and death can ensue. In the mid-1940s, the antibiotic 'streptomycin' was discovered, and by the mid-1950s antibiotic therapy became widely available in the developed world, leading to a sharp decrease in the incidence of tuberculosis in subsequent decades in countries where treatment was readily accessible.

During the 1920s and 1930s, tuberculosis was a dreaded disease: there was no guaranteed cure and there was a high likelihood of death. Tuberculosis was a disease endemic to most European civilisations. In 1925, one expert estimated that as many as one in 160 people in Australia was infected.[12] Between 1900 and 1925, pulmonary tuberculosis was the single greatest cause of death in young and middle-aged adults.[13] It was not only feared because of the high mortality rate, but because of its devastating social consequences. Young families were particularly hard hit by the disease because it incapacitated breadwinners and child-bearers, and consequently brought unemployment, poverty and social ostracism in its train. Tuberculosis cut across class and occupation, but it had a particularly devastating effect on the poor because the slow debilitating progression of the illness resulted in lost employment over many years. For men, invalidism and their families' slide into destitution brought with it the additional stigma of unemployment and economic dependence.

How did soldiers contract tuberculosis? Given that the condition was extremely widespread in the general population, many men with tuberculosis certainly joined the AIF completely unaware, or in denial, about their condition. Upon enlistment, new recruits were asked whether they had the disease but they were not given a sputum test, a practice which, when introduced, saw a lower rate of TB among Australian soldiers during the Second World War. Occasionally, soldiers were discovered to have tuberculosis during training in Australia, and were not allowed to embark for active service overseas. Others were found to have the condition shortly after arrival in the Middle East or Europe. Some men, however, were certainly exposed to infection for the first time during military life, in the close quarters of the trenches, on overcrowded troopships or in military hospitals. The privations, squalor and unsanitary conditions of battle undoubtedly facilitated the transmission of the bacilli, awakened 'old tubercules' in soldiers' lungs, and accelerated the progression of TB to the active stage.[14] Indeed, epidemiological studies suggest that tuberculosis has traditionally flourished among soldiers during wartime.[15] During the Great War, there was wide popular acceptance that gas poisoning exerted a 'malignant influence' in the lungs, producing a 'fertile soil for the propagation of the tubercle bacillus'.[16] Yet tuberculosis could not be traced directly to gassing in all instances. Pilots and sailors also developed the disease. In 1922, one sailor at the

Bedford Park Sanatorium declared that his condition was attributable to spending many hours in a frozen sea after being torpedoed.[17]

Despite the varied origins of their infection, tubercular soldiers had one thing in common – they formed a new class of 'spreaders' who carried a 'foul tide of infection' into their family homes.[18] Australians welcomed home tubercular soldiers apprehensively because they knew that the 'white demon' they carried in their lungs was a potential threat to homefront communities. During the war, most people understood that tuberculosis was an infectious disease transmitted by germs, an idea which had all but superseded an earlier belief that it was a hereditary condition.[19] The acceptance of germ theory saw a shift in medical and popular responses to the conceptualisation of tuberculosis and popular attitudes towards sufferers. While the eugenically 'unfit' had been the subject of public anxiety in the nineteenth century, by the First World War it was 'spreaders' who were the danger, wherever they were to be found.[20] Indeed, by 1916, the Committee Concerning the Causes of Death and Invalidity in the Commonwealth confirmed that the most 'serious element of danger' was posed by carriers who actively transmitted the condition through personal contact.[21] The demise of heredity as an explanation relieved sufferers and their families of the old eugenic 'stain' of tuberculosis. Modern germ theory, however, brought with it a new nightmare – 'that being consumptive, *you were yourself* the source of danger to your family'.[22] It is ironic that at the very time when the Anzac soldier came to represent the epitome of citizenship, having 'given birth' to the nation, returned tubercular soldiers were gaining a reputation as dangerous carriers of 'the greatest "killer" in our national life today'.[23]

Tubercular soldiers survived the war only to return to Australia with a disease that was considered a 'menace to the country'. In the early twentieth century, amidst widespread anxieties about the falling birth rate and concerns to strengthen the 'racial fitness' and health of the new nation, the 'white plague' was perceived as a serious threat because it destroyed family units. Australian governments had already taken strong action against its spread. Tuberculosis officially became a notifiable disease in Victoria and New South Wales in the first two decades of the twentieth century, and immigrants to Australia with 'definite signs and symptoms' of tuberculosis faced deportation.[24] In May 1917, it became widely known that a number of Sydney soldiers had returned to their homes untreated, and a public panic ensued. 'Is it right', Miss Vera Bax of the Girls' Liberal League wrote angrily to her local member of parliament, 'that these men should endanger the lives of their own and other families?'[25] The government considered the mandatory detention of tubercular soldiers, but chose not to proceed because 'it hardly seems fair that discharged soldiers should be singled out' while civilian tuberculars were able to remain at liberty.[26] As a consequence of the government's attempt to shield Australia's heroic Anzacs from the stigma of tuberculosis, an unknown number of families was exposed to the danger of infection.

Upon their arrival in Australia, tubercular soldiers were encouraged not to return to their families straight away because of their perceived contagiousness. While the wounded often went home or were allowed to receive visitors in open hospital wards, tubercular soldiers were typically sent directly to military sanatoriums, or special wards in repatriation hospitals, where they were isolated and treated.[27] There was no compulsion to remain in a sanatorium. A number of soldiers, however, prudently chose to complete a course of treatment. Voluntary isolation was a central principle of the government's approach to the management of tubercular soldiers, as it recognised that 'one infective tubercular uncontrolled [was] a greater menace to the public health than 1000 tuberculars under adequate supervision'.[28] At repatriation sanatoriums, visiting hours were severely restricted, and patients were ideally discharged only when their condition was deemed neither detrimental to themselves nor dangerous to others. The main goal of sanatorium treatment was to reduce a soldier's infectiousness to a safe level through a regimen of bed rest, fresh air and a nutritious diet. Some soldiers progressed to the debilitating advanced stage of the disease, but many 'active' cases were successfully 'arrested' and discharged back into the community with no sign of the bacilli in their sputum. Yet the lack of an effective cure for tuberculosis meant that a soldier could relapse and become infectious after his return home. For this reason, sanatoriums placed a considerable emphasis on instructing patients on how to minimise the dangers of infection.

A FAMILY DISEASE

Tuberculosis experts believed that the home was the 'centre of infection'.[29] Accordingly, a key part of the education endeavour was the modification of personal and domestic practices. Soldier patients were encouraged to live with the disease in a self-disciplined manner, and to take responsibility for regulating any habits that could lead to infection. They were given lectures, demonstrations and leaflets with a view to encouraging them to keep their disease 'in subjection when once arrested'. As a measure to protect families as yet unformed, single tubercular soldiers were recommended not to marry 'for a year or two' to avoid the danger of infecting their wives and children.[30] This was no doubt difficult advice for some men. The official repatriation archive reveals little about how many veterans abstained from matrimony for the prescribed period, or how many married without fully disclosing their tubercular status to their spouse. Conversely, we do not know how many young women spurned the advances of returned soldiers with tuberculosis on the grounds that such an alliance was to be avoided.

Once treatment ended, tubercular soldiers were discharged, knowing that they carried not an individual disease, but a 'family disease'.[31] They were usually relieved to be reunited with their kin, as many experienced the sanatorium environment as restrictive and depressing. After rejoining his family, one patient declared, 'I personally am fighting the good fight at home under hygienic conditions and in pleasant surroundings'.[32] Within the domestic sphere, the first task of tubercular soldiers and their families was to create an environment suitable for the veteran's recovery, and one that minimised the transmission of germs. Medical experts advised that the home environment should be clean, light and airy to discourage the growth and activity of the tubercle bacilli outside the human body. Some tubercular ex-servicemen decided to relocate permanently or temporarily to a warmer climate. In 1926, after a period of convalescence in his parents' home in Tasmania, Harold Kenworthy moved to live with a cousin in East Moree in New South Wales, an area known for its dry, hot weather. He frequently sunbathed on the edge of a local water hole in the heat of the day, informing his father 'it will help bring my strength back'.[33]

Other soldiers remained in the family home but altered the domestic architecture. The Repatriation Department provided financial assistance for ex-servicemen to construct a 'sleep-out' on the verandah, which was usually enclosed by canvas blinds. Sleeping alone in a well-ventilated space, preferably outdoors, was thought to 'cool' the sufferer's body to fight infection more effectively, and lessen the number of germs in the communal household air. Men without verandahs sometimes used the payment to purchase a tent which they pitched in the back yard. For husbands and wives, the departure of a tubercular man from the marriage bed reduced the possibilities for emotional and sexual intimacy. Some couples, however, may have believed this to be prudent, as according to some experts, sexual relations 'hasten[ed] the progress of the disease'.[34]

In addition to segregated sleeping quarters, tubercular ex-servicemen and their family members were advised to adopt a range of bodily and domestic practices to prevent the spread of infection. The greatest risk was posed by the sputum of men in the 'active' phase of the disease. In 1921, the *Tassie Digger* warned that actively infected soldiers should 'never indulge in kissing'.[35] Even 'arrested' ex-servicemen were advised to live as though passing on the infection was a possibility. Sputum was to be expectorated into a receptacle, not a handkerchief, and beards and moustaches were to be cropped, as they were potentially laden with germs.[36] Ordinary shared household objects were also believed to be hazardous because they could harbour bacilli. Tubercular soldiers were advised to use separate cutlery and crockery, and to clean their teeth in a separate bowl, so that family members were not exposed to any lurking germs. In their capacity as household managers, women played a key role in the elimination of rogue bacilli in the domestic sphere. In 1918, the *Everylady's Journal* declared that it was a wife's duty to keep a tubercular home in a state of 'scrupulous cleanliness' because germs thrived in damp and dirty environments.[37] Tuberculosis demanded vigilance and the implementation of infection prevention practices that altered the household dynamics and reduced the freedom with which kin were able to interact. The health and safety of veterans' families depended on these practices to prevent germs from breaching their bodily boundaries.

Within the home, family members were involved not just in disease prevention, but in the daily care of tubercular veterans. Wives and mothers were responsible for providing nutritious meals and fortifying remedies to bolster their soldier's resistance to illness. Tuberculosis was an incurable disease, and its treatment lay not in medication, but in the restoration of physical strength and the management of symptoms. High protein foods such as dairy products, bacon and roast meats were recommended, and patients were encouraged to eat 'as much food as you can'.[38] Patrick Rouhan's wife Dora was a dedicated home nurse and prepared a diet mainly of milk and eggs, and administered 'tonics & all & every kind of patent food' to restore his strength.[39] She even developed her own rhubarb and soda mixture, which provided considerable relief from coughing. Large quantities of nutritious foods were expensive, especially for households with an unemployed breadwinner on a pension. In 1920, the RSSILA noted that a 50 per cent pension of £1/10/- per week was 'inadequate to furnish a TB with the necessaries of life which are absolutely essential to men suffering from this complaint'.[40]

PHTHISIOPHOBIA AND INVALIDISM

Tubercular soldiers frequently struggled to support their households financially. Like other physically disabled soldiers, many could only manage 'light jobs' and were prone to absenteeism due to chronic ill health. Tubercular soldiers, however, faced a unique threat – phthisiophobia, or the fear of tuberculosis. For example, in 1926, Jim Molloy responded to an advertised vacancy at a local cold drink factory in Adelaide, but on applying, he found that 'they would not entertain the idea of a T.B'.[41] During the 1920s, the Sydney City Council allowed limbless soldiers to staff newspaper kiosks on street corners, but was reluctant to issue licences to tubercular servicemen, a discriminatory practice that was supported by the police.[42] In factories and offices, it was not only employers, but fellow employees who objected to having tuberculars in their midst. The sacking of a tubercular soldier struck fear into the hearts of his family members. In 1928, one wife in 'tearful distress' reported to the Tubercular Soldiers' Aid Society explaining that her husband had been dismissed after disclosing his status to his employer.[43] Given the hostile labour market, finding another job was no easy task. Nonetheless, while some tuberculars were trapped in an uncertain employment cycle, others did find and retain suitable jobs. Beryl Nelson's father, Walter Marks, was hired as an outworker for a local factory and inserted wicks into kerosene lamps by hand at the kitchen table.[44] Working at home, he could set his own hours and did not have to exert himself physically. Importantly, although he visited the factory to pick up the lamps, he was separated from the other workers, and posed no direct threat of infection.

Tubercular soldiers' employment difficulties meant that families often relied heavily on a war disability pension for their survival. In theory, there was a special fixed 100 per cent pension rate for 'TBs'. In the eyes of some returned men, however, the Department's interpretation of the legislation 'was such as to make it practically useless'.[45] The prevalence of tuberculosis among civilians meant that 'war causes' could be difficult to prove. Moreover, men with delayed-onset TB often struggled to secure a pension because the link between infection and war service was hard to establish as the years passed, especially if the veteran had experienced periods of good health. Most tubercular veterans were on partial pensions which were reassessed every six months, resulting in fluctuations in their payments that did not necessarily coincide with employment opportunities. Notably, the *Australian Soldiers' Repatriation Act* did not recognise phthisiophobia as a barrier to employment. The Department was simply concerned with measuring scientifically the physical impairment of veterans, not the level at which they had been socially disabled. Although the Department assessed many tubercular soldiers as 33 or 50 per cent incapacitated, employers generally viewed them as a 100 per cent risk.

The combined economic and social effects of tuberculosis could be tragic. 'It is no exaggeration', lamented one commentator, 'to say that thousands of homes are wrecked yearly by this scourge'.[46] The disease had an inescapable presence in the home. The lack of an effective cure meant that family members were intimate witnesses to the slow physical decline of soldiers. The sound of a persistent hacking cough was common in the households of TB soldiers. As Beryl Nelson recalls, 'He used to cough a lot. He used to bring up a lot of phlegm, it's not very nice talking about that, but he used to do that, you know'.[47] While limbless soldiers could recover some of their physical function with prostheses, tubercular soldiers were at the mercy of a progressive illness which consumed the sufferer internally over time. Some family members spent years caring for chronically tubercular veterans, often knowing that they were on the road to a 'lingering death'. In the final stages of the disease, kin observed their loved ones enduring painful and distressing symptoms, such as the coughing of blood. Family members were not only witnesses to tubercular soldiers' physical demise, but the mental depression that commonly accompanied the disease. Tuberculosis often led to partial, prolonged or complete invalidism that could lead sufferers to feel hopeless about their circumstances. As the Tubercular Soldiers' Aid Society (TSAS) noted in its magazine the *Optimist*, 'his illness is usually a very slow one. He feels weak and miserable and worried'.[48]

Tuberculosis was a disease over which the sufferer had little control: it affected the basic functioning of the whole body and limited the capacity to engage in social events. Men had to accept that the disease diminished their ability to participate in activities that confirmed their masculine identity, such as physical labour and sport. For returned soldiers, the physical limitations of tuberculosis were keenly felt, and many struggled to adjust emotionally to their 'delicate' state and its attendant invalidism and dependence. 'Circumstances seem to force him to become a constant receiver' wrote one tubercular soldier, who stated that he had been 'robbed of the opportunity to give'.[49] Tubercular soldiers often found it emotionally difficult to adjust to an invalid's lifestyle and became 'depressed and debilitated individual[s]'.[50] Many lost hope about the possibility of recovery, and despaired about the future of their families. Others turned to alcohol even though abstinence was part of their treatment. The uncertain and terminal nature of the disease often engendered despair within households, and created heavy emotional burdens for both the sufferer and his kin.

Family members received some respite when tubercular soldiers were admitted to hospitals or sanatoriums for treatment. A stay in a country sanatorium offered patients the chance for uninterrupted bed rest away from the worries of home. In the minds of some ex-servicemen, however, sanatoriums were not places of cure, but depressing, overcrowded and unsanitary environments where consumptives were sent to spend their last days.[51] Patients were also separated from family members and the support they offered. Most sanatoriums had no accommodation for families, although married quarters were established at some facilities in an effort to entice men to treatment. Family separation came with its own stresses. 'I feel sorry for Mr Major being separated from his wife', wrote the Matron of the Angorichina Hostel in the Flinders Ranges, 'Today he spoke as if she longed to be with him, and he made me feel quite sad'.[52] Indeed, some men left sanatoriums mid-treatment because of worry about their family members and duties at home. For those who stayed, a full course of sanatorium treatment offered families hope that their loved one would return home in improved health. Yet for some, treatment only yielded short-lived benefits. In 1927, Mr Steven's health declined after he returned home from the Angorichina Hostel. As the secretary of TSAS noted, 'Mr Steven has not been at all well; in fact, his family is very worried about him. I am afraid he only has a small chance of escaping TB'.[53]

INTRA-FAMILY TRANSMISSION

Tubercular soldiers and their families had much to worry about – unemployment, discrimination, invalidism and death. One of their biggest anxieties was intra-family transmission. It is unclear exactly how many family members were directly infected by ex-servicemen because the Repatriation Department did not keep detailed information or statistics on the health of soldiers' relatives. Similarly, popular sources rarely quantified the problem, and tended to refer to the plight of wives and children infected by returned men in generalised terms. Arguably, this was because of a reluctance to 'blame' ex-servicemen for the suffering of their family members, or publicly stigmatise them further. Yet there is sufficient evidence from veterans' medical files and the records of organisations, such as the Red Cross and TSAS, that an unknown number of family members was infected by returned soldiers. As early as 1922, the Red Cross Aftercare Department which assisted ex-servicemen and their kin observed 'we have entire families that are suffering from the disease'.[54]

Soldiers who posed the greatest danger to their families were those who did not take adequate infection prevention measures. These included men who refused sanatorium treatment, or returned prematurely to their homes before they were pronounced 'arrested'. Some men believed that confinement in a sanatorium publicly advertised them as a consumptive and turned down treatment, while others resented being separated from family and friends. A number of these men were reckless with regard to their own infectiousness. In 1917, one army medical officer reported 'a large percentage' of patients released from the MacLeod Sanatorium in Melbourne 'have tubercle bacilli in their sputum and they spit it about indiscriminately'.[55] Men with such a cavalier attitude undoubtedly posed some level of danger to those with whom they came into close contact. Other soldiers dutifully remained in repatriation sanatoriums, but did not strictly adhere to infection prevention guidelines on their release. My interview with Beryl Nelson suggests that although servicemen may have been educated about their condition, there was some variation in the degree to which they implemented the recommended practices, which potentially created opportunities for the spread of disease.

During the 1920s and 1930s, Beryl lived with her parents, her four sisters and two grandmothers in a small two-bedroom house in Brisbane. Her father, Walter, was a tubercular soldier, and was awarded a 100 per cent TB pension in the 1930s. As a child, Beryl was not directly informed about her father's tuberculosis, nor did she understand the nature of the disease until she was in her late teens. Beryl now realises that some aspects of her early family life were shaped by his efforts to prevent infection. Walter shared his repatriation-issue cod liver oil and malt extract remedy with his children. Beryl was dosed up with 'that bally malt stuff' every week, which she believes her father administered because 'he knew what he had, and he didn't want us to have it'.[56] Yet Walter did not use separate eating utensils and crockery, nor sleep alone. The household used communal plates, glassware and cutlery, and the entire family slept in a sleep-out built on the long verandah, apart from the two grandmothers who were allocated the indoor bedrooms. This suggests that he had a discretionary approach to domestic infection prevention, which may have reflected the emotional significance of particular acts.

It is conceivable that Walter chose not to sleep alone on the verandah because he had a close relationship with his wife, Clarinda. Faced with permanent exile to the sleep-out, Walter may have negotiated with Clarinda to sleep outdoors together rather than be separated. Screening off the children's beds at the opposite end of the verandah was a creative solution to a space problem, and also allowed their lungs to be fortified with fresh air as a preventive measure. Beryl spoke tenderly about the enduring bonds within her family, and suggested that these sleeping arrangements were 'probably why we kept together'. Given the closeness of the family, it is not surprising that Walter chose not to use different cutlery and crockery. He may have preferred to participate in mealtimes without feeling constrained by the use of separate utensils, or perhaps he felt awkward explaining to his young children why he used 'special' plates and cups. The reluctance of Walter and Clarinda to inform the children about their father's disease suggests that they feared revealing it might frighten or alienate them. Arguably, the desire to feel emotionally part of, rather than separate from, one's family, was a powerful factor which influenced the degree to which infection prevention practices were followed. Walter died from tuberculosis in the 1940s, and neither Clarinda Marks nor her daughters ever became infected.

Although Walter adopted some infection prevention strategies, other tubercular soldiers took no action. In some instances, this was because they had no idea they had the disease. A number of veterans were discharged from the army without symptoms, and did not seek treatment until it had been allowed to progress to an advanced stage in civilian life. In its early stages, tuberculosis was easily mistaken for a cough or bronchitis, and some men may have assumed that their 'chest troubles' were a chronic respiratory problem, especially if they had been gassed. Others may have suspected they were infected with tuberculosis, but lived in a state of denial about their danger to others and never sought treatment. A number of veterans deliberately chose not to disclose their status to wives and family members because of the stigma attached to tuberculosis, which only increased the opportunities for transmission. One public health expert pointed to a number of tragic cases of family infection resulting from soldiers' mistaken belief that 'war-time TB' was different from the civilian condition. These men knew they had tuberculosis but did not believe themselves to be contagious, and 'refused to submit to a family investigation' or accept medical advice.[57] While this misapprehension does not appear to have been widespread, it is further evidence that social and emotional factors influenced the ways in which soldiers managed their infectiousness, and that the possibilities for transmission varied significantly between households.

Returned soldiers' wives and children sometimes contracted tuberculosis from actively infected men. In some instances, this occurred shortly after soldiers' discharge, but in other cases transmission happened well after the Armistice. By the late 1920s, the Red Cross announced 'it is true that many soldiers' wives have contracted the illness'.[58] In 1929, the RSSILA was so concerned about the danger to wives that it recommended to the Repatriation Department that they were periodically examined for the disease.[59] Wives were usually observers of the malady in their husbands. Once they had been infected, however, their roles reversed, and servicemen became witnesses to their wives' suffering. Veterans no doubt carried a heavy burden of guilt about their culpability as transmitters, and worried about the fate of their loved ones. In practical and economic terms, a wife's invalidism could bring a tubercular soldier's household to a standstill. In 1927, Angus Triffitt left the Angorichina Hostel because his tubercular wife was struggling to manage their dairy farm alone. He was 'just about distracted with worry' about how they would face the future both affected by the disease.[60] Given the dependence of TB soldiers on their wives, the shared invalidism of a married couple could completely devastate their household.

Tubercular soldiers also posed a danger to their children because, as one medical expert warned, 'the great majority of infections occur in childhood'.[61] Actively infected servicemen were advised not to have any contact with children because they were believed to be more susceptible to germs than adults. Anti-tuberculosis literature alerted parents to the dangers for infants. 'Never let your baby live in a house with someone who has active tuberculosis', warned one booklet for new mothers.[62] Some tubercular soldiers and their wives arranged for the regular testing of their children to monitor their health. After the death of her ex-soldier husband from TB in 1933, Mrs Gladwin took her daughter to a health clinic: 'The Dr said there is nothing to worry about with her as she is quite alright & not infected in anyway with the complaint her father suffered from. I am pleased as we can never be too careful about some things'.[63] Not all families were as fortunate. In 1935, the wife of one tubercular veteran, Mrs Elise Crellin, reported that one of her children was affected by tuberculosis and had started to cough up blood.[64]

OFFICIAL AND CHARITABLE RESPONSES

Despite evidence that war-related tuberculosis could be transmitted within ex-servicemen's families, the Repatriation Department would not accept any financial responsibility for the screening, treatment or care of soldiers' relatives. Repatriation sanatoriums only catered for soldiers, and family members had to pay for their own treatment in state or private civilian facilities. In Adelaide, low income families sought assistance at the home for consumptives on North Terrace. This institution was reportedly damp, cheerless and housed patients in small dreary rooms, which one commentator called 'death cells'.[65] The cost of sanatorium treatment for family members was an added burden for already struggling households. In 1929, TSAS was alerted to the case of Mr James, himself a tubercular soldier, who could not afford £5 per week to pay for his wife's treatment in a sanatorium.[66]

The Repatriation Department consistently rejected calls from the RSSILA and TSAS to provide free examinations and treatment for the wives and children of returned men with war-related TB. In 1929, the Minister for Repatriation, Neville Howse, claimed that there was no 'logical basis' on which family infection could be recognised, as it was not always traceable to contact with the soldier.[67] He insisted that the primary role of the Department was to educate the tubercular soldier to 'preclude the transmission of the disease to his relatives', and that any unfortunate family members were eligible for treatment within a 'very efficient' civilian system. The *Australian Soldiers' Repatriation Act* only allowed for the care and compensation of individual servicemen, not family units. Moreover, although the Act formally recognised TB as a war-related disability, the legislation contained an inbuilt bias towards measuring and compensating wounds, rather than communicable diseases. Accordingly, there was no mechanism for the recognition of the spread of TB in soldiers' families. In the eyes of the government, the official responsibility of the Department ended with the education of the tubercular soldier.

Given the reluctance of the Repatriation Department to respond to the spread of tuberculosis in soldiers' families, many turned to the Red Cross and other voluntary organisations, such as TSAS, for financial and social support. Such organisations recognised the effects of tuberculosis on veterans' kin and holistically responded to entire family units, serving both 'the stricken soldier and his dependants'.[68] Tubercular soldier associations flourished in the postwar period, and were among the most 'powerful and active' of all disabled soldier organisations, arguably because they served a large constituency of families which the Repatriation Department ignored.[69] In South Australia, TSAS provided a lifeline for struggling families. TSAS was a highly organised group of about 200 volunteers which broke away from the Tubercular Soldiers' Association (TSA) in 1921, to provide direct welfare support to TB veterans and their families, leaving the public political work of lobbying for pensions to the TSA. This dual structure was not evident within other disabled soldier populations, which suggests that there was a particularly high demand for support services among the families of tubercular soldiers.

TSAS provided financial assistance to 'necessitous cases', particularly to veterans who were officially rejected or received no pension. They paid, or provided loans, for items needed by tubercular families, including canvas blinds to enclose verandahs, foodstuffs such as eggs and milk, and assistance with the payment of private doctors' accounts for wives and children. TSAS dealt with distressing cases of family breakdown and helped to organise respite and permanent care for children whose invalid parents could no longer care for them. In 1929, it arranged for one of its volunteers to look after Mr Creed and his children during his wife's hospitalisation. TSAS feared that the young ones would be 'neglected' and not receive 'proper nourishment' in her absence.[70] In other cases, tubercular soldiers asked TSAS to find accommodation for their children on an ongoing basis, in private homes or institutions. In 1926, TSAS took responsibility for placing Ned Adams' children into the care of the Methodist Children's Home in Adelaide because he was too sick to continue caring for them in the absence of his wife, whom we can only surmise had died or was herself an invalid.[71] Adams' extended family members may have been reluctant to take potentially tubercular children into their own homes, fearing the infection of their own offspring. In other cases, TSAS arranged for children to be sent to orphanages upon the death of their tubercular parents.

The care of children of tubercular soldiers was also taken up by the Red Cross. In the early 1920s, the Red Cross established two 'preventoria' in the Blue Mountains west of Sydney for 'sickly and delicate children', who were sent there to have their health 'built up by rest and skilled care'.[72] Preventoria were institutions for 'pretubercular' children designed to stop the disease taking an active hold in their young bodies. During the early twentieth century, tuberculosis became increasingly redefined as a childhood disease and many preventoria were established across the developed world by anti-tuberculosis and child health campaigners.[73] Given fears about the falling birth rate and the racial health of white Australia, children became the new object of attention among health professionals. They represented the starting point for the prevention of disease and the cultivation of good hygienic habits. Shuna, Australia's first preventorium, opened in the Blue Mountains in March 1924. It housed 20 daughters of tubercular soldiers who spent from four to six weeks playing in the fresh country air, receiving nutritious food and plenty of milk, and sleeping on open verandahs.[74] In April 1925, Juong opened its doors to the sons of TB soldiers.[75] Children from poor homes were usually given preference, because it was believed that poverty and malnutrition heightened their chances of contracting TB.

In its annual reports, the Red Cross proudly described the wonderful transformation of children during their stay at preventoria:

> One tiny girl of five, pathetically weak and debilitated after months in hospital, weighed only two stone five pounds when she went to 'Shuna', and could not stand for weakness. A fat rosy little mortal who has put on twelve pounds in weight returned to her delighted parents after a stay of thirteen weeks in the Home.[76]

The Red Cross noted that many children at Shuna and Juong were not only physically weak but showed signs of 'nervous strain'. They warned that children of tubercular soldiers came from home circumstances that were 'by no means normal'.[77] Part of the role of preventoria was to relieve the emotional stress on young children caused by poverty and living with a chronically ill father. By 1928, 800 children had stayed in Red Cross preventoria and respite homes for children of returned soldiers in New South Wales.[78] It is notable that the Red Cross provided a whole tier of welfare and supported accommodation to tubercular soldiers' families without any direct financial help from the Repatriation Department. Indeed, the Department rarely acknowledged the ongoing work of the Red Cross for disabled soldiers' families in its annual reports or public statements.

COMMUNITIES OF UNDERSTANDING

Voluntary organisations such as the Red Cross and TSAS provided crucial material support to tubercular soldiers' households. For many families, they also offered a community of friends and 'fictive kin' that buffered them against social stigma and phthisiophobia. Tubercular soldiers and their kin were vulnerable to social ostracism as a consequence of the popular misapprehension that the disease was exceptionally contagious. Many people avoided the homes of affected men, and neighbours waved and called hello from across the street, rather than visit. Some quite literally ran away from tubercular ex-servicemen. One military medical officer recalled witnessing

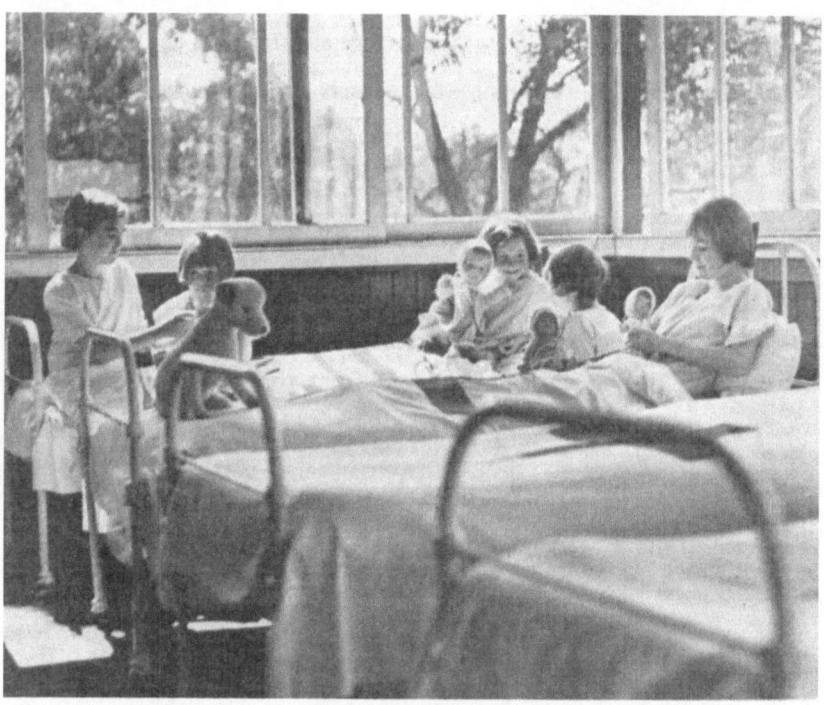

Young patients at the Shuna Red Cross Preventorium in the Blue Mountains, New South Wales in 1934. Red Cross, NSW, *Annual Report*, 1934–35. Image courtesy of the Australian Red Cross National Archives.

people 'scurry out of a railway compartment' on a train 'when a sufferer used a sputum bottle' on the way to a Blue Mountains sanatorium.[79] Understandably, many kept their status hidden. This could be stressful at social functions because the use of separate crockery and the embargo on kissing alerted others to their condition. The management of stigma and rejection, as well as the concealment of chronic illness were heavy psychological burdens for tubercular veterans, and led many to feel like outcasts. In some instances, soldiers and their families were shunned by their relatives because of the fear of infection.

In this context, tubercular soldier organisations, such as the TSA and TSAS, provided much needed social opportunities, sometimes replacing extended family networks: 'The T.B. soldier needs a friend and the T.B. Soldiers' Aid Society means to supply that need as long as it exists'.[80] At gatherings of the TB Women's Association in Adelaide, the wives, sisters and mothers of veterans, who had often first met during sanatorium visits, had the chance to gain personal strength from other women whose husbands were stricken with tuberculosis. As one observer noted, 'tragedy is rife in the lives of the members, but on their meeting day cares are forgotten, and we delve into someone else's worry and care, and learn thereby'.[81] TSAS was like a big extended family, and many members were in constant contact with the organisation over many years. Indeed, some tubercular soldiers preferred to join the TSA, rather than the RSSILA, because of the understanding they found in the company of tubercular veterans. For example, Beryl Nelson's father never joined the RSSILA, but was a loyal member of the TSA. She suggested that he did not fit into to the dominant culture of the League partly because of his ill health: 'he never went to [the RSL], because he never drank or smoked you see, so he didn't mix in with other people like where they go and have a drink and all that sort of thing'.[82]

The TSA and TSAS organised social events that welcomed people with tuberculosis, and provided them with a safe space, free from phthisiophobia. These functions were important for families, because they could socialise freely in the company of other people who understood their circumstances. When Beryl Nelson was a child, her mother accompanied her and her sisters to church and social events, as her father 'never went in amongst people'. Yet every year he proudly took the children to the annual Australia Day family picnic organised by the TSA in Brisbane. They were a highlight of her childhood because of her father's presence and the treats she received:

> Dad used to take us, the two or three of the older ones you know. And we used to go down the bay in Brisbane directly in a boat, the 'Otter', I remember it as well as anything. And we used to get free things on that boat, you know the call would go around, 'they're going to give out apples' or something. And we'd all queue up, and you'd have to go up this side of the boat, and around the other side, and they'd be 'round the other side giving out the apples, you know, and all that sort of thing. And then there'd be something else on, a bag of lollies, or something, you know.[83]

These events provided children with a happy occasion in a sometimes difficult childhood. The provision of free gifts was important for large families in difficult financial circumstances. Importantly, tubercular soldiers and their wives could forget about the disease for an afternoon, and interact without being overly self-conscious. Tubercular associations arranged social functions for members' children to a much greater extent than other disabled soldier organisations. Each year, 500 children 'looked forward with eagerness and expectation' to the annual TSAS Christmas party in Adelaide. It was on this day, reported the *Optimist*, that the organisation 'opens its arms and gathers its flock' to give families 'the brightest and most thrilling treat of the year'.[84]

A CHIVALROUS BATTLE

One of the most important roles of tubercular soldier organisations was to teach ex-servicemen and their families how to live with a disease that had such devastating consequences. TSAS named its magazine the *Optimist*, and encouraged tubercular soldiers to face their difficulties with a cheerful outlook, rather than dwell on their troubles. In 1926, TSAS posted 10 000 copies of the *Optimist* to its readers around Australia.[85] It continued to publish the magazine well into the late 1930s, which suggests that a large and loyal readership valued its advice. In the magazine, TSAS transformed tuberculosis from a menacing disease into an opportunity for self-improvement. Soldiers were encouraged to adopt a 'nimble' mental attitude and 'fight the poison' with a sense of hope.[86] The courageous battle against TB was a standard feature of the civilian literature on tuberculosis. This discourse suited returned soldiers particularly well because it reconfigured them as men actively engaged in a battle *against* tuberculosis, rather than as 'soldier spreaders'. The *Optimist* cast tubercular soldiers as manly protagonists in their own lives, and transformed them into active agents in charge of their own recovery, not passive victims consumed by illness. It suggested that 'TBs' were still capable of the same resilience and determination they had shown on the battlefield, and that their fight against the disease was worthy of respect.

The *Optimist* did recognise that tubercular soldiers were a threat to the health of their families. Rather than using the language of contagion or fear, however, TSAS adopted a chivalrous discourse about 'protecting others'. Returned soldiers were encouraged to take charge proactively and defend the health of their own families. While the advocates of shell-shocked soldiers claimed that war neuroses were different from civilian insanity, TSAS did not assert that the 'war time' tuberculosis was distinct from civilian TB.[87] It realised that infection blurred the boundaries between soldiers and their civilian family members, and that their efforts were best directed towards preventing the spread of infection rather than distancing themselves from civilians. Indeed, it even suggested that soldiers were more vulnerable to the disease because their 'powers of resistance' had been reduced by the hardships of war.[88] TSAS adopted the universal symbol of the anti-tuberculosis movement, the double-barred cross, which symbolised its commitment to halting the spread of disease.

Tubercular soldiers returned to Australia with a war disability unlike any other. As the *Optimist* reflected, they did not have the honour of 'losing an eye or a limb, or receiving a visible mark of conflict'.[89] Their disability was invisible, infectious and insidious, and a potential danger to their kin and other civilians. Ex-servicemen with TB and their families faced many of the same struggles as other disabled soldier households. Some of their challenges, however, were particular to the disease. The infectiousness of tuberculosis meant that within the domestic realm, soldiers and their kin partitioned themselves from one another through household practices to stop the spread of the bacilli. Family members were intimate witnesses to the slow physical demise of their loved one, and the lack of an effective cure meant that they lived with the constant anxiety that he may die. The disease could damage the economic and social worlds of the sufferer and his family. Within the labour market, soldiers faced the challenges of phthisiophobia and many struggled to secure suitable employment or gain a pension commensurate with their level of invalidism. Tuberculosis often brought despair and depression into tubercular soldiers' homes because of the degenerative nature of the disease, social stigma and chronic poverty. In some cases, ex-servicemen transmitted tuberculosis to those dearest to them. Yet the Repatriation Department was steadfast in its resolve not to treat or assist infected family members: it was still determined to section off war disability as a 'military experience'. The Department defined war disability as an impairment in the body of an ex-serviceman, and regarded his family members as merely 'civilian sufferers'. It afforded them no official status other than veterans' dependants, and took no responsibility for their wellbeing. This task was left to voluntary organisations such as the Red Cross and tubercular soldier associations.

The 1930s ushered in new challenges for tubercular soldiers and their families. The incidence of TB among returned men continued to increase, and in 1934, the RSSILA claimed that in Victoria alone more than one ex-serviceman was dying each week from the disease.[90] As tubercular veterans approached middle age, they became more susceptible to the symptoms of the disease. Moreover, the onset of the Great Depression meant that the economic struggle of their households became harder, and it became more difficult to purchase nourishing foods and to pay for private sanatorium treatment for family members. It was not just the families of tubercular veterans who faced such problems. During the 1930s, ex-servicemen with other war disabilities often found that their wounds were starting to deteriorate and they struggled to compete against able-bodied workers in a depressed labour market. For many disabled soldiers of the Great War who survived the 1920s, the 1930s proved to be a difficult decade. The next chapter explores how disabled soldiers and their families negotiated the new challenges that faced them during the Great Depression as veterans 'burnt out' and households found themselves in the midst of a dramatically different economic context. During that decade, 'manly independence' became an ever more elusive ideal and disabled soldiers became increasingly reliant upon the support and care of their family members.

CHAPTER 7

burnt out soldiers and the 1930s depression

> I am youth! Brim full of vigour,
> Unhampered by the weight of years:
> Ambition soaring higher, bigger,
> Unconquered by experienced fears.
>
> I am age – grown grim and hoary,
> Crackling bones full of fears:
> War-worn. I tell another story,
> Learn'd in the span of so few years.
>
> Duckboard, May 1926.[1]

During Melbourne's 1935 Anzac Day parade, three returned soldiers collapsed and died. Newspapers reported that many had found the strain of the march too severe, and described how thousands had dropped out along the way, 'many leg weary and tired'.[2] The march started at the Shrine of Remembrance and concluded at the Exhibition Building, a journey of some 2 miles (3.2 km), which entailed a long uphill climb along Bourke Street towards Parliament House. Some returned men complained that it was a 'very strenuous day for men over 40' and urged a reduction of the length of the march, or at least a downhill route.[3] One, signing himself 'Gassed' of Toorak, wrote to the *Herald* declaring that 'the present march is too severe for anyone suffering from a disability'.[4] Although newspaper reports optimistically emphasised the 'amazing spirit' of the diggers and insisted on their heroic youthfulness, the deaths of these Anzacs brought home the truth that Australia's returned soldiers were ageing and 'burning out'.[5] In 1915, the Anzacs had been described as superb specimens of manhood who had been baptised by fire at Gallipoli. Twenty years later, Anzac Day spectators watched men who had succumbed to the 'strain of the war years' and the 'nerve-racking and disease-spreading conditions' of the battlefield.[6] The following year, the Melbourne march was shortened and re-routed downhill to make it easier for the ageing Anzacs with grey hairs and bent shoulders, and the *Argus* proclaimed that 'time was marching with them'.[7]

By the 1930s, disabled soldiers and their families faced a range of challenges that they could have only distantly imagined when Australia's wounded warriors returned home from the battlefields of Europe. Young men who had enlisted in their twenties were now middle-aged men. In many instances, families lived with veterans whose wounds had degenerated, and whose physical or mental health was failing. Some households were touched by war disability for the first time as soldiers who had returned 'fit' started to suffer from war disabilities which 'almost unsuspected, were breaking through their health'.[8] Disabled soldiers' family members were also ageing. Parents and wives, many of whom had provided financial and emotional support to their soldier for years, were growing older and frailer. Veterans' children born shortly after the war entered their adolescence with the worry that their fathers' health was likely to 'deteriorate long before their time'.[9] The 1930s ushered in a dramatically new economic context.

As the Great Depression hit, ageing ex-servicemen found themselves unable to compete in a shrinking labour market, and wage earning opportunities for their kin also diminished. For many disabled soldier families, the Depression years increased the already considerable challenges they had confronted in the 1920s, and a significant number of households faced an unprecedented struggle for survival.

Yet, despite the greater vulnerability of ex-servicemen's families in the 1930s, the government did not increase its financial support. Faced with responding to mounting numbers of civilian unemployed, the government no longer viewed rewarding ex-servicemen as a national priority. Indeed, it actually reduced its economic investment in disabled soldiers in 1931 through a range of pension cuts. At the outbreak of war, new recruits and their families had been promised that the repatriation system would cater to 'every possible want of the soldier' and that incapacitated men would be looked after 'so long as treatment may be necessary'.[10] By the 1930s, however, it was clear that the government no longer had the political will, or adequate funds, to realise such idealistic wartime commitments. Consequently, as disabled soldiers aged, the economic climate worsened and the government tightened its belt, and many families of disabled soldiers were called upon to make even greater sacrifices than they had done in the 1920s.

This chapter examines the experiences of disabled soldiers and their families during the 1930s, a period still little understood by historians of the aftermath of 1914–18. Scholars' interest in repatriation, rehabilitation, and the emergence of disabled soldier organisations has seen a chronological bias towards the war years and the 1920s. The 1930s is often treated as a postscript: an era in which disabled soldiers were simply 'forgotten', even as the RSSILA consolidated its cultural position in Australian life.[11] Such conclusions echo disabled soldiers' own political claims that they had become 'forgotten heroes' who no longer received public sympathy and were victims of the government's broken repatriation promises.[12] But not all Australians were guilty of forgetting disabled soldiers. For the families of these men, war disability was not a fading memory, but a daily reality which saw increasing demands placed upon them: they could not forget. During the 1930s, as disabled soldiers received less financial compensation from the government and the significance of their sacrifices diminished in Australia's collective public memory of the war, the domestic burdens on thousands of ex-servicemen's families grew in magnitude.

BURNT OUT SOLDIERS AND THE GREAT DEPRESSION

During the 1930s, disabled soldiers' families lived with men whose physical and mental impairments had changed since their return from war. By 1933, returned soldiers constituted about 14 per cent of the adult male population over thirty, and their average age was about forty-four.[13] While some men's disabilities had improved or stabilised since the war, others experienced a deterioration of their impairments. Gunshot and shrapnel injuries created vulnerabilities within muscles, bones and organs, which became subject to secondary complications. Injured body parts became less supple as men aged and old wounds started to 'flare up'. An 'internal derangement of the knee joint' in 1916 could become painfully arthritic by 1929.[14] War injuries were subject to the strain of daily use and the internal interconnectedness of the body's systems, and even men whose disabilities were 'stationary' rather than 'progressive' could not escape the effects of time. One limbless soldier reported that he was 'unable to wear his artificial limb because of pain', and observed that the ankle of his 'sound leg' was also 'giving way'.[15] The health of shell-shocked and tubercular veterans was also subject to further deterioration, and the Red Cross continued to divert the bulk of its charitable assistance to TB and 'nerve cases'.

By the late 1920s, Australia's disabled soldiers were joined by a new population of ailing ex-servicemen. These veterans had no apparent battlefield injuries but reported to repatriation clinics for the first time, claiming that they had developed conditions due to 'the exposures and privations of war service'.[16] They commonly described the delayed onset of non-specific symptoms such as 'thinness and debility', 'periodical attacks in the chest and stomach caused from the effects of gas', 'weakness', and increasing 'dizziness and trembling'. This cohort of men steadily grew, and by 1931 a significant statistical shift in the composition of Australia's population of disabled veterans had occurred. 'Wounded' soldiers represented only 42 per cent of war disability pensioners.[17] The remaining majority had no apparent 'wounds' but exhibited a myriad of physical and mental ailments attributable to

Ageing patients at the Prince of Wales Military Hospital, Sydney. ABOVE L–R George Gregory, fifty-four, Robert McGregor, sixty, BELOW L–R Phillip Stapleton, thirty-three (the youngest patient), and Donald Sutherland, seventy-five (the oldest patient). *Reveille*, 1 August 1935. Image courtesy of Newspaper Collection, State Library of Victoria.

the 'blast of war' which, they asserted, had undermined their health.[18] By 1933, there were about 75 000 officially recognised disabled soldiers – one third of all surviving returned men – all incapacitated to a greater or lesser degree, and an additional unknown number of veterans whose health problems were not accepted by the Repatriation Department.[19]

In the early 1930s, the term 'burnt out soldier' came to prominence as a way to denote soldiers whose disabilities had 'gone bad', as well as those who developed health problems as a result of the 'intangible effects' of war.[20] The RSSILA was quick to respond to this concern and undertook a campaign around the figure of the burnt out soldier to gain more liberal pensions for ageing veterans. It asserted that *all* returned soldiers had a heightened vulnerability to disability and disease because their constitutional resistance had been weakened by war. Importantly, the League claimed that veterans 'had not as long to live' as civilian men. Unfortunately, the fear of premature death had some foundation. The comparative census data of 1933 (released in 1940) demonstrated that returned soldiers had a 13 per cent higher mortality rate than civilian men, which equated to approximately four years, although this claim was disputed by some.[21] Ironically, it appears that returned soldiers were 'burning out' just as decades of public health initiatives were delivering increased health benefits to Australians, and a larger number of people were reaching old age than in previous generations.[22]

Disabled soldiers of the First World War entered middle age as the effects of the Great Depression began to bite. The international economic collapse of 1929 had 'immediate and savage' consequences for the Australian economy, and ushered in the longest period of declining output and rising unemployment that the capitalist world had ever seen.[23] In Australia between 1929 and 1932, the gross national product fell 31 per cent, and unemployment rose from 10 per cent to 28 per cent.[24] The *Age* reflected in the winter of 1932 that behind the unemployment figures lay a 'tragedy of dispirited men and wan women and children'.[25] The human impact of the Great Depression in Australia has been well documented and debated by historians.[26] During the 1930s, employment was a key determinant of the well-being of Australian families. Households headed by breadwinners in secure full-time employment were able to remain relatively financially secure. Families of the jobless tended to face periods of protracted financial hardship because once people lost their job they tended to remain unemployed for a long time. The fortunes of disabled soldier families were similarly shaped by the employability of their breadwinners. Although not all ex-servicemen's households faced ruin during the 1930s, the diminishing employment prospects for ageing workers who were physically or mentally incapacitated meant that many were in a less stable financial position than they had been in the 1920s.

BURNT OUT WORKERS

Throughout the 1920s, employers had been reluctant to take on disabled employees, because of fears of reduced productivity and absenteeism. The onset of the Depression only made employers more cautious of hiring men who were not 'fully efficient'. Disabled ex-servicemen's increased age also made them more vulnerable to unemployment than they had been in the 1920s. As one burnt out digger lamented in 1931, 'the councils want able-bodied men, not wrecks'.[27] Few were willing to hire 'ageing mentals', particularly those with a history of institutionalisation. One patient at Bundoora resignedly wrote in 1931, 'there exists a very natural reluctance amongst employers of labour to engage an ex-patient from a mental hospital'.[28] Only a decade earlier, disabled soldiers had been eligible for vocational training and education programs to assist their re-entry into the workforce. By the mid-1920s, however, these schemes had been largely dismantled. During the 1930s, the Repatriation Department showed little interest in funding the retraining of ageing veterans. For disabled soldiers with limited skills and education, employment opportunities in new occupational fields were not plentiful. In an employment market characterised by an oversupply of labour, disabled soldiers not only had to compete with their able-bodied counterparts, but the next generation of skilled and educated workers rising through the ranks.

Disabled soldiers were often the first to be 'let go' if a business needed to cut costs. But ex-servicemen's vulnerability to dismissal did not always reflect their true capacity to work. For instance, during the 1920s, many disabled soldiers were employed in the federal public service on a temporary basis after failing the medical test for permanent employment. In the early 1930s, these men were sacked because of their temporary status, rather than a demonstrated failure to perform.[29] Despite their ability to work, they were easier to shed because they had never been securely employed. For such ex-servicemen who joined the dole queues during the 1930s, the competition for 'light work' intensified greatly.[30] Some government agencies that had offered 'light' positions during the 1920s were unable to meet the demand. In 1932, the Sydney City Council cut its capital works projects and declared that it was 'no longer capable of finding "light work"' for disabled men, including its own injured employees.[31] In this context, many burnt out soldiers found it hard to start again and were pushed to the fringes of the labour market.

While some burnt out ex-servicemen struggled to find employment during the Depression years, others had secure jobs and more easily provided for their families. Margaret Cramond's family was relatively well off because her limbless father, Alfred Plane, had an office job with an insurance company.[32] In 1932 the household income actually increased when Alfred received a promotion. Similarly, Joan Wishart reflects that the economic downturn 'didn't affect us that much' because her father was employed as a public servant in a specialised technical job in the growing area of radio, which offered him some protection from unemployment.[33] The Hargreaves were the only family in their street with a car, and Joan realises that the family's circumstances would have been very different if her father had been unemployed. Joan believes that he managed his mental depression by throwing himself into his work and keeping busy with other projects at home. The family not only benefited financially from John's employment, but it also had a positive effect on his mental health and their home life. During the Depression years, employment continued to offer disabled veterans financial and psychological rewards, and assisted them to gain self-esteem as breadwinners.

Families of securely employed disabled soldiers had the opportunity to lead a life of relative financial prosperity during the 1930s. Wages largely remained the same in real terms but the cost of living dropped, which meant that those with full-time jobs could take advantage of lower prices in food, clothing, housing and household goods. Even though the salaries of federal public servants, like John Hargreaves, were reduced by the Scullin government, these families were still financially advantaged because of the low cost of living. Some mildly disabled men in employment felt secure enough to give up their pensions in response to a government appeal in 1932, targeting veterans 'holding good positions'.[34] The lives of the securely employed, however, were characterised by a sense of wariness about the future. They witnessed the struggles of the unemployed, and lived with the fear that they may be the next to lose their job.

FAMILIES' PENSION STRUGGLES

During the Depression years, war pensions became crucial to the survival of the families of disabled soldiers, whose employment prospects were precarious. Between the early 1920s and the early 1930s, the number of families dependent on war pension payments had increased considerably. Over 80 per cent of all returned soldiers had married, and the number of pensioned veterans' dependants had almost doubled.[35] Although the majority of disabled soldiers continued to receive only a partial pension, it provided a small regular income which could be supplemented with other earnings. Importantly, the official acceptance of veterans' disabilities also relieved families of medical costs and meant that men were eligible for treatment in repatriation hospitals. During the 1930s, ex-servicemen applied for war pensions with a heightened awareness of their declining health and mortality, as well as the broader economic context. Some anticipated the day they would succumb to their injuries, and applied so that their dependants were not left in indigent circumstances after their death.[36] Returned soldiers sometimes came in for criticism by the civilian unemployed, particularly younger jobless men, because of the perception that 'old diggers' received an unfair economic advantage.[37] In their eyes, by providing ex-servicemen and their families with greater financial security than those on the dole, the government ignored the economic sufferings of a new generation of able-bodied Australian breadwinners.

During the 1930s, the number of war disability pension applicants increased, and by 1937 about 43 per cent of all returned soldiers had applied.[38] The deterioration in veterans' health prompted the rise in claims but the increased vulnerability of 'war worn' men to unemployment was also a factor. The Repatriation Department was critical of men who turned to the pensions system apparently because of unemployment, rather than their disabilities. During the Great Depression some unemployed disabled soldiers no doubt exaggerated their ill health to gain higher rates of payment. Repatriation doctors were wary of such men, and recorded their suspicions in the files of 'cunning' applicants who appeared overly knowledgeable about their symptoms, having 'read or been advised about' them.[39] The Department's heightened awareness of fraudulent claims meant that such claimants were not always successful. Furthermore, returned soldiers were statistically less likely to be granted a disability pension than ever before as the Repatriation Department tightened up the system to save money.

Despite the rising number of new applications, the total number accepted between 1930 and 1934 fell from 13 650 to 2792, and the number of pensions in force declined as the Department sought to reduce its expenditure.[40] During this period, the majority of appeals to the newly established War Pensions Entitlement Appeal Tribunal and War Pensions Assessment Appeal Tribunal were also rejected.[41] Those most at risk in the pensions system were soldiers who had not consulted repatriation doctors since they had been discharged from the army. The Department placed a premium on documentation, and viewed any gaps in a man's official medical history as an indication that the complaint was civilian in origin. Many years after a soldier's discharge, it was difficult to quantify the degree to which health problems were caused by war service or civilian life. The *Australian Soldiers' Repatriation Act*, written over a decade earlier, said little about measuring the degeneration of wounds over time, quantifying the effects of ageing or determining the cause of ailments delayed in their onset. During the 1930s, ageing soldiers felt betrayed if their claims were dismissed. 'It is very hard to think you are not intitled to some help when you know in your own heart that your sufferings were the result of happenings while on service', wrote one rejected applicant.[42]

Table 7.1 Between 1933 and 1935 the number of soldiers receiving war disability pensions decreased.[43]

Year	War disability pensions in force
1929	73 436
1930	74 578
1931	75 316
1932	75 646
1933	75 244
1934	75 037
1935	74 998
1936	76 337
1937	77 076
1938	77 315
1939	77 151

The Repatriation Department's strict implementation of pension legislation meant that it developed a reputation for being unsympathetic to burnt out soldiers and their families. This perception was reinforced when the Scullin government reduced dependants' payments by 22.5 per cent under the *Financial Emergency Act 1931*.[44] This was a blow to the combined income of families, and meant that households had to survive on significantly less. In a letter to the *Sydney Morning Herald* in March 1932, 'Disabled Digger' described how the cuts had affected his family:

> My lungs are gone through gas. Not bad enough for the special pension, but bad enough for £2/2/ weekly. I was ordered extras by a specialist, but through the reduction I have had to forgo them or see my children go short. I have had to move into a cheaper house. The house was cheaper because it was in a damp locality.[45]

Some women viewed the reduction in dependants' allowances as a particular affront because it devalued the support they provided to disabled soldiers in the home. The wife of one limbless soldier, Mrs Margaret Scott, asserted the importance of remunerating women's domestic labours as carers. She insisted that 'it must be remembered that … wives have the care of sick men (many of whom are very sick indeed). To have these men cared for in hospital would cost much more than the meagre war pension allowance'.[46]

The *Financial Emergency Act* contained another harsh measure for families. The government ceased paying dependants' allowances to the 'new' wives and children of war pensioners altogether. After 1931, disabled soldiers who married for the first time or remarried had to survive on a single man's payment alone. This was financially devastating for men who relied solely upon pension income. The measure explicitly deterred ageing disabled veterans from (re)marrying, and attributed less social worth to their new wives and offspring. It put single, widowed and divorced disabled veterans at a disadvantage in the marriage market, and reduced their chances of finding a younger partner who would care for them in their old age. This legislation was bitterly resented because it divided disabled soldiers' families into two classes.[47] Arguably, the embargo was designed to prevent opportunistic women from marrying elderly veterans and subsequently claiming a widow's pension in order to live an independent life at the expense of the state after his death. Yet it effectively punished disabled soldiers who had delayed marriage because of their impairments, and those who no longer had the assistance of their first wife. Given the unpaid support provided by wives to disabled soldiers in the home, the exclusion of 'new' wives and children from pension remuneration was particularly parsimonious.

Between 1930 and 1932, the government introduced a raft of other cost-cutting measures to reduce its pension expenditure on disabled soldier families. Veterans' employment income was taken into account for the first time and the entitlements of dependants deemed to have an adequate means of support could be reduced or cancelled, depending on the circumstances of each case.[48] Burnt out soldiers and their families did, however, receive some relief in 1936. In that year, the government amended the pensions system and introduced a Service Pension for all veterans over sixty, the tubercular, and the permanently unemployable, irrespective of the cause of the disability.[49] This mirrored the burnt out soldier legislation in Canada and Britain, which offered special pension benefits to ailing veterans. Tubercular soldiers welcomed the Service Pension, and constituted the largest single group who were deemed eligible for the payment. Many burnt out men, however, were unsuccessful in their applications because it was tough to meet the criteria. In its first year of operation, 2346 men were accepted but even more were rejected.[50] The pension was means tested, and men under sixty who applied on the grounds of being 'unemployable' had to prove that they were *permanently* unemployable, and accordingly

The pension income of disabled soldier families dropped when dependants' allowances were cut during the Depression. *Mufti*, 1 July 1934. Image courtesy of Newspaper Collection, State Library of Victoria.

the Act excluded those who were able to undertake casual work or who suffered intermittently from a disability or illness. While the Service Pension appeared to be generous, in reality its scope was severely limited.

AGEING SOLDIERS, AGEING FAMILIES

During the Depression years, disabled soldiers and their families found themselves in a changed economic context, and were faced with a pensions system which generally delivered lower benefits than they had received in the 1920s. As the years passed, families' personal circumstances also changed. Invalidism, the loss of income and family breakdown saw disabled soldiers and their kin living in a diversity of household arrangements. Some married men resided with their nuclear families, while others were taken in by extended family because they could not generate a sufficient income to live independently. Severely incapacitated men were often still residents of Anzac hostels, or spent lengthy periods of time away from their families in hospital. Other men lived alone and had never married, or were separated or divorced. A number still resided in the homes of their parents. The configuration of households varied greatly, but disabled soldier families had one thing in common – across Australia, ex-servicemen had all grown older. By the 1930s, the domestic labours of family carers were shaped, to a greater or lesser degree, by the ageing process and the deterioration of disabled soldiers' health. Importantly, the ageing of carers themselves also saw a shift in families' experiences of war disability.

During the war, the parents of disabled soldiers tended to be in their forties and fifties; but by the 1930s they were in their sixties and seventies. Parents were often the 'greatest friends' of disabled soldiers because of their loyalty to their sons as the years passed.[51] Some were a source of support during rehabilitation and periods of ill health, while others had been the primary carers of their sons since their arrival home. Some twenty years after the return of their sons, however, many struggled to provide home-based care. During the late 1920s, Clara and John Stephens were carers for their shell-shocked son in their home in central Victoria. Herbert was forty years old and had never married. He was unable to live independently because of his mental difficulties, and had spent the early 1920s in Mont Park Hospital. After an apparent improvement in his condition in 1926, Herbert was granted permission to return home. The Stephens' new life with their middle-aged son was difficult because he was 'not normal'.[52] He slept erratically and walked about the house at all hours of the day and night. Clara's and John's lives were dominated by Herbert's needs, yet they loyally continued to support him, insisting that 'the home is always here for him'. They fed and clothed him, and helped him establish a small bee farm to earn some extra money. Before the war, they may have looked forward to grandchildren and expected that their son's salary would help provide for them in retirement. Instead, as a middle-aged man, Herbert was still economically and emotionally dependent on them. Clara wrote to the Repatriation Department hoping that he would be favourably considered for a higher war pension, pointing out that 'his father is 73 years and I am 65 years'.[53] Like so many parents of disabled soldiers during the 1930s, the Stephens were tiring of the burdens of care in their old age. As Clara wearily reflected 'it has been a long war to us'.[54]

War disability cast an increasing shadow over the households of disabled ex-servicemen. During the 1930s, kin like Herbert and Clara Stephens often found that the demands on them for practical and emotional support grew. Wives continued to provide nursing care for their ailing husbands, although they too were growing older. In 1936, Ada Greer attended to the injuries of her fifty-year-old husband by 'fomenting his leg day & night to ease his pains'.[55] The burden of home care became heavier for the wives and mothers of shell-shocked soldiers because military mental institutions had become overcrowded. Yet women were also under pressure to generate income outside the home to supplement partial pensions. In 1932, Mrs Ingram gave evidence to support her husband's claim for an increased pension, stating that 'she has to work to keep him'.[56] For many of these women, such labours were not new, and there was a degree of continuity in the support they had provided to their disabled soldier since the war. And yet for other households, new demands emerged as their veteran's health declined. Extended family members were sometimes called upon for the first time to provide domestic support to ageing invalid men. Shortly after the onset of the Great Depression, Beverley Broadbent's aunt moved from Melbourne to the Mallee in rural Victoria to assist her brother, John Stubbs, and his young family, when it became clear that his health was deteriorating.[57] In order to assist ageing and infirm ex-servicemen, families became more inventive in the ways they collaborated to stretch their shrinking resources.

As soldiers' physical and mental condition broke down, their families also had to adjust to new regimens of medical treatment and hospitalisation. Between 1922 and 1939, the number of men seeking treatment at repatriation clinics and hospitals more than doubled, from 21 432 to 49 157.[58] This population consisted of men whose disabilities had been apparent immediately after the war as well as those whose health problems had been delayed in their onset. The recently invalided joined long-term patients in repatriation institutions, some of whom had not moved far from their hospital beds for up to eighteen years.[59] For some families, household life was significantly disrupted by periods of hospitalisation. In 1936, one ailing digger sadly observed: 'I am unable to make a permanent home through being forced to go to hospital at regular intervals'.[60] The interruption and anxiety caused by hospitalisation was more pronounced within families unused to the absence of their soldier. During visiting hours, relatives of the 'newly crippled' anxiously joined the kin of long-standing Repat patients as they called upon their loved ones in hospital.

GROWING CHILDREN

By the 1930s, the children of disabled soldiers, who were born in the 1920s, played a more prominent role in their fathers' lives. They were able to participate in hospital visits, as well as provide support to their fathers within the home and assist their mothers with domestic tasks. In the late 1930s, Henry Nugent's son had the responsibility of telephoning the Repat when his fifty-four-year-old father had a 'turn'.[61] Some youngsters helped their ailing fathers by assisting them with income-generating activities. During the 1930s, Joyce Muir's father was a ganger for the Victorian Railways and the family lived in the station master's house of a regional train station. Each morning, Joyce helped her father inspect the tracks before the trains came through. She now reflects that 'he was getting to the stage where he couldn't do the heavy work' because of his lung problems.[62] Joyce's assistance took some of the physical strain off her father, and allowed him to do a full day's work repairing the tracks. A father's declining health could come at an emotional cost for youngsters. Even at a young age, some children feared their father's life would be shortened as a consequence of his war disabilities. During her childhood, Beverley Broadbent was surrounded by war disability. Her uncle Rae returned gassed, her uncle John lost a leg, her uncle Wilson came back with shrapnel in his brain, and her own father Eric suffered from lung problems. She recalled that there was a sombre feeling within both her nuclear and extended family that these men had 'lost ten years of their lives' as a result of their war service.[63]

By the 1930s, the impact of war disability on soldiers' children had become a focus of concern for charitable agencies and returned soldier organisations. In 1929, the Red Cross expressed its fear that disabled soldiers' children were vulnerable to a 'reflex of troubles' traceable to their fathers' war disabilities.[64] The RSSILA was also anxious that 'an abnormal number' of veterans' children born since the war suffered from nervous diseases and chest complaints due to their fathers' service.[65] At the heart of these concerns was the belief that disabilities such as tuberculosis and mental unsoundness could be passed to children through hereditary or environmental mechanisms, and that ex-servicemen's physical, psychological and economic problems generally conspired to create an 'unsuitable' home environment. In July 1932, the Children's Health Bureau at Anzac House, Melbourne, opened and saw 3714 children in its first five years of operation.[66] The League's concern to monitor the wellbeing of disabled soldiers' children was informed by the growing child health movement, which asserted that intervention in early childhood led to a healthy adulthood. The services of the Bureau were free, and were used by parents unable to pay private medical fees. Notably, the Repatriation Department took no steps to monitor the health of disabled soldiers' offspring, nor to recognise the increasing strain experienced by family members as veterans' health declined during the 1930s.

TURNING TO CHARITY

During the 1930s, families were caring for burnt out soldiers at the same time as their household economies were coming under increasing financial pressure. Households often did not have sufficient savings or assets to see them through extended periods of unemployment, especially if the veteran had been unable to sustain a full-time job during the 1920s. The general increase in unemployment meant that opportunities for wives and older children to earn extra income outside the home were harder to come by. The cost of feeding, clothing and schooling children put a strain on the household purse. As children born after 1920 became young adolescents, they often cost more to keep but brought no income into the home. For large families with more mouths to feed, unemployment and inadequate pensions could spell disaster. Many disabled soldiers had already become dependent on extended kinship networks for financial and housing support during the 1920s. As veterans' economic prospects decreased during the Depression years, their reliance on kin often increased, and a new population of men moved in to the homes of more prosperous family members.

In 1934, Victor Whatley and his wife were 'forced to live with relatives' because he could not get a job.[67] Whatley had been wounded in the head by a bullet at Villers Bretonneux in April 1918 and was discharged with a small pension for deafness. He was a skilled draper and remained employed during the 1920s, holding several positions as head draper. As he aged, however, his hearing problem gradually worsened and eventually started to interfere with his work. By the 1930s, he was almost completely deaf and could no longer gain employment in his trade. The Repatriation Department steadfastly refused to award a higher pension rate. In 1934, Whatley commented that his injury placed him 'at a great disadvantage in competing with others when a job offers'. As one former employer observed, defective hearing was 'a great drawback' in an occupation that involved personal interaction with customers.[68] Eventually, Whatley and his wife had little choice other than to 'accept charity from my people', an arrangement about which Whatley felt intensely uncomfortable.[69] His pride in his skills, his service to his country and his identity as a breadwinner were all compromised as he was reduced to dependence on his relatives.

As the Depression worsened, increasing numbers of disabled soldier families looked outside their family support network and turned to charitable organisations. By 1936, the Red Cross noted that as soldiers reached middle age, they and their dependants became 'an increasing responsibility' for the organisation.[70] In one year alone, between 1929 and 1930, the Red Cross Aftercare Department in Sydney assisted 15 167 dependants of returned soldiers, some of whom were requesting assistance for the first time.[71] As children grew, families also looked to the Soldiers' Children Education Scheme and Legacy to provide educational opportunities for their children that they could not afford. 'Owing to my disability I have not been in a position to help my daughter in any way further than my pension would allow', wrote a veteran to the administrators of one educational fund.[72] While some philanthropic organisations were able to assist families, others could not always provide the desired level of support. During the Depression years, many charitable agencies found it difficult to raise funds, and their capacity to provide financial aid was typically reduced. To make the best use of their resources, patriotic funds and disabled soldier organisations often restricted their assistance to unpensioned disabled soldiers. For households whose pensions had already been cut by the 1931 *Financial Emergency Act*, and for whom dependence on charity was an undesirable alternative, the loss of occasional assistance from charities was keenly felt.

In some respects, the material hardships and survival strategies of disabled soldier families who had fallen on hard times were not dissimilar to those evident in the households of the able-bodied unemployed during the 1930s. Both suffered poverty and fell back on alternative sources of income. Mavis Floyd's ailing veteran father sold empty beer bottles that he collected after football matches at the MCG, and the family saved money by walking rather than catching trams.[73] Such stories of resourcefulness were common among poor families headed by able-bodied men.[74] Over time, however, families that were headed by a disabled breadwinner (soldier or civilian) were often under greater material and emotional strain than the households of non-disabled men. For most able-bodied men, there were few barriers to accepting the offer of a casual labouring job. By contrast, disabled veterans sometimes had to decline employment, such as seasonal farm work, which could exacerbate their disabilities and take them away from the family carers so central to their daily lives.

FAMILIES UNDER STRAIN

Many disabled soldiers on low or no pensions found themselves in a poverty trap which was damaging to their health. A lack of income reduced disabled soldiers' capacity to buy nourishing food, which also contributed to their 'health downfall'. Sometimes unemployment and financial troubles precipitated a nervous breakdown, particularly among shell-shocked men whose psychological state was already fragile. After almost two decades of supporting disabled soldier families, the Red Cross became increasingly willing to make public the plight of these households. In 1935, it described its work with burnt out soldiers who had 'los[t] their grip on life, both mentally and physically' as the result of a cycle of unemployment and mental depression.[75] Although it still affirmed the heroism and sacrifices of disabled soldiers, it no longer shied away from revealing the private struggles of wives who lived with their husbands' loss of dignity as they were rejected for pensions or jobs. Despair reverberated within the households of thousands of disabled soldier families. Financial and emotional hardships sometimes placed a strain on marriages. Perhaps it is no surprise that the 1933 census exposed a markedly higher divorce rate among returned soldiers than within the civilian community.[76] In 1936, the despondency of one burnt out soldier was so great that he told his wife that the men who had died on the battlefield 'had the best of it' in comparison to those who had returned disabled.[77]

Some wives burnt out themselves because of the ongoing stress. The Red Cross saw many women who had developed 'nerve trouble' as a consequence of their financial woes and associated problems that could be traced to their husband's war disability.[78] During the 1930s, Furlough House, the Red Cross seaside home for dependants of returned soldiers, continued to offer respite to the wives and children of unemployed disabled men 'who have borne the strain of the war years and the depression'.[79] It provided such kin with a fortnight's health-restoring respite from their daily burdens, free of charge. Other family members were grateful for a break in their own homes when their soldier was admitted to a hospital or institution. In 1931, the sister of one ailing returned man wrote to the Red Cross expressing her appreciation for being relieved of her caregiving responsibilities for a while. 'Thank you for gratefully receiving our Soldier Brother into your convalescent Home. He is so happy there. I shall never forget when I arrived at the Red Cross and you said you would be able to help him, and how my load has become lighter.'[80]

While many disabled soldiers received the continuing support of their families, some had no living kin to provide care, or had become estranged from their kinship networks by the time they entered middle age. These men became heavily reliant on the repatriation system. Those whose disabilities were officially rejected, however, often spent their last days in benevolent homes for the aged. 'Mental diggers' were particularly at risk of losing family support, and a number became 'homeless and apparently friendless' and had no relatives willing to support them.[81] Psychological problems sometimes created behavioural difficulties and strained men's capacity for communication and intimacy, which could lead to a deterioration of family relationships as the years passed. Ageing 'mentals' who had never married could easily become 'single lunatics' once their parents had died, especially if siblings or other kin would not take on the responsibility of their care. Sometimes family members ceased to visit their institutionalised loved ones, and despaired that they had lost the man they had once known. In 1930, Mrs Dorothy Clements asked the Inspector-General of the Insane whether she could 'go into the country with her children' because she felt that she could no longer 'do anything' for her husband, a patient at Mont Park.[82] For these men, mental institutions became a substitute home. Patients were provided with a bed, three meals a day and protection from the harsh economic realities of the Great Depression. In 1931, one shell-shocked veteran sought readmission, stating that he had been 'very foolish to leave one of your Institutions. The life is much harder on the outside'.[83]

BURNT OUT SOLDIER SETTLERS

In rural Australia, the 1930s was a particularly difficult decade for disabled soldier settlers and their families. By 1927, there were about 35 000 soldiers on the land, and the failure of the Soldier Settlement Scheme, particularly in Victoria, was generally acknowledged.[84] Tragically, the 'burning out' of settlers coincided with the onset of the Great Depression. Men struggled to turn a profit as their health declined. As one ailing fruit grower at Merbein stated in 1936, 'hard work is absolutely beyond me now'.[85] Soldier settlers often burnt out more rapidly than veterans in the city because of the physical strain of agricultural labouring. As early as 1923, one settler was reported to have the appearance of a man 'well up in years'.[86] By the 1930s, war-related health problems were plaguing settlers. The recurrence of the effects of injuries, the decline of physical wellbeing, and the emergence of mental disorders were common problems. But impairment was not always the sole cause of failure. In the 1930s, all settlers were at risk of reduced profits due to depressed prices, and increased debt if loan repayments could not be made. Even some properties owned by able-bodied veterans, which had formerly been regarded as show places of the district, were in arrears and experiencing diminished returns.

The Soldier Settlement Scheme had been attractive to disabled soldiers because it offered them the opportunity of an independent rural lifestyle that they could structure according to their impairments. They could work outdoors in the fresh air, set their own pace, rest if they became ill, and utilise the labour of their wives and children. By the 1930s, however, many were indebted to the state and had little control over their livelihoods, as their profits were eaten up in loan repayments. Farm work was often much harder than they had anticipated, and required physical endurance over many years. Ageing had particular implications for disabled settlers. They increasingly had to employ labourers for 'heavy jobs', which further reduced their profits. The Closer Settlement Board had ultimate control of the lease, owned the land and kept families under surveillance to monitor their efficiency and returns. Many families found themselves in desperate situations. To meet basic living expenses, some settlers took jobs away from their farms. Others turned to illegal activities, such as selling farm produce under a false name to avoid liens. Veterans, disabled and non-disabled, abandoned their blocks, or were asked to leave their land because they could not meet their loan repayments.

In some cases, however, pensioned veterans were at a slight financial advantage over the unpensioned. Thomas Fielder had his right leg amputated in France and was granted a pension of £1/17/6 per fortnight.[87] In 1922, he was granted land and the family sank heavily into debt. Yet they were able to remain on their block throughout the Depression years. It seems Fielder's pension provided an important and reliable source of income that allowed the family to scrape by. Pensions for 'permanent' injuries, such as limblessness, were relatively high and not subject to review or cancellation. But war disability pensions were not always a safeguard against financial hardship. The majority of disabled soldiers lived with less stable health problems that were subject to monthly medical reviews. If a veteran's health improved, his pension may have been reduced or cancelled, despite the unprofitability of his block and the market for produce remaining unchanged.

For disabled soldiers, failure on the land was experienced as a double loss. Men who had lost their health during the war now lost their optimism, money and liberty. Wives and children became witnesses to the emotional blow of failure, veterans' anger at the scheme, and the struggle to start again. In the 1930s, the Falconer family was thrown off their soldier settlement block in Western Victoria. Frank's chronic head pains had troubled him since the war, and made life as a farmer very difficult, but it was the slump in wool prices in the mid-1930s that dashed the family's hopes of success. Frank was faced with starting again in a depressed labour market which favoured the able-bodied. After an unsuccessful stint as a dairy farmer, he took a job with the Country Roads Board as a labourer. Despite the reassurance of a wage, the shift to a lower status job and the loss of his career prospects had a negative psychological effect. Keith Falconer recalls that his father suffered an enormous sense of personal failure and a loss of expectation about the future: this grief was felt by the whole family.⁸⁸ The 1930s was a difficult time for disabled soldier settlers to lose their land. Veterans were no longer young wounded heroes, but middle-aged men rendered physically and mentally weary by their experiences. The psychological stress of debt and 'bitter servitude' of the scheme was too much for some disabled soldiers to bear, and a number committed suicide, leaving their families in considerable debt and with lasting emotional wounds.⁸⁹

In 1922, the Repatriation Department confidently declared that the extent of war disability among returned soldiers was known and finite. It stated that no new cases were expected to emerge because

The Falconer family before they left their soldier settlement block at Lang Koop, Western Victoria in the mid-1930s. After the war, Frank struggled to work his block because of headaches resulting from a severe head injury sustained at Camiers in 1916. Left to right Colin, Keith, Donald, Mary and Frank. Image courtesy of Keith Falconer.

'the length of time since the Armistice has fully disclosed the physical condition' of the majority of soldiers.[90] The Department was optimistic about the potential for each disabled man to overcome his impairments and become a self-supporting citizen as time passed. By the 1930s, however, the Department found itself overwhelmed by an increasing number of ageing soldiers seeking medical treatment for a range of war-related health problems. Many burnt out soldiers were at an increased risk of unemployment, yet the pensions system tightened its criteria and consistently rejected cases where any doubt existed as to 'war causes'. In the early twentieth century, men looked forward to old age as a time of 'delayed reward' during which they would reap the benefits of their contribution to society in their lifetime.[91] But those who had served in the Great War faced a very different old age. Burnt out soldiers felt that the war had robbed them of their health. Together with their families, they struggled to cope with an uncertain financial future, and contemplated their own accelerated journey to the grave.

FORGOTTEN FAMILIES

During the 1930s, the combined effects of veterans' ageing, their deteriorating disabilities and the Great Depression were felt in homes across Australia. Families typically found that the economic and emotional burdens upon them had increased, and that disabled soldiers were more dependent on their relatives than ever before. Ageing parents and wives continued to care for veterans in the home, growing children became involved in the support of their fathers, and extended kinship networks became even more crucial to the survival of households. Yet, as families' burdens increased, the government's financial commitment to disabled soldier households actually decreased. Many ex-servicemen and their kin were left to turn to extended family networks and charitable organisations for material aid. At the very time when veterans' families needed greater assistance from the government, financial support was simply not forthcoming.

By the 1930s, disabled soldiers had, in many respects, become 'forgotten men'. We must remember, however, that disabled soldiers were not the only 'forgotten' ones: the sacrifices of their family members continued to receive little formal government recognition despite their increased economic and emotional burdens. Although families saved the government an incalculable amount on the mounting repatriation welfare bill during a protracted economic crisis, their unpaid domestic labours went unrewarded, both financially and symbolically. The government still insisted on treating disabled soldiers as breadwinners with the capacity for self-reliance, rather than as interdependent members of families, even though the ideal of 'manly independence' became even less realistic as veterans aged.

For many disabled soldier families, the 1930s represented the lowest point in the 'long war' they had endured since their 'changed man' had returned home. Over the subsequent years, some families continued to struggle with the consequences of disablement. For others, however, the 'long war' ended when their loved one died prematurely as a consequence of his war disabilities. During the 1920s and 1930s, thousands of returned soldiers succumbed to their impairments and illnesses, and a number took their own lives as a result of psychological and financial troubles. For the bereaved kin of these men, the death of their loved one saw the burden of domestic care lifted from their shoulders, and a new burden of grief take its place.

CHAPTER 8

postwar death, grief and memorialisation

> That war service was the cause of his untimely death, must be some consolation to those he has left behind.
>
> Comrade of an ex-serviceman who died from his wounds, June 1934.[1]

In 1926, Harold Kenworthy lay dying in the Randwick Repatriation Hospital, Sydney. Harold had experienced numerous health problems during the war, including heart troubles and shortness of breath, and in 1919 he was finally discharged as medically unfit. After persistent poor health in the early 1920s, he was diagnosed in 1924 with tuberculosis of the throat and lungs, which the Repatriation Department accepted as wholly war-related.[2] By April 1926, Harold's condition had rapidly deteriorated, and he was admitted to Randwick as an urgent case. His cousin shared the bleak prognosis with Harold's father in a letter: 'Harold wishes me to tell you that his case is bad ... I think that he understands that his case is practically hopeless'.[3] On 21

August 1926, Harold died from war-related tuberculosis at the age of thirty-six: ten years after he had enlisted. Two days later, his parents placed a death notice in the *Hobart Mercury* lamenting the loss of their 'youngest beloved son' and proudly noted that he was 'late [of the] A.I.F. 30th Battalion'.[4]

Harold Kenworthy was one of thousands of returned soldiers who died slowly during the 1920s and 1930s as a consequence of their war-related disabilities. Although his death was officially pronounced 'war caused', his family grieved in the knowledge that he was not publicly afforded the same status as the soldiers who died on the battlefield during the war. On the war memorial in his home town of Latrobe, Tasmania, Harold was never to be listed under the heading 'These Died', but named as a soldier 'Who Served'. At local Anzac Day memorial services, speakers rarely mentioned postwar casualties such as Harold, but focused on paying tribute to his comrades who had made the 'supreme sacrifice'. In 1940, Harold's sister requested that his name be added to the nation's Roll of Honour at the Australian War Memorial. But it was never inscribed.[5] During the postwar years, the deaths of disabled ex-servicemen, like Harold Kenworthy, were largely unheralded in public forums. Their families mourned men whose passing had an uncertain place in the nation's collective memory of war and public commemorative practices.

This chapter examines the meaning of the war-related deaths of disabled soldiers in the 1920s and 1930s. It explores family members' experiences of loss and grief and investigates how they expressed their sorrow within funeral and burial rites and other memorialising rituals available to them. Families' experiences of grief after a veteran's death in the postwar period were markedly different from those who lost a loved one between 1914 and 1918. During the war, kin endured a 'distant grief' after their loved one was killed on the battlefields of Europe, and mourned with the anguish of knowing that his body would never be returned to Australia for burial.[6] By contrast, disabled soldiers who died from their injuries after the war often passed away surrounded by family members, in repatriation hospitals or their own homes. Yet, although families of the disabled dead had the comfort of grieving in the presence of a body, their experiences of loss found limited public acknowledgment. Dead ex-servicemen were seldom named on war memorials among the 'gallant fallen', and official Anzac Day speakers rarely made reference to veterans' slow and painful demise. Within Australia's national commemorative traditions of war, the steadfast focus on the 'supreme sacrifice' of the battlefield dead served to overshadow the 'lingering sacrifice' of damaged ex-soldiers who died after their return home.

This had a profound effect on families of the postwar dead: it disenfranchised their grief. At the very time when public validation may have strengthened these relatives emotionally, the dominant 'grieving rules' of war commemoration did not adequately acknowledge the specific character of their loss.[7] As a consequence, they were left with a sense of being an underclass of grievers without honour or privilege.[8] Although such exclusion was sometimes a source of bitterness and frustration, these post-1918 mourners often actively worked to enfranchise their grief in positive ways through alternative strategies and forums. Many found meaningful validation of their losses through personal commemorative acts and community-based practices. For instance, kin frequently enlisted the help of local RSSILA branches to create specific funeral rituals for them, which affirmed their loved one's passing as a 'war death'. After the death of a disabled ex-serviceman, his family's burdens of grief involved negotiating a relationship with powerful patterns of remembrance within which they were marginalised. Although their 'labours of loss' were submerged within Australia's dominant commemorative traditions, they often found ways to mediate, publicly and privately, their grief and engaged sympathetic partners within their communities to do so.

Such is the power of the 'fallen' in the historical imagination that scholars have had relatively little to say about the deaths of returned soldiers after the war. Most studies begin with the premise that the war dead died 'at' and 'during' the war. Although ex-servicemen's deaths were a familiar and constituent part of postwar life, few historians examine veterans' deaths *after* their return home.[9] Our conceptualisation of the cost of war for Australian families shifts dramatically when we consider deceased ex-servicemen part of 'the war dead'. Moreover, the number of families touched by war-related death becomes much larger than we usually recognise. These families constituted a distinct community of mourners whose grief had its own particular contours. Their history prompts us to reconceptualise the spatial and temporal boundaries of 'war death' and its attendant grief, and challenges us to think beyond the limits of Australia's 60 000 'fallen'. Importantly, it enriches our understanding of the impact of disablement on families by drawing attention to the final phase of impairment for many soldiers – death.

A NEW POPULATION OF 'WAR DEAD'

The Armistice of 11 November 1918 signified the cessation of hostilities, but it certainly did not mark the end of war-related deaths. A new population of dead emerged, whose fate we must signal by adding the prefix 'postwar'. Gaps in Repatriation Department statistics prior to 1925 make it difficult to accurately determine the total number of postwar deaths. We do know, however, that between 1925 and 1940, 13 595 ex-servicemen pensioners died from officially accepted war causes, which equated to about two to three veterans each day.[10] Some, however, believed that the real number was much higher, because the Department did not include men whose deaths had been rejected as war-caused. In 1937, the RSSILA claimed that the true number of soldiers who had died from the effects of war wounds had surpassed the 60 000 who were killed on the battlefield between 1914 and 1918.[11] While such high estimates are not sustainable – the 1933 census showed that only 38 000 returned soldiers had died since their return – the symbolic weight of these claims remains important.[12]

During the 1930s, commentators argued intensely about the number of war-related deaths and the significance of soldiers' physical sacrifices on and off the battlefield. Some likened the 'returned dead' to Jesus, who was crucified slowly by his enemies and suffered a 'drawn out dying' in order to redeem others.[13]

Ex-servicemen died of an enormous range of war-related conditions. Some succumbed to the effects of deteriorating war wounds and chronic diseases, while others descended into alcoholism or took their own lives because of mental instability. Of course, not all disabled soldiers' deaths were war-related. Some died from 'natural' causes, unrelated illnesses or as a result of civilian accidents. Among returned soldiers, however, there was a heightened awareness of 'premature death' as a consequence of war. In 1930s Australia, men aged thirty could expect to live until sixty-nine, and a proportion of veterans was simply not reaching old age.[14] During the late 1920s and 1930s, returned soldier magazines carried lists of ex-servicemen under headings such as 'In Hospital' and 'Last Post' which updated veterans on the fate of their comrades.[15] These were the casualty lists of the postwar years. They listed the names, not of young Anzacs cut down in their prime, but middle-aged ex-servicemen whose wounds and impairments had finally taken their toll. In 1928, the *Sydney Morning Herald* described the death of Frank Healy, who had been paralysed at Gallipoli. 'Sapper Healy Dies: 13 Year Ordeal', cried the headline as the article described how he had lain 'helpless on an aircushion' since 1915.[16]

POSTWAR WAYS OF DEATH

During four years of war, the youthful 'fallen' suffered untimely and violent deaths as members of the AIF in the face of enemy fire. By contrast, disabled soldiers died as civilians, often in the company of their families, and their deaths stretched out over many decades. For many, the process of dying was gradual and often anticipated by their families. For some, however, the grieving process began the day their

THE DEATH OF "WALLY" GUY

Brave Soldier Passes

PATIENT SINCE 1922

Another story of the Great War —and a very gallant one—closed at Caulfield Military Hospital yesterday with the passing of Walter Henry Guy, one of the pioneers of the 14th Battalion. "Wally," as he was known to the hospital, was aged 38. He had been there since 1922.

Today his comrades at the hospital told of the wonderful cheerfulness of "Wally" during the time he was a patient. It is a story which reached its climax yesterday morning, when he was being wheeled into the operating theatre for the last time.

Turning in his cot, he wished his fellow patients "Cheerio" with a smile and a wave of his hand. The nurse who brought him out of the theatre again says that he was quite conscious. Scarcely able to command his smile, he gave her his last greeting—with a wink.

"Wally" Guy

During the late 1920s and 1930s, newspapers reported on the increasing numbers of returned soldiers who died from their war disabilities. *Herald*, 6 October 1932. Image courtesy of Newspaper Collection, State Library of Victoria.

soldier returned home. Alexander Cameron was already dying when he was invalided to Melbourne after being crushed by an ammunition wagon near Baupame in 1917. His sisters nursed him until he died in 1919 at their Surrey Hills home, three days after Christmas.[17] Like the Cameron sisters, many family members watched as returned men struggled with impairments which inevitably led to death. The spectre of death loomed large in some families, and children grew up knowing that time spent in their father's company was precious. In 1922, the wife and children of one soldier suffering a war-related heart condition cherished their daily life together as it was soon to pass – 'he is likely to die at any minute' observed one visitor.[18]

After the war, ex-soldiers' 'ways of death' were very different to those of their fallen comrades of 1914–18. During the war, soldiers sometimes died alone on the battlefield or in military hospitals surrounded by their mates or unfamiliar nursing staff. Their families received official telegrams containing only the most basic information, such as 'killed in action', or 'died of wounds'. Relatives waited anxiously for letters from chaplains, nurses and comrades which described the death and subsequent burial. By contrast, ex-servicemen's physical experience of death after the war occurred within the intimate world of the family – kin watched and waited. The 'medicalisation of death' meant that veterans often died at the local repatriation hospital.[19] Family members were encouraged to attend the soldier in his last days, and often had an understanding of his prognosis as well as a personal relationship with nursing staff. Other men passed away in the family home. In 1943, at the age of eleven, Diane Nicholas discovered her father's body: 'I took my father's breakfast to him, and he didn't wake up ... I knew he was dead really, but I wasn't going to admit it ... but my mother leapt out of bed and said "Oh, he's dead!"'[20] Here, most powerfully the presence of the body was experienced by kin. Diane's father died peacefully within the comfort and familiarity of his own bedroom, far from Pozières where he had sustained the chest wounds, to which his death was partly attributed.

The death of a disabled soldier had emotional and financial consequences for families which varied greatly according to the type of death. A quick death was arguably emotionally easier for kin than one which involved the gradual physical or mental demise of their loved one. The passing of severely disabled men who had endured years of 'living death', however, often came as a relief for families, as death brought finality to their physical suffering and loss of independence. Death also released family members from the burden of nursing invalid soldiers in the home and managing the challenging behaviours of mentally disturbed ex-servicemen. As households started their new rhythms, kin also had time to reflect on 'what once was' and 'what might have been' had their soldier never gone to war, or returned home wounded. For some, physical artefacts such as medicine bottles and walking sticks reminded them of the challenges of their shared life together. When Harry Spreat died from war-related tuberculosis in 1924, his wife and two children were left with the 'sleep out' he had constructed on the verandah.[21]

Suicide was one of the most difficult types of death experienced by ex-servicemen's families. Here, the grieving process was complicated, because their loved one had chosen to abandon his kin.[22] Distressed families were also left with the shame and stigma of suicide. The Department of Repatriation kept no formal record of the rate of suicide among returned soldiers, and it can be difficult to discern, from soldiers' medical files, the extent to which their actions stemmed from their war service or from financial or domestic difficulties in civilian life. There is, however, some evidence that ex-servicemen were more prone to suicide than civilian men.[23] It is clear that some men's traumatic wartime experiences left them emotionally vulnerable. In 1931, Clem Barrett 'went to pieces' and his wife described how he had become increasingly 'irritable and difficult to understand' since returning from war.[24] Clem tried to gas himself, but his daughter discovered him in the kitchen and turned the oven off. Shortly after this, he informed the family, 'I am done, I am useless, I have nothing to live for', and committed suicide with a razor.[25]

OFFICIAL RESPONSES AND PENSIONS

Disabled soldiers' deaths had significant financial implications for their surviving family members. During the war, dependants of the battlefield fallen were virtually guaranteed a pension because the war-relatedness of soldiers' deaths was rarely in question. In the postwar period, bereaved dependants of disabled soldiers were eligible only if the death was officially deemed war-caused. After a veteran died, the Department ceased his pension and commenced an investigation into the cause of death. This process could take weeks. The immediate loss of pension income was a shock for many families. Some struggled financially until a pension was granted or alternative income arrangements were in place. Families waited anxiously for the official pronouncement of the cause of death. Not all disabled soldiers, however, were deemed to have passed away as a consequence of their war disabilities. In some instances, disputes arose when families strongly believed that the death was attributable to war service, but this could not be clinically proven because of insufficient medical evidence. In death, as in life, the Department was obliged to apply rigorously the criteria of the *Australian Soldiers' Repatriation Act*. If a death was accepted, the soldier's widow, children and dependent parents were eligible for a modest pension. If a death was rejected, no pension was awarded and kin were no longer considered the financial responsibility of the Department.

The continuation of pensions for surviving dependants was essential for households that could not generate a sufficient livelihood, particularly those composed predominantly of women debarred from earning a male breadwinner's wage, and those with young children to support. Families who relied on a pension while the disabled serviceman was alive generally had an even greater need after his death. While some families had a small nest egg, the precarious employment patterns of many disabled soldiers meant that households often had little in the way of savings on which surviving family members could draw. The loss of pensions and the soldiers' employment income could be disastrous, and some households lost the capacity to function as an independent unit. Such families often turned to extended family networks. In 1935, Mrs Frances Kelly was living with her son-in-law because she was unable to manage on her small pension after her husband died from war-related tuberculosis.[26] Others sought assistance from voluntary associations. The Red Cross provided 'comforts' to families of the disabled dead, and TSAS made ongoing weekly payments to unpensioned widows of tubercular soldiers, regardless of whether the death had been officially accepted.[27]

In some instances, families split up after the death of a disabled soldier if they were unable to survive financially. In 1931, Mrs Ethel Chamberlain wrote to the Repatriation Department regarding her nephews, who were orphaned after the suicide of their soldier father. Charles Chamberlain had been a 'nervous wreck' since his return from war.[28] During the 1920s, he lost his tramways job and failed to make a success of his soldier settlement block at Bendigo. In the late 1920s, Charles' wife died, leaving him with four children under the age of six, and two months later he took his own life. In the eyes of the Repatriation Department, Charles' suicide was triggered by the loss of his wife, and accordingly his death was not deemed war-related. The Department immediately ceased financial assistance to the family. The rejection of Charles' suicide meant that Ethel could not afford to raise the children in her own home because no dependant's pension was awarded. The four children were placed in the St Vincent de Paul Orphanage and raised at the expense of that organisation.

For family members, the rejection of a death from physical or mental war disabilities not only had financial implications, but often had an emotional cost. Official rejection denied family members the peace of mind that the death had been purposeful. Mrs N Fletcher's husband died in 1929, and her anger and frustration were still palpable in 1936:

> He suffered intense pain at times with his leg ... and pieces of bone were taken out at intervals, and I really believe that all the pain he suffered was partly responsible for his death. I am sure it must have been, but the Repatriation Department wanted me to prove it and I said God only knows and I could not prove it any more than anyone else ...[29]

Official rejection became a stumbling block to the effective resolution of grief, as well as causing financial hardship. While some relatives were content to accept that their soldier's death was not war-related, others appealed vigorously and continued to fight for pension justice for months or even years.[30] These 'unaccepted' mourners entered a kind of bureaucratic and emotional purgatory. Surviving wives struggled to claim a 'war widow' identity in the light of their unrecognised postwar sacrifices and those of their husbands.[31] Similarly, families of 'unaccepted' mental soldiers who died in civilian asylums were left with the ineradicable stigma that was publicly attached to the insane. Officially rejected kin were perhaps the most disenfranchised of all grievers, because doubt formally remained over the true cause of their loved one's death, which they were powerless to resolve.

After an ex-soldier's death, his family members had to begin their lives again. Bereaved wives were left to deal with the solitude of widowhood. In 1936, Iris Mead, the widow of a TB soldier, was 'becoming almost afraid of the loneliness of the house' and took in a lady boarder for company and to earn extra income.[32] Diane Nicholas told me that her mother found it difficult to socialise without her husband: 'widows weren't wanted amongst married couples in those days', she reflected, 'there was just one couple who stuck by her, otherwise they all dropped her'.[33] In addition to this, remarriage was difficult for middle-aged widows because few eligible bachelors remained from the First World War generation. Widows sometimes looked to Legacy to assist them to rebuild their social networks, and provide opportunities for their fatherless children.[34] Legacy was an organisation that supported families of the war dead, and provided programs for children, such as physical education classes, literary and social events, and 'big brother' schemes. Immediately after the war, however, Legacy generally only assisted families of servicemen whose deaths had been officially accepted. While most branches had relaxed this rule by the late 1920s, a small number of branches were fearful of being 'overwhelmed by the large number of "unaccepted children"' and excluded them well into the 1930s.[35]

COMMEMORATIVE EXCLUSION

During the postwar era, war-related death assumed vastly different forms to those experienced by Australian families between 1914 and 1918. Families' patterns of grief were shaped by ex-servicemen's modes of death and the intersection of personal and public 'loss contexts'. One of the most significant factors affecting their experiences was their secondary status within Australia's postwar commemorative traditions. Veterans' deaths and their families' attendant grief had little place in the nation's conspicuous public cultures of remembrance. For instance, on the war memorials that came to dominate the civic landscape, deceased ex-servicemen's names were virtually never inscribed: that honour was reserved for those who 'nobly fell'. This is perhaps not surprising. In the immediate aftermath of war, such monuments acted as surrogate graves for thousands of families whose loved one's body had never been returned home.[36] Yet, while war memorials were powerful 'sites of memory' for kin of the wartime dead, they acted less successfully as places of mourning and remembrance for families of the postwar dead.

In the early 1920s, most Australian towns and suburbs erected a war memorial. These typically included a roll of honour which named all who served, and paid particular tribute to the 1914–18 dead under headings such as 'The Heroic Dead'.[37] During the design process, local communities debated the merits of listing the returned dead alongside the fallen. Dead ex-servicemen, however, were difficult to memorialise publicly. Most committees were not prepared to leave an ominous space for those 'yet to die', nor argue about the inclusion of those whose deaths had not been officially 'accepted'.[38] War memorials were constructed from imperishable materials, which made inscriptions expensive and difficult to amend in the future. Moreover, in the eyes of some, it was best that the postwar dead remain nominally separate from the 1914–18 dead. Some relatives of the fallen felt their loss demanded a higher order of public acknowledgment than families whose sons 'were more fortunate and had come back'.[39] Although war memorials were 'creations of communities', many of which had first-hand experience of veterans' deaths, the demands of the wartime bereaved and the structural and temporal exigencies of monument construction, typically saw postwar deaths rendered invisible.[40] War memorials immortalised 'the fallen' by inscribing their names in stone, thereby providing a physical focus for families' grief. The names of those who died after the war, however, were also frozen in time – they remained forever listed among the 'living' returned.

There were some exceptions. For example, the University of Queensland War Memorial was unveiled in 1925, listing the names of thirty-three staff and students 'who died on the field or as the result of illness or injuries received after enlistment'.[41] Among those named was John Fryer, who had died as a result of gas poisoning in February 1923. Fryer was a much loved member of the English Department whose death was deeply mourned within the University community. The University's decision to adopt a comparatively broad definition of war death was no doubt made with Fryer's passing in mind, and reflected the esteem with which he was regarded by his colleagues. The naming of Fryer, however, while admirable, potentially created problems for the families of the other seventy-seven returned university men, some of whom surely died from war-related causes in subsequent years.

The naming of the postwar dead was also a vexed question for the management committees of larger state war memorials. These monuments took much longer to plan and construct. Many were only officially opened in the late 1920s or early 1930s, by which time a larger number of ex-servicemen had died. Yet the decisions of state committees varied. The Western Australian State War Memorial committee ambitiously decided to honour all who died on service as well as men who later died from injury or illness.[42] The Melbourne Shrine of Remembrance Committee similarly recommended in 1929 that a 'special tablet' be erected to perpetuate the memory of 'those who died as a result of war injuries subsequent to discharge' but this was never realised.[43] Despite a growing public awareness of the challenges facing ageing and invalid veterans, the 1914–18 dead remained the symbolic focus of most state memorials. Arguably, this was because these monuments were designed to transform battlefield death from a mortal condition into a sacred, noble and immortal state. Through its use of ancient Greek temple design principles, for instance, Melbourne's Shrine of Remembrance reminded visitors that the 'gallant fallen' had transcended their suffering and been made perfect in death.[44] There is no evidence that its architects were instructed to take into consideration the needs of disabled ex-servicemen. Indeed, each Anzac Day veterans in wheelchairs sat in front of the large stone staircase which encircled the Shrine while their comrades easily walked up to the sanctuary area. Such monuments were built with the integrity of the soldier's body in mind – to celebrate his masculine beauty before he fell – not to remind visitors of the damage that modern artillery could wreak upon men's bodies when they were 'unsuccessfully killed'.

ANZAC DAY

It was not only upon civic monuments, but in the public rituals of Anzac Day that the losses of families of the disabled dead found inconsistent validation. During the 1920s and 1930s, the primary focus of Anzac Day memorial services was to preserve the memory of the 'glorious dead' of 1914–18. Familiar rites were repeated (the Last

Post, the laying of wreaths), which allowed the bereaved to participate in a larger collective memory of loss during the war years. Such ritualisation helped forge a common narrative of the past which served to unify national memory about the battlefield dead and the meaning of their deaths.[45] Once the boundaries of remembrance had stabilised, however, it became difficult to accommodate newer narratives of loss. Speakers sometimes made a token mention of the men who had come back 'broken in health and spirit', but rarely mentioned those who died after the Armistice.[46] The 'backward gaze' of Anzac Day ensured that its commemorative focus was *memories* of wartime death.[47] It was neither a day to lament the struggles of disabled soldiers, nor to mourn the passing of returned servicemen, lest this detract from families' memories of the 'gallant fallen' whose heroic deeds had become a permanent part of the nation's history.

By the mid-1930s, as Anzac Day gradually shifted from a day of mourning to a day upon which returned servicemen celebrated their own war service and sacrifices, the grief of kin was further displaced, including that of families of the postwar dead.[48] Indeed, it is almost impossible to find any public acknowledgment of their losses in newspaper reports on Anzac Day events during the 1930s. This was an era in which the RSSILA increased its support to 'decrepit diggers', and commentators called for greater recognition of the 'returned wounded'.[49] Yet the youthful image of the fallen soldier – not dead veterans – remained at the centre of mainstream commemorative events. This is perhaps because, as historian Jay Winter reminds us, public commemoration infuses death with ideas of citizenship.[50] Within Australia's burgeoning national foundational narrative of Anzac, the battlefield dead had, as the *Brisbane Courier* put it, 'given their mortal bodies, in the belief that, by their sacrifice, freedom and liberty would be enshrined in the annals of the nations of the earth'.[51] By contrast, veterans did not inspire these meanings through their delayed deaths. They had not perished in the glorious act of securing nationhood: rather they had returned to their families and died as civilians.

On Anzac Day, families of the wartime dead became a community of mourners whose grief was 'entitled'; that is, its dramatisation was socially permitted within common commemorative narratives.[52] By contrast, mourners of the postwar dead constituted a community which had not yet completely formed, and whose diverse experiences of trauma and loss on Australian soil were awkwardly submerged in public memorialising endeavours. The resulting disenfranchisement of their grief is usefully understood with reference to broader shifts within cultures of mourning. There is a consensus among historians that the highly expressive public rituals for military deaths during the First World War were replaced with a 'model of suppressed or silent grief' which constrained mourners of the civilian dead after 1918.[53] As Pat Jalland has argued, the tragic mass deaths of young soldiers, whose bodies were never returned home, rendered the 'domesticated deaths' of individual civilians relatively insignificant.[54] As grievers of civilian men, rather than soldiers, kin of the postwar dead were perceived as less deserving of public acknowledgment, and as Jalland suggests, any claim to greater recognition, may have been perceived as 'self-indulgent and even immoral'.[55] Bereaved families of the postwar dead were caught in a shift between an old and a new context of mourning. Their grief was trapped between the past and the present. Families mourned a contemporary loss, but their sorrow and desire for memorialisation had its roots in the war years. This chronological misalignment of loss and grief, along with the diverse and 'unfinished' nature of postwar death, meant that public commemorative cultures seldom spoke to their experiences.

Little evidence remains of the 'private readings' of Anzac Day services. The feelings and reactions of the kin of postwar dead are difficult to uncover in the archives. It is clear, however, that some rituals simply did not make sense in the context of postwar death. Speakers' desire to remember 'the deathless army whose bodies lie on Gallipoli and other fields of the Great War' was at odds with families' visceral memories of suffering and death in Mentone, Mossvale and

Marrickville.⁵⁶ While sentiments such as 'Age shall not weary them/ Nor the Years condemn' may have consoled families of young men killed in action, such words hardly reflected the demise of soldiers who had died slow deaths from their war disabilities – age *had* wearied them, and the years *had* condemned them. There is evidence that some relatives of the 'fallen' chose not to attend Anzac Day services in order to protect their private memories of their loved one.⁵⁷ It seems equally as likely that some families of the postwar dead avoided official ceremonies because they felt alienated by rituals and rhetoric designed to honour the 1914–18 dead. We must not, however, assume that all kin bereaved in the postwar period were unable to engage with Anzac Day traditions. Some identified strongly with the heroic and immortalising language of Anzac Day, believing that their veteran had taken an equal place in heaven alongside his comrades who had died during the war.⁵⁸ Others uttered 'Lest we forget' to evoke memories of a 'broken' soldier rather than a 'fallen' soldier, thereby selecting and reinterpreting relevant parts of the proceedings in light of their particular circumstances. Yet, this is precisely the work of disenfranchised grievers: to assert the legitimacy of their losses within commonly accepted commemorative narratives.

LOCAL RITES OF MOURNING

Although families struggled with public cultures of memorialisation, they were often more able to articulate their experiences of loss and grief at local, community and family levels. In the first instance, the presence of a body meant that they could exercise a high degree of control over funeral and burial arrangements. During the war, families of the dead had little say over the burial of their loved one, and could only imagine how he was laid to rest, or request an official photograph of the grave. By contrast, relatives of the postwar dead were custodians of their loved one's body, and agents of the rituals of death. Although funerary customs gradually became less grandiose during the 1920s, families could still choose to bury or cremate their loved one with some degree of ceremony. In May 1920, Mrs Ida Kerin's husband, Ambrose, died at the Caulfield Military Hospital, and she decided on a padded coffin in polished kauri wood with a breast-plate bearing a crucifix mounted on the front.[59] At this time, funerals varied in price between £10 and over £60, depending on the quality of the coffin and the elaborateness of the services provided.[60] Mrs Kerin appears to have used her Repatriation Department funeral grant of £10 towards a rather expensive funeral which cost £24/5/0. Two years later, she still owed the balance of £14/5/0, which the funeral director wrote off as a bad debt.

The high cost of funerals often left bereaved families with a large financial outlay to manage, especially if the bill arrived before the veteran's cause of death had been officially declared. Fortunately, the RSSILA provided financial advice and assistance to the kin of ex-serv-

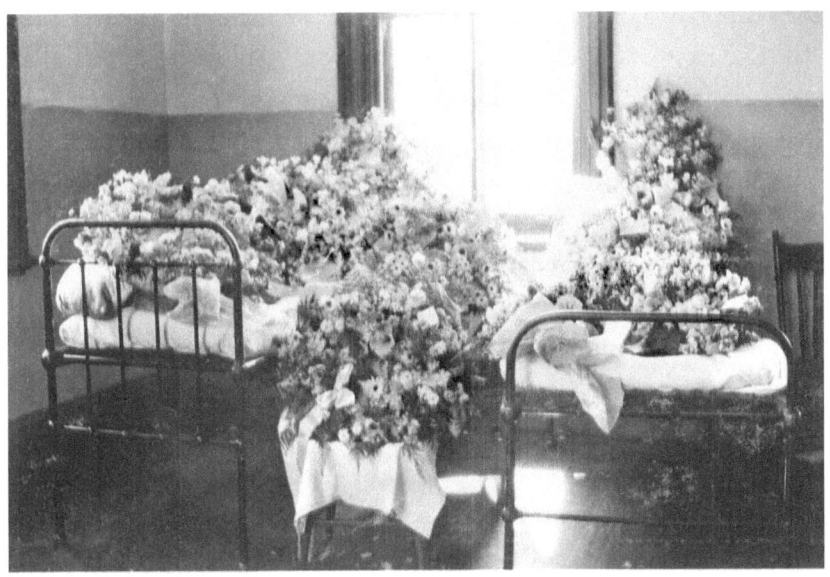

Floral tributes fill a room at the Keswick Repatriation Hospital after the death of a returned soldier, c. 1925. Australian War Memorial negative number P03845.004.

icemen during their grief. During the 1930s, Beverley Broadbent's father Eric was the secretary of the Caulfield RSSILA and was regularly called on to assist bereaved widows who had been 'conned into getting very expensive coffins' by the local funeral parlour. Eric would contact the undertaker to 'make more reasonable arrangements'.[61] The RSSILA, and other disabled soldier organisations, also provided funds to families unable to bear the cost of soldiers' funerals, especially those whose deaths were rejected by the Repatriation Department. One of Diane Nicholas' strongest memories of her father's death in 1943 was her mother's feelings of frustration and powerlessness at not being able to pay for his funeral.[62] In her grief, Mrs Nicholas turned to the RSSILA, who provided funds, which relieved her anxiety enormously.

In death, as in life, community organisations such as the RSSILA formed an important network of support for the kin of ex-servicemen. Through the provision of practical, emotional and financial assistance, they responded to families in need, and paved the way for the enfranchisement of families' grief at the community level. The RSSILA not only helped families financially, but was often called upon to incorporate formal League rituals into funeral services. These included draping a flag across the coffin, displaying soldiers' medals on top, and providing red poppies to mourners. Sometimes a League representative gave a speech acknowledging the effects of war upon the soldier. Such rituals allowed mourners to express their solidarity and fellowship with the family. For rejected families, those locked in protracted administrative battles with the Repatriation Department, and surviving kin of men who had taken their own lives, a formal RSSILA funeral provided a quasi-official setting in which kin could declare the death a 'war death'. In some instances, it was clergy, rather than departmental officials who most eloquently and publicly asserted the meaning of the death to the family. After the suicide of VC winner Hugo Throssell in 1933, the chaplain insisted at his funeral that Throssell had 'died for his country as surely as if he had perished in the trenches'.[63]

FUNERALS

At ex-soldiers' funerals, families had the opportunity to make meaning of their losses openly, and express a range of feelings in front of a sympathetic audience of friends and extended kin. They could grieve not only over the death, but for other losses they had experienced in the postwar period. After the death of her limbless soldier uncle in 1929, Beverley Broadbent recalled the profound sense of sorrow among mourners at his funeral.[64] Their sadness related not only to his death and the tragic circumstances, but to the struggles he had experienced after being invalided home without a leg. John Stubbs failed to make a success of his soldier settlement property at Manangatang and experienced increasing health problems during the 1920s. He eventually developed an ulcer from the physical strain of labouring, which burst and killed him before a doctor could be summoned to the farm. At his funeral, the family grieved not only for John's death, but the loss of his dream to become a self-sufficient farmer, and for the emotional and financial anguish of his wife and two boys, which continued after his death.

For the kin of shell-shocked men, funerals evoked a particular kind of 'double grieving' because these men had, in a sense, already died an earlier psychological or social death.[65] In 1943, Betsy Burchett's mother, Rene, decided on a low-key funeral after the death of her husband, John, at the Caulfield Repatriation Hospital. As Betsy recalls, 'it was a very private funeral, very private' at which family members reflected on John's life, without rituals which insisted upon the purposeful nature of his wounds.[66] Instead, they made sense of his war-related mental breakdown on their own terms. Betsy has overwhelmingly positive memories of her father as a popular, charismatic man with a wonderful personality, a view her mother encouraged her to cherish. At the funeral, the family focused on honouring the man they wished to remember. Rene Brown perhaps decided against an RSSILA funeral because she wanted to forget selectively some of the painful memories associated with her husband's war neurosis. Like

Betsy's mother, many next-of-kin decided against RSSILA funerals and some even rejected the official government funeral grant.[67] This may have been because they wanted to reclaim their loved one from his military past and any suffering associated with it.

GRAVES, HEADSTONES AND CEMETERIES

As families made funeral arrangements, they also needed to decide on the type of grave in which they would bury their loved one. Disabled soldiers whose deaths were officially accepted were eligible for military graves in Australia. These bore a headstone in marble, bluestone or granite of similar design to those in European war cemeteries, and were erected by the Defence Department at the request of the family. Yet not all eligible families applied. Such kin were perhaps reluctant to inter their loved one under a 'standard issue' headstone that forever identified him with his war service and diminished the significance of his civilian and family life. In some instances, relatives took no action to erect a military or civilian headstone, perhaps for financial reasons or because their relationship with the deceased had deteriorated over the years.[68] If the death was officially rejected, the family was obliged to bear the full cost of a civilian grave and headstone.[69] This was a cost that some families simply could not afford, particularly during the Depression years, and local RSSILA branches were active in raising money for dignified graves for ex-servicemen.[70]

For many eligible families, a military grave was important because it recognised ex-servicemen's sacrifices and validated the military origins of death. Although Betsy Burchett's mother declined an RSSILA funeral, she was adamant that John should be honoured with an official headstone because it meant that he 'was safe and sound ... that he was safely buried', and was peacefully resting as a soldier.[71] Betsy believes that an official grave also helped her mother to put her disagreements with the Repatriation Department behind her because finally, John had received an 'honest deal' from the government. Once families were informed of their eligibility for a military grave, they were invited to submit a short epitaph for the headstone. Most chose simple Christian sentiments such as 'Forever with the Lord', 'In the Love of Our Saviour King', or 'Peacefully Sleeping'.[72] Others, however, adopted the heroic language associated with battlefield death to affirm a sense of continuity with the 1914–18 fallen. In 1920, William Starke's relatives buried him under a headstone that read 'He faced death & fatal illness with equal courage'.[73] A few inscriptions point to the burdens that disability had placed on the family after the war, and the difficulty kin had in finding purpose in the death. In 1926, Claude Hancock's family decided on 'Sometime, someday we will understand'.[74]

Given that national public 'sites of mourning' seldom recognised postwar death, the graves of the ex-servicemen became important places of mourning for many relatives. Veterans' gravesides became a parallel world of intimate commemoration in which the bereaved remembered their loved one's return from war, his suffering and passing, without explicitly being reminded that he was not one of the 60 000 'noble dead'. Each Anzac Day, community organisations supported families' acts of memorialisation in local cemeteries. RSSILA branches arranged for soldiers' graves to be 'spruced up', and conducted special ceremonies at which a boy scout laid a wreath of rosemary and the Last Post was played.[75] The Anzac Fellowship of Women placed wreathes on the graves of returned soldiers whose wives and mothers were unable to travel to other districts.[76] Such local rituals at the grave were important for relatives, whether or not they were able to integrate successfully their own grief into the heroic pageantry of mainstream commemorative events. Again, it was community organisations such as the RSSILA, rather than official government agencies, that recognised families' emotional connection to returned soldiers' graves.

Indeed, the official care of military graves in Australian cemeteries often left much to be desired. During the 1920s and 1930s, the Imperial War Graves Commission developed a reputation for the

'His Duty Nobly Done': Major Harry Arnall died from war-related causes in August 1920 and was buried in a military grave at the Waverley Cemetery in Sydney. Australian War Memorial negative number H11674.

meticulous care and fastidiousness with which it tended the overseas graves of Australia's wartime dead. By contrast, the Department of Defence became known for its haphazard management of war graves in Australia, some of which were reported to be neglected and 'overrun with grass and weeds'.[77] While some military graves were well tended, the disregard of others became the source of complaint.[78] In 1935, Peter Soutar wrote to the authorities about the unkempt state of the Northern Suburbs military graves in Sydney: 'Many of the graves have <u>no headstones</u>, <u>no flowers</u>, [and are] painful to look at ... People returning from the Battlefields of France Flanders etc. have told me of the well kept graves and beautiful flowers trees etc. I ask Sir why all this neglect at the Northern Suburbs cemetery?'[79] In such instances, families of the postwar dead were forced to put up with second-class graves which publicly diminished veterans' sacrifices. For relatives who valued the symbolism of a military grave, the lack of government attention further disenfranchised their grief.

After the burial of their loved one, family members adopted various strategies at the personal and community level to ensure the remembrance of their soldier as the years passed. In 1926, seven years after the death of her son, Mrs Elizabeth Cameron belatedly applied for an official 'In Memoriam' badge.[80] It was important for Mrs Cameron to remember Alexander's passing as a 'war death'. She perhaps also sought identification with the community which mourned the 1914–18 dead, and wished for a kind of symbolic kinship with women who had experienced different 'ways of grief'. Indeed relatives' organisations, such as the Friendly Union of Soldiers' Wives and Mothers, catered to the needs of families affected by wartime and postwar death. Their members were both divided and united by their experiences of loss. In some cases, an individual's 'grief work' entailed coming to terms with both modes of death. On the eve of Anzac Day 1937, Mrs Fanny Maddern placed an 'In Memoriam' notice commemorating the death of a son in 1917, the death of another son in 1920, and a brother in 1932:

> MADDERN-BOWEN – In loving and proud memory of
> my sons and brother …
> What though their crown a bandage
>   Stretcher or cot their throne;
> Splints or a crutch their sceptre,
>   The Anzac name is their own.[81]

Relatives like Mrs Maddern were highly sensitive to the kind of memory of war enshrined by Anzac Day tradition, and that which it excluded. They were aware of the dangers of challenging it, and carefully worked towards integrating their own experiences into it. By claiming 'the Anzac name' for all her loved ones, she was attempting to close the gap between the past and the present, and assert the transcendent and inclusive potential of that commemorative tradition.

THE AUSTRALIAN WAR MEMORIAL

Although relegated to the periphery of Australia's dominant commemorative culture, families had one great hope for the public recognition of their loved ones' deaths – that their names would be inscribed on the Roll of Honour at the Australian War Memorial. The national war memorial in Canberra was one of the last war memorials to be completed in Australia. It took until 1961 for the bronze panels of the Great War Roll of Honour to be put in place. While local and state war memorials erected in the early 1920s rarely named the disabled dead, the management of the Australian War Memorial had much grander plans. Its policy was to name all who had been killed during the war, as well as those who died from their disabilities afterwards. In 1928, the *Sydney Morning Herald* confirmed that 'every Australian who died as a result of war sickness or injuries' would be included.[82] This reflected the view of the Director of the Memorial, Major Treloar, and Official War Historian, CEW Bean, that an honour roll consisting only of the names of those killed on the battlefield would discriminate against returned men whose deaths were a direct result of their war service.[83]

From the late 1920s onwards, the Australian War Memorial began the massive task of systematically collecting the names of the postwar deceased. In addition to receiving monthly lists of 'accepted' deaths from the Repatriation Department, the Memorial also encouraged kin to report deaths personally and, during the 1940s, it provided them with a circular to confirm the details of their deceased soldiers. Many family members wrote to the Memorial with a sense of restrained pride at the prospect of having their loved one's name inscribed on the honour roll. In 1936, Dulcie Kear reported the name of her brother, Percival, who died in 1929 from the effects of injuries and gassing: 'I heard your appeal over the A.B.C. Radio stations, & hasten to send our Dear One's, honoured name, for inclusion in the Rolls'.[84] Mrs Emma Vawser requested the naming of her son, Percy, writing 'I with others would esteem it an honor to have our departed soldiers name there'.[85] In some instances, family members proudly sought the naming of loved ones who had died over a decade earlier. In 1936, Mrs Law wrote regarding her son, who had died in the Caulfield Military Hospital in July 1919.[86] It was most commonly women who took the responsibility of writing to the War Memorial, and many adopted a quasi-sacred tone to convey the solemnity of their request.

Some family members composed letters in which they expressed their grief and explained the circumstances of death at length, while other kin wrote short factual epistles. In 1928, Mrs M Montgomery wrote twice seeking the inclusion of the name of her 'fond late husband' who had died 'through the effects of war' the year before; her grief was palpable. In her second letter, she wrote with an emotional effusiveness and heightened sense of religiosity, alluding to her husband's transcendence into heaven: 'Around the throne of Heaven/ Thousands of Children Stand Singing/Glory Glory Glory/Amen'.[87] Others simply stated the facts of death and the date without revealing their feelings about the loss. In 1936, Mrs J Deardon wrote plainly that her brother had 'died from war effects' eight years ago. '[I]n fact', she bluntly stated, 'he committed suicide'.[88]

The gathering of names created a strong expectation among family members. Relatives expressed gratitude that their loved one's name would be inscribed – 'trusting his name will be put on [an honour roll] plate thanking you'.[89] Some were fearful of missing the deadline. In 1940, Mrs McDonald anxiously wrote: 'Will you kindly do your utmost to have the name of my husband included as I fear on account of the delay [of this letter] it may arrive late for inscription'.[90] War Memorial staff individually acknowledged the letters: 'thank you; your brother's name has been included'.[91] The naming of their loved ones was emotionally significant for many families, especially because their deaths had not been memorialised on local monuments. A complete listing of all the 'war dead' on the Roll of Honour in Canberra allowed families to feel that their sons' suffering and death in the postwar period was as important as the deaths of the 'fallen'. Importantly, through the inscription of names, families stood to become part of a larger community of kin whose grief was 'entitled', and whose experiences of disability and loss were part of the national memory of war.

Some families, however, responded with mixed feelings when they were invited to confirm their soldier's details. For some, memorialisation was tinged with sorrow about how their soldier's life had been affected negatively by war disability, bitterness about his perceived poor treatment by the government, or a deep discomfort about whether his sacrifice had ultimately served any purpose. In 1941, Mrs Rebecca Hinds lost her husband to war disability but saw little value in adding his name to the Roll of Honour: 'I am not in favour of all this kind of thing, as we wives and mothers do not need them to remind us of those we have lost ... they gave their lives, 'tis true and I often wonder what for'.[92] Some kin of the disabled dead were angry about the expenditure of money on 'another stone monument' to the dead instead of a 'comfortable hospital' for ailing veterans.[93] Such comments echoed public debates of the early 1920s about whether memorials should be utilitarian or symbolic in character. Family members now brought the weight of many years' painful experience to bear on such considerations. A number of widows valued the symbolic honour shown to their husbands by the War Memorial, but were bitter about the financial peril in which they found themselves. Violet Aiken wrote, 'I appreciate my husband's name being erected in the "Hall of Memory" immensely but what about those left behind?'[94] For some, the 'living memorial' of a pension was a more valuable legacy than the symbolic inscription of their soldier's name on an honour roll, particularly during the economic depression of the 1930s.

In their letters, family correspondents sometimes complained about their poor treatment by the government. In 1936, Mrs N Fletcher vented her anger about the official rejection of her husband's death seven years earlier. She declared: 'I think he deserves to be put on the Honour Roll for fighting for his country. He should at least have that honour'.[95] War disability had cast a shadow over Mrs Fletcher's life. In 1929, her husband had died, and her brother 'nearly died of malaria & dysentery' during the war and 'looks older now than he really is'. She wanted the postwar suffering in her family to be acknowledged by the War Memorial, and asked: 'Are you getting a list of those who are still living? Or do you only want a list of those who have died?' Even though her debilitated brother was alive, she believed that 'he deserves to be on the roll'.[96] The policy of the War Memorial, however, was to include only the names of deceased soldiers whose deaths had been officially accepted. Only in death – and an appropriate death – would the Memorial record a soldier's sacrifice.

By 1941, the Australian War Memorial had collated and confirmed approximately 90 000 'eligible names' but the Roll of Honour was far from complete, and was proving a much more formidable task than anticipated.[97] During the 1940s, the memorial management remained committed to honouring the 'equal sacrifice' of all Australians who gave their lives for their country. By October 1952, however, it had changed its policy because of the complexity of collecting the names of the postwar dead, many of whom had not yet died. Furthermore, the Second World War had radically altered the priorities of the Memorial. There was simply not room to inscribe the names of all soldiers who died during and after both wars. It was decided that the cut-off point would be 1 April 1921, the official date of the disbandment of the AIF, and that the details of those who died after that date would be recorded upon cards, for inscription in a supplementary roll in book form which would be placed on display and updated as time passed.[98] These cards remain in storage to this day – they form something of a hidden honour roll for the postwar disabled dead.[99]

Today, the Australian War Memorial Roll of Honour is popularly perceived as a complete listing of the 'war dead'. Its comprehensiveness and accuracy are a source of pride for the Memorial, as one of its publications asserts: 'Australia is one of the few nations to name its war dead so completely'.[100] Yet, it does not name ex-servicemen who 'lingered on' and died from their war wounds and impairments after 31 March 1921. Had the original 1920s proposal for the Roll of Honour been pursued, the War Memorial would be a much longer building. The commemorative area would stretch up Mount Ainslie in order to incorporate the tens of thousands of names of those who died after their return to Australian shores from all wars. At present, for the descendants of these veterans the national War Memorial in Canberra is more a 'site of forgetting' than a 'site of memory'. It places a higher value on commemorating the deaths of those who made the 'supreme sacrifice' rather than the postwar struggles and deaths of disabled soldiers. In 2004, Diane Nicholas told me that while she does not 'put much store by things like honour boards' the inscription of the names of ex-servicemen who died of their war disabilities, such as her father, would allow visitors to the War Memorial to gain a more realistic idea of the 'scale of the slaughter' of the Great War.[101]

The Roll of Honour at the Australian War Memorial does not list names of First World War service personnel who died from war-related causes after March 1921. Australian War Memorial negative number P02169.002.

A DIFFERENT WORLD OF GRIEF

Australian soldiers who died from their war wounds and impairments during the 1920s and 1930s laid down their lives as surely as the 'fallen'. The families of the postwar dead also experienced a deep sense of loss and grief. They were, however, to remain a population of invisible mourners. Their disenfranchisement saw them wounded three times: they lost their loved one, their grief was publicly marginalised, and the significance of the sacrifices they had made while their disabled soldier was alive were also diminished. For although, in the context of war, killing and death do not always occur contemporaneously, a 'cult of the fallen' sat at the heart of the Anzac culture of commemoration.[102] After 1918, Australians' desire to mark war's end and to make sacred the traumatic deaths of its 'fallen' saw a higher commemorative worth placed on wartime death than postwar death. The wartime dead represented the 'end of sacrifice', but the postwar dead represented the perpetuation of suffering and death.[103] Accordingly, dead ex-servicemen were sidelined in collective social memory, and their families came to inhabit a different world of grief to the kin of the 1914–18 dead.

In response to their disenfranchisement, relatives of the postwar dead did not organise politically, nor agitate publicly for greater recognition of their losses. Instead, they sought acknowledgment in more subtle, practical and local ways, often acting with the assistance of sympathetic community organisations. Some embraced the Anzac tradition of remembrance, while others resisted memorialising narratives which privileged the battlefield dead. The contours of their grief reveal the fraught process of making sense of a 'war death' within the limits of national codes of commemoration. Their history reminds us that the 1920s and 1930s was not simply an era during which memories of the 'fallen' were sustained, but an era productive of experiences of war-related death and grief, which saw newer memories compete with older memories of loss for public recognition.

CONCLUSION

the shared legacies of war disability

War disability forever changed the shared lives of Australian soldiers of the First World War and their family members. Yet families' experiences of disablement and war-related death have been accorded virtually no place within Australia's dominant collective memory of the Great War. To most Australians, public remembrance of 1914–18 focuses on commemorating the 60 000 battlefield fallen, and affirming the centrality of their sacrifices in the national foundational narrative of Anzac. Within this powerful commemorative tradition, Australia's more than 90 000 'shattered Anzacs' have a secondary status, and the sacrifices of veterans' families are all but invisible. Yet, for damaged ex-servicemen and their kin, the legacies of war were profound and lasting. Behind each 'changed man' who faced the future with 'the burden and impediment of an impaired physique', a family's life was transformed, as soldiers and their kin reconciled themselves to living with the consequences of disablement.[1] Although the Repatriation Department insisted that disabled ex-servicemen could successfully regain their 'manly independence', many families lived with men who were, in reality, dependent on kin for their social, emotional and economic wellbeing. As Victoria's Inspector-General for the Insane observed of one shell-shocked man in 1925, 'he will always be somebody's responsibility'.[2]

This book has exposed the interior of family life in order to bring to light Australian families' hidden experiences of war disability during and after the First World War. It has argued that families' experiences need to be reinstated into the history of that conflict, for although disabled soldiers bore the wounds of war, their kin shouldered significant burdens as a result of veterans' disablement. In doing so, it has proposed a family model for the analysis of war and its aftermath which calls us to evaluate the impact of conflict not only on the 'nation', but also on the private spheres of kinship within which ordinary people lived and made sense of their experiences in relationship with one another on a daily basis. By examining families' experiences, the damaging reach of war into the social fabric well after 1918 becomes apparent. The First World War wounded not just combatants, but their fathers, mothers, wives, siblings and children, in very different ways. Families were the building blocks of the nation; and it was within families that the painful legacies of war were really managed.

Yet historians have been slow to understand war disability as a family experience. Most have followed the soldier-centred focus of the repatriation archive, rather than questioning it. Official records do not comprehensively document family life: that history exists in the margins of case files and within families' own collective memories. Indeed, the bureaucratic structures of the 'Repat', which were organised around the rehabilitation and pensioning of the individual soldier, obscure our present-day view of the private structures of support that ex-servicemen found within their own families. To uncover families' experiences, we need to listen to the 'silences' in the archives, engage with the oral histories of descendants, and explore the human relationships that sustained veterans: not simply trace the pensions paper-trail. Ex-servicemen's relationship with the state was only one dimension of the repatriation experience. Once we are alert to the power and significance of the family in veterans' lives, we can begin to understand how 'repatriation' was a dynamic process, with official and private aspects, which took place within a tripartite relationship between the soldier, his family and the repatriation bureaucracy. By adopting a family perspective, we can also see how an invisible tier of family-based welfare propped up the formal repatriation system, and how the state relied upon, yet neglected, the sacrifices of family caregivers.

THE SECOND REPATRIATION SYSTEM

Families' experiences of war disability reveal the limits of Australia's repatriation system. Although the *Australian Soldiers' Repatriation Act* of 1917 ushered in a new and revolutionary era in the history of the Australian welfare state, the repatriation system did not replace the family as the key provider of care and support for ex-servicemen. During and after the First World War, families remained a primary locus of emotional, social and economic support for disabled soldiers. Under the Act, family members were officially designated passive 'dependants' of ex-servicemen. However, they played an active role in the lives of veterans whose independence was compromised by war disability. The dependence of disabled soldiers upon their kin was not the exception: it was commonplace. The type of support offered by kin was unique to each family and of a highly personal, responsive nature that arguably could never have been replicated by state agencies. In family homes across the nation, the wellbeing of disabled soldiers was secured as much by the collective endeavours of family members as it was by the Repatriation Department. The skilled unpaid caregiving labour of family members formed a publicly invisible second repatriation system, without which the nation would never have 'recovered' from war.

Family support was vital to ex-servicemen's emotional and material wellbeing, and their shared lives were shaped by the affection and stress that accompanied familial obligation. Although some ex-servicemen were able to become independent breadwinners, a proportion remained reliant on their kin. These families were characterised by significant levels of emotional, economic and social interdependence. Home-based care was overwhelmingly women's work, and the bulk of responsibility fell disproportionately on them. Fathers and male relatives played important roles in generating additional income, and advocating for shell-shocked men who could not represent their own interests. Ex-servicemen depended on the assistance of their immediate and extended families, and in some cases, households merged in order to survive. We must not forget that the return of a disabled soldier could lead to tensions within the home, as well as the breakdown of relationships and the estrangement of kin. War disability had different and diffuse effects on Australian households that changed as time passed. The final burden for many was the death of a 'shattered' loved one who had survived 1914–18, but did not live to see 1939–45.

Despite the reach of war disability into Australian families, the Repatriation Department was consistent in its disavowal of any responsibility for the welfare of ex-servicemen's kin. The government's wartime promises that soldiers, if incapacitated, would be 'well looked after', extended only to members of the AIF: not to their families. The Department sectioned off war as an exclusively 'military' experience, and asserted a repatriation model in which soldiers were to regain their independence in a one-to-one relationship with the state. It took little interest in the welfare of kin because they had not 'served'. Paradoxically, it relied on families as a 'natural' source of support for veterans, but did not recognise publicly the value or cost of that care, and took for granted the service of caregivers within the home. Wives were left alone to deal with the myriad behavioural problems of shell-shocked men – including violence and depression – and seek their own treatment for war-related tuberculosis and venereal disease. It is perhaps unfair to critique with hindsight the narrow focus of a repatriation system that was rapidly established and sustained with limited funds. But it needs to be recognised that the system implicitly relied on women's unpaid caregiving, yet never publicly acknowledged their service and sacrifice. Instead, the Department insisted on ex-servicemen's capacity to regain their economic independence through their own efforts, even though this ideal was patently a fiction for many men. Thousands of disabled soldiers never became successful breadwinners and, despite the strength of their family relationships, were burdened with the public stigma of dependence upon their kin and charitable organisations.

THE BURDENS OF SACRIFICE

The sacrifices made by family members to support their disabled loved ones often came at a personal cost – war 'disabled' the lives of kin as well as soldiers. Wives and mothers sometimes found their freedom to pursue employment and personal interests restricted by their caregiving duties. Looking back on her married life in 1966, one wife recalled this difficult reality: 'I spent most of my time looking after my husband so I could not go to work'.[3] Others found that the rhythms of family life were interrupted by illness and hospital treatment, while the absence of an able-bodied breadwinner created ongoing economic hardship for some households. Families' experiences were shaped by the nature of their soldier's impairments as well as their class, wealth, composition, the extent of their pension and employment income, and the personal capacity of soldiers and their kin to reconcile themselves to disablement. War disability transformed the lives of Australian families unevenly. Yet there is a common theme in families' experiences: after they 'gave their sons' to war, they were expected to give of themselves again by picking up the pieces afterwards.

In the absence of adequate support from the Repatriation Department, charitable organisations played a critical role in supporting disabled soldier families. Associations such as the Red Cross, the RSSILA and TSAS provided aid to 'unaccepted' disabled soldiers and responded holistically to family units. These groups understood that returned soldiers' welfare was fundamentally connected to that of their families, and in response households formed important alliances with them. Relatives' organisations, such as the Sailors' and Soldiers' Fathers Association, also provided kin with a supportive space in which to validate their sacrifices as caregivers. The charitable sector provided an additional layer of welfare for Australian families which complemented the formal repatriation system. Notably, the activities of these organisations were not restricted by the *Australian Soldiers' Repatriation Act*. Charities took on family units, not just the veteran, as the 'client', and acknowledged the vulnerabilities and strengths inherent in their interdependence.

Despite the challenges that war disability brought into Australian homes, many families responded with considerable resilience and resourcefulness. For a number of women, the act of caregiving allowed them to develop skills as healers and experience a sense of 'human stewardship' for their loved one's health.[4] Housebound soldiers who took responsibility for raising children often fostered close bonds within their families. Within some homes, veterans' physical disablements became a source of humour and were incorporated in their play with their children. Disabled soldiers' children recall varying levels of resilience among their own family members. Betsy Burchett effectively lost her father to shell shock in the late 1920s, but her mother's insistence on maintaining a positive outlook fostered in her a keen sense of hope. Buoyed by fond memories of her father and a family culture of optimism, Betsy now reflects that despite the impact of her father's war disability, 'I was really fortunate and have been a fortunate person'.[5]

War disability challenged families. It revealed the dependence of kin on one another, and tested their capacity to respond to traumatic injury together. Yet this history of 'domestic heroism' does not fit easily into Australia's commemorative traditions of war. Within the Anzac legend there is little room to valorise 'shattered diggers', much less pay tribute to the 'maternal sacrifice' of their mothers or 'marital sacrifice' of their wives. In the national memory of war, the iconic Anzac soldier – a young independent bushman with a perfect physique – stands alone in the absence of family relationships, eternally enacting a story of individualism, independence and mateship. Stories at odds with this narrative, such as the struggles of physically or mentally disabled soldiers, their dependence on families and charities, and the valour of female caregivers have been marginalised or forgotten. Yet in reality, disabled soldiers of the Great War were not 'familyless' individuals: they were sons, husbands and brothers whose impairments had significance for their kin as well as themselves.

In the present day, the Department of Veterans' Affairs (the successor to the Repatriation Department) gives much greater recognition to the therapeutic role of kin in ex-servicemen's lives, and acknowledges the personal cost of war disability for family members.[6] Although war pensions are still 'medically' calculated on the basis of the extent of damage to the individual's body, ex-servicemen are no longer encouraged to strive for 'manly independence' but to consider their own health, and that of their family members, in holistic terms. Medical and allied health researchers are increasingly promoting the need to support veterans and their carers across the life course.[7] Historians can usefully draw upon such contemporary family-based approaches to war disability in order to comprehend how Australians responded to the personal and national trauma of the First World War. For during the 1920s and 1930s, hidden beneath Australia's first repatriation bureaucracy, and overshadowed by its individualistic rhetoric about war disability, was an intricate world of family support, struggle and survival.

For historians, the recognition that war disability is a family experience has the potential to open up new avenues of enquiry in related areas of research. An awareness of the challenges faced by disabled soldiers' families can enrich our understandings of the welfare state, unpaid labour, gender, caregiving, charity, marriage, childhood, grief and loss, and family life in the 1920s and 1930s. Questions about the impact of war disability on families are equally applicable in the aftermath of more recent wars, such as the Second World War and the Vietnam War. Family models can also usefully be applied to the study of disability within civilian populations. Paradoxically, while many disability historians have championed 'social models' of disability over 'medical models', most remain focused on disability as an individual experience, rather than one which had profound social implications for kin with whom disabled people's lives were, for better or worse, inextricably entwined.

In the decades after 1914, thousands of Australian families had their lives turned upside down by the disablement of a loved one during the First World War. Today, painful memories continue to be aroused as children of these disabled soldiers reflect on the impact of war disability on their families. The selective nature of Australia's national memory of war means that the sacrifices of disabled soldiers and their kin have largely been suppressed within the public domain. Families have possibly been hesitant to assert with greater force their stories within cultures of commemoration because of concerns about the dignity and privacy of veterans. For their part, official historians and custodians of the Anzac tradition have perhaps been reluctant to validate families' stories publicly, for doing so would mean accepting that the Great War not only damaged thousands of soldiers, but thousands of families and the individuals who comprised them. It is time to acknowledge the burdens of sacrifice carried by Australia's 'shattered Anzacs' and their civilian kin. The trauma of wounding and disablement was experienced by soldiers within webs of intimate family relationships. Managing the physical and emotional legacies of war was a massive task that demanded the adjustment and reconciliation of entire households. For these families – and for the nation to which they belonged – repatriation was a process that was never truly complete, and still continues for many Australians today.

APPENDIX 1

recruitment methods for oral history informants

The eleven children of disabled soldiers I interviewed for this book were recruited through a combination of advertising and word-of-mouth referrals. Some responded to an advertising flyer circulated by the Melbourne headquarters of the RSL and Legacy throughout their Victorian branches. It was titled 'Soldier Disability in the 1920s and 1930s – Do you have childhood memories of a family member who returned from the Great War with a Disability?' The flyer called for informants over the age of seventy who would be happy to discuss their experiences of a disabled soldier family member with a physical or mental disability, which did not necessarily have to be recognised officially by the Repatriation Department. Through these advertisements I recruited a handful of urban and regional informants, many of whom subsequently encouraged their friends to contact me. For instance, after I spoke with Gwen Summers, she introduced me to Betsy Burchett, a friend who lived in the same retirement village. Two other informants, Mary Reddrop and Joyce Muir, were recruited through family and friendship networks.

It is important to remember that the informants who participated in this study represent a cohort of people who were willing to talk about growing up with a war-disabled father. A number had strong links with the RSL and Legacy, which may have given them the confidence to respond to my advertisement because they had already told their story many times to friends within the veteran community. Indeed, aspects of some informants' narratives were already well-formed when I interviewed them. I was concerned, however, only to interview people who 'self-selected' into the study and were happy to work with me. Given the age of my cohort, I did not want to interview reluctant subjects for whom the telling of their story would create an unacceptable level of emotional vulnerability. There were clearly a greater number of people who chose not to participate in my research. While their reasons are unclear, their hesitancy may reflect an unwillingness to retell difficult family experiences from their early lives to a stranger, or a fear that 'opening up' may unsettle established memories of their father or other family members.

APPENDIX 2

profiles of oral history informants

BEVERLEY BROADBENT (b. 1929)

Interviewed 6 October 2004

Beverley is the daughter of John Eric Broadbent (known as Eric), born in 1893, who served in the Middle East with the 4th Machine Gun Squadron, 4th Light Horse. Eric was one of four sons the Broadbent family sent to war, three of whom returned with disabilities. Eric was wounded in the arm and experienced respiratory problems, Rae received gunshot wounds to his hand and was gassed, and Wilson came home with shrapnel lodged in his brain which caused his death at the age of thirty-six. The fourth brother, Alan, was only twenty when he was killed shortly before the Armistice. On the other side of the family, Beverley's uncle, John Stubbs, returned from France without a leg. He was given a soldier settlement block in the Mallee which proved difficult to make profitable, and he died at the age of thirty-two, leaving a widow and two sons. After Eric returned to Australia, he became active in the RSSILA and became the secretary of the Caulfield branch in Melbourne. Beverley spent her childhood not only witnessing the effects of war disability within her own family, but observed her father's efforts to assist other returned soldiers and their families through the League.

BETSY BURCHETT (b. 1922)

Interviewed 3 November 2004

Betsy Burchett is the daughter of John Godber Brown who joined the AIF in August 1915 at the age of twenty-nine. He served as an officer with the 6th Field Artillery Brigade and survived the war without being physically wounded, receiving the Military Medal for bravery in 1917. He married shortly after returning to Australia in 1919. Betsy, an only child, was born in 1922. In the late 1920s, John had a nervous breakdown, which the Repatriation Department accepted as war-related. He became a permanent resident at the Bundoora Convalescent Home for returned soldiers. He died at the Caulfield Repatriation Hospital in 1943.

MARGARET CRAMOND (b. 1927)

Interviewed 29 September 2004

Margaret Cramond is the daughter of Alfred Agnew Plane of the 15th Battalion AIF. She grew up with a father, uncle and grandfather who all suffered from war disabilities. Alfred, her father, was born in Melbourne on Christmas Day 1891 and enlisted in August 1914 at the age of twenty-three. He served in New Guinea, Egypt and France. On 9 August 1916, Alfred was wounded at Pozières and was transferred to London where he had his right leg amputated below the knee. After returning to Australia, Alfred married in 1926, and Margaret was born in 1927. Alfred died in 1984 at the age of ninety-two. Margaret's uncle was severely gassed and died at the age of forty-nine, leaving a young family. Her grandfather, an army chaplain, was invalided home to Australia after having a nervous breakdown at Gallipoli and took a number of years to recover from his experiences.

KEITH FALCONER (b. 1924)

Interviewed 20 October 2004

Keith Falconer is the son of Frank Falconer, who joined the AIF in January 1915 at the age of twenty-two. Frank served at Gallipoli with the 23rd Battalion and was severely injured in France in June 1916, sustaining multiple shrapnel wounds to the head and back. He was invalided to England for medical treatment and had a steel plate surgically implanted in his head to protect his brain. During an extended period of convalescence, he met his wife, Mary Ann, an English VA, who nursed soldiers on his ward. Frank returned to Australia in March 1919, and Mary Ann followed as a war bride shortly afterwards. After his return, Frank was unable to take up his former job as a factory engineer because he suffered from chronic headaches and could not bear the noise. Desiring a quieter life, he applied for a soldier settlement block and was granted 1000 acres (405 ha) in far western Victoria in 1920. However, his migraine headaches made farm labouring extremely difficult. Keith was born in 1924 and witnessed the struggles of his parents to make a success of their holdings.

MAVIS FLOYD (b. 1924)

Interviewed 25 November 2004 and 6 December 2004

Mavis is the daughter of John Gordon Mackay (known as Gordon) who served with the 2nd Machine Gun Battalion. At the outbreak of war, Gordon was a married man with a young family who lived in Richmond, Melbourne. He was a man of poor physical condition as a result of childhood rheumatic fever, and for this reason he did not enlist at the outbreak of war. In May 1916, however, he finally succumbed to the pressure to enlist after receiving a white feather in his letterbox. Despite his health problems, the army deemed Gordon 'fit' for active service, even after his brother wrote a letter advising them not to accept him. On the Western Front, Gordon was hospitalised on numerous occasions for ill health and was also injured in the knee. In May 1919, he was discharged, and Mavis, who was one of ten children, was born in 1924. After his return to Australia, Gordon never worked due to chronic ill health. The family survived on a small pension, and during the 1930s Mavis' parents battled with the Repatriation Department to have the rate increased.

JOYCE MUIR (b. 1928)

Interviewed 5 April 2005
Joyce Muir is the daughter of Gerald Muir, who enlisted in Melbourne in February 1915 at the age of twenty-two. Gerald was medically invalided back to Australia in 1917 with a chronic lung condition. Upon his return he married and was extremely violent towards his wife and children during the postwar decades. Although he was never formally diagnosed with shell shock, Joyce believes that Gerald's aggressive behaviour can be traced to wartime experiences at Gallipoli and on the Western Front which left him psychologically disturbed. Joyce Muir was interviewed by me on the understanding that neither she nor her family would be identified in this book. 'Joyce Muir' and 'Gerald Muir' are pseudonyms.

BERYL NELSON (b. 1923)

Interviewed 27 April 2005
Beryl is the daughter of Walter John Marks who served with the 9th Battalion. He was a Queenslander and enlisted at Mackay in January 1917. During a year of service overseas, he experienced a recurring bronchial illness and arthritis and spent a significant amount of time in hospital. Walter returned to Brisbane in 1919 and married

shortly after his discharge from the army. Beryl, the second of five daughters, was born in 1923. During the early 1920s, it became apparent that Walter had tuberculosis, which the Repatriation Department accepted as being war-related. He received treatment for this condition for many years and died at the Rosemount Repatriation Hospital in 1945.

DIANE NICHOLAS (b. 1932)

Interviewed 12 October 2004

Diane Nicholas is the daughter of Philip Nicholas who enlisted in September 1916 at the age of twenty-three. Philip arrived in France in May 1917 with the 2nd Pioneer Battalion and four months later was seriously wounded in the abdomen and lungs. After medical treatment and an extended period of convalescence in England, he was invalided back to Australia in August 1918. Philip never recovered completely from his injuries and his lungs were permanently affected in the postwar years. He married Nellie Whitelaw in 1926 and Diane was born in 1932. Philip died at home in 1948, and the Repatriation Department deemed his death partly attributable to his war injuries. The letters he wrote home during the war are held in the State Library of Victoria.

MARY REDDROP (b. 1928)

Interviewed 27 September 2004

Mary Reddrop is the daughter of James Henry Roberts who was born in Seymour, Victoria in 1894. James, known as Jim, enlisted in March 1916 and served with the 37th Battalion in France. After being at the front for only a matter of weeks, he was severely wounded in the leg in February 1917 and transferred to England. He was invalided home to Australia in mid-1917 and discharged in November of that year after receiving further medical treatment in Melbourne. He married in

1921 and had five children, of whom Mary is the third. Jim's youngest daughter, Margaret, born in 1938, is the author's mother. Jim's injuries were not debilitating, but he experienced recurring leg pain.

GWEN SUMMERS (b. 1922)

Interviewed 28 October 2004

Gwen Summers is the second child of Wilfred Albert Davey who was born in 1895 and came to Australia as a migrant in 1913. Wilfred enlisted in the AIF in January 1916 at the age of twenty, and served with the 8th Light Horse Brigade. He was wounded at the Battle of Beersheeba and sustained mild facial injuries as the result of a gunshot wound to the ear. He was discharged as medically unfit in August 1919. When Gwen was about nine, she discovered a letter on the kitchen table from the Repatriation Department which revealed that her father was receiving a small pension for war neurosis. The family never talked at length about Wilfred's war service, and he kept any emotional difficulties he experienced relatively well hidden.

JOAN WISHART (b. 1926)

Interviewed 9 August 2004

Joan Wishart is the daughter of John Alfred Hargreaves, who enlisted in July 1915 at the age of eighteen. John was sent to the Western Front and served with the 7th Battalion at Pozières, where Australian casualties were extremely heavy. In September 1916, he was buried by a shell and admitted to a military hospital in Belgium with shell shock. He was transferred to England for treatment and invalided home to Melbourne in September 1916, in a 'mental stupor' without the capacity for speech or movement. After treatment at the Caulfield Military Hospital and Royal Park Hospital for the Insane, John was discharged in a much improved condition and successfully resumed his career with the Postmaster General's Department. In February 1919, he married

Caroline Walker, whose parents disapproved of the match because of the stigma attached to the time John had spent in a mental hospital. Joan was born in 1926. John went on to become Officer-in-Charge of Radio Australia, and after his retirement was awarded the Imperial Service Medal for his pioneering work in Australian shortwave broadcasting.

notes

INTRODUCTION

1. ARCS, NSW, *Annual Report*, 1925–26, p. 17.
2. *Herald*, 26/4/1921, p. 1.
3. *Herald*, 25/4/1925, p. 3.
4. *Crosslight*, April 2007, p. 10.
5. Ken Inglis, *Sacred Places*, p. 97.
6. AG Butler, *The Official History*, vol. 3, pp. 880 & 896. Butler notes that this statistic represents the number of 'woundings' not the number of 'wounded men', as some men were wounded on more than one occasion, see p. 894.
7. ibid., p. 963–64; Department of Repatriation, *Annual Report*, 1938–39, p. 15.
8. AG Butler, *The Official History*, vol. 3, p. 880.
9. ibid., p. 965 & 930. This can be attributed partly to advances in orthopedic surgery.
10. These were typically less outwardly visible conditions such as 'nerves' and tuberculosis. See NAA, AWM 41, 730 & NAA, AWM 41, 724. For a history of the Repatriation Department, see Clem Lloyd & Jacqui Rees, *The Last Shilling*.
11. See Deborah Stone, *The Disabled State*.
12. *Australian Soldiers' Repatriation Act 1920*, Part III, Section 23.
13. On social models of disability see Michael Oliver, *The Politics of Disablement*.
14. On early twentieth-century families, see Michael Gilding, *The Making and Breaking of the Australian Family*; Kerreen Reiger, *The Disenchantment of the Home*.
15. Alfred Derham to his family, 15/5/1915, UMA, 67/6, Box 7/2/1, Folder 7/2/2/28–76.
16. Letter to AWM, undated, received 20/11/1940, NAA, AWM 164.
17. Kay Saunders, "'Specimens of Superb Manhood'", p. 99.
18. This stands in contrast with a larger

number of studies in the context of World War Two and the Vietnam War. See John Raftery & Sandra Schubert, *A Very Changed Man*; John Raftery, *Marks of War*; Joy Damousi, *Living with the Aftermath*; Michael McKernan, *This War Never Ends*.

19 See Clem Lloyd & Jacqui Rees, *The Last Shilling*; Richard Lindstrom, 'The Australian Experience'; Kate Blackmore, 'War, Health and Welfare'; Stephen Garton, *The Cost of War*; Joanna Bourke, 'Shell Shock and Australian Soldiers'; Joanna Bourke, 'The Battle of the Limbs'; Joy Damousi, *The Labour of Loss*, pp. 85–102; Michael Tyquin, *Madness and the Military*. There are some exceptions, see Richard White, 'War and Australian Society', p. 413–17; John McQuilton, *Rural Australia and the Great War*, pp. 119–37; Stephen Garton, *The Cost of War*, pp. 196–206; Janet McCalman, *Journeyings*, pp. 80–81. Also see Judith Allen's study of domestic violence in *Sex and Secrets*, pp. 130–56.

20 The overseas literature on disabled soldiers after the First World War is extensive and includes Robert Weldon Whalen, *Bitter Wounds*; Seth Koven, 'Remembering and Dismemberment'; Joanna Bourke, *Dismembering the Male*; Desmond Morton & Glenn Wright, *Winning the Second Battle*; David Gerber (ed.) *Disabled Veterans in History*; Deborah Cohen, *The War Come Home*; Paul Lerner, *Hysterical Men*; Jeffrey Reznick, *Healing the Nation*; K Walter Hickel, 'Medicine, Bureaucracy, and Social Welfare'. On 'the body': see Roxanne Panchasi, 'Reconstructions'; Sabine Kienitz, 'Body Damage'. Some international historical studies do foreground the role of families: see Janis Lomas, '"Delicate Duties"'; Jessica Meyer, '"Not Septimus Now"'; Peter Barham, *Forgotten Lunatics*, pp. 167–80 & 340–54;

Reinhard J Sieder, 'Behind the Lines'.

21 Jay Winter, *Sites of Memory*, p. 45. Also see John McQuilton, *Rural Australia and the Great War*, p. 134; Stephen Garton, *The Cost of War*, p. 177.

22 Stephen Garton, *The Cost of War*, p. 202; Richard White, 'War and Australian Society', p. 409.

23 RH Fetherston, *Report on 1. Australian Army Medical Services Overseas*, p. 63.

24 See *Repatriation*, September 1920, pp. 8–9; ARCS, Victoria, Caulfield Branch, *Red Cross Record*, 1/1/1918, pp. 9–10; W Fitzpatrick, *The Repatriation of the Soldier*. Also see Peter Cochrane, *Simpson and the Donkey*, pp. 74–81.

25 See Joy Damousi, *The Labour of Loss*; Tanja Luckins, *The Gates of Memory*; Bart Ziino, *A Distant Grief*; George Mosse, *Fallen Soldiers*; Jay Winter, *Sites of Memory*. See chapter 8 for additional literature.

26 On the relationship between war memory and oral history see Penny Summerfield, *Reconstructing Women's Wartime Lives*; Alistair Thomson, *Anzac Memories*.

27 See Mark Priestly (ed.) *Disability and the Life Course*; Philip M Ferguson, 'Mapping the Family'.

28 Letter to Chairman of AWM, 28/11/1936, NAA, AWM 93, 2/5/19C, Part II.

CHAPTER 1

1 Letter, 17/8/1916, AWM, PR00643.
2 Letter to Edna Tooney, 23/10/1917, AWM, PR02027.
3 Letter to aunts, 21/11/1917, AWM, PR02027.
4 Letter to Edna Tooney, 22/2/1918.
5 Letter to Charles Goddard, 6/10/1916, SLV, MS 13106, Box 3777/4.

6   Letter to Ellen Derham, 25/5/1915, UMA, 67/6, Box 7/2/1, File 7/1/1 a and b.
7   AG Butler, *The Official History*, vol. 3, p. 890.
8   See William Peach to his mother, 14/7/1915, NLA, MS 929.
9   Interview with Mavis Floyd, 25/11/2004; Attestation Paper, 3/5/1916, NAA, B2455, MACKAY JG.
10 LL Robson, 'The Origin and Character of the First AIF'. See also LL Robson, *The First AIF*; Richard White, 'Motives For Joining Up'.
11 Returned soldier in 1966, quoted in JNI Dawes & LL Robson, *Citizen to Soldier*, p. 151.
12 *Age*, 11/8/1915, p. 8. Also see Peter Cochrane, 'Deliverance and Renewal', p. 18.
13 *Argus*, 2/5/1916, p. 8. Also see Lloyd Robson, *The First AIF*, p. 79.
14 Charles Bazeley, 7/1/1916, NAA, B6525, FINANCIAL/BUSINESS-A.
15 Letter to family, 26/3/1917, AWM, PR03407.
16 *Age*, 7/6/1916, p. 12.
17 *Recruiting Campaign No. 2 Organiser's Manual*, Director-General of Recruiting, Victoria, 1917, p. 12.
18 See New South Wales State Recruiting Committee, 'A GOLDEN RULE', AWM RCO 2291, 5/5/3, Sydney, c.1914–1918.
19 'Honour, Opportunity, Cash', Recruiting Leaflet, South Australia, undated, AWM, 5/5/9.
20 ibid.
21 Harold Hinckfuss, *Memories of a Signaller*, p. 3.
22 Diary of Arthur Richer, 8/5/1916, published as Lyn McKay (ed.) *Diary 1916–18*.
23 Letter to Alfred Derham, 28/10/1914, UMA, 67/6, Box 7/2/1/1–7.
24 Bart Ziino, *A Distant Grief*, p. 9. Also see Susan R Grayzel, 'Defining the Geography of War'.
25 *Our Empire*, 19/8/1918, p. 2.
26 Letter to Jim Keast, 17/8/1916, AWM, PR00643.
27 *Soldier*, 25/5/1917, p. 21.
28 *Soldier*, 31/8/1917, cover page.
29 Joy Damousi, *The Labour of Loss*, p. 21.
30 *Our Empire*, 19/8/1918, p. 2.
31 Isabella Walker to Ellen Derham, 23/5/1915, UMA, 67/6, Box 7/2/1, File 7/1/1/ a and b.
32 *Age*, 18/8/1915, p. 7; *Sydney Morning Herald*, 2/8/1916, p. 11; *Argus*, 25/4/1916, p. 7.
33 *Rules for Censorship of the Press*, 1918, p. 13.
34 Peter Cochrane 'Deliverance and Renewal', p. 28; Peter Cochrane, *Simpson and the Donkey*, pp. 74–81. See Advertisement for Dr Sheldon's New Discovery, *Argus*, 28/9/1916, p. 11.
35 Letter to mother, 30/7/1915, NLA, MS 929.
36 AG Butler, *The Official History*, vol. 3, p. 896; Michael Tyquin, *Gallipoli*, p. 12–28.
37 Diary of EM Trantner, 3/2/1917, SLV, MS 10786.
38 AG Butler, *The Official History*, vol. 3, p. 896–97.
39 Letter to parents, 13/8/1916, UMA, 81/81.
40 Letter to sisters, 30/5/1917, SLV, MS 10434.
41 AG Butler, *The Official History*, vol. 3, p. 896. On feigned illness see Diary of J Green, 10/8/1916, ML, MS 1838.
42 Letter to his family, 8/9/1915, AWM, PR03407.
43 Michael Roper, 'Maternal Relations', p. 302.
44 John Lindsay Ross, 'An Explanation', 1932, SLV, MS 12541, Box 3407.
45 Martha Hanna, 'A Republic of Letters', p. 1341.
46 Michael Roper, 'Maternal Relations', p. 300. Also see Joy Damousi, *Labour of Loss*, p. 48.
47 Martyn Lyons, 'French Soldiers and

their Correspondence', p. 90.
48 Corporal WC Mayne to his wife and children, 31/7/1916, AWM, 3DRL/0866. On postal delays see Joy Damousi, *The Labour of Loss*, pp. 19–20; *Argus*, 7/8/1915, p. 18.
49 Letter to Charles Goddard, 23/10/1916, SLV, MS 13106, Box 3777/1.
50 ibid.
51 NG Cullen to Thomas Derham, 15/5/1915, UMA, 76/6, Box 7/2/1, File 7/1/1 a and b.
52 Isabel Williams to Ellen Derham, undated (mid-May 1915) UMA, 76/6, Box 7/2/1, File 7/1/1 a and b.
53 See letter from Ellen Anderson to Ellen Derham, 15/5/1915, UMA, 67/6, Box 7/2/1, File 7/1/1 a and b.
54 Letter to sister, 13/5/1916, AWM, PR00643, File 3/11.
55 On literacy rates see Amanda Laugesen, 'Australian Soldiers and Print Culture'; Martin Lyons & Lucy Taksa, *Australian Readers Remember*, p. 197.
56 Letter to family, 19/8/1917, published in Mary J Chandler (ed.) '*Dear Homefolks*', p. 84.
57 Letter to mother, 20/10/1918, UMA, 88/109.
58 Letter to husband, 6/10/1916, SLV, MS 13106, Box 3777/4.
59 Letter to husband, 6/10/1916, SLV, MS 13106, Box 3777/4.
60 See NAA, B2455/1, WORTH W. On relatives' responses, see *Age*, 8/5/1915, p. 14; *Age*, 15/5/15, p. 12.
61 Douglas McMurtrie, *The Disabled Soldier*, p. 98.
62 Letter to mother and sister, 14/8/1915, AWM, PR02057.
63 Letter to mother, 18/1/1917, quoted in Ron Blair & James Affleck, *For King and Country*, p. 60.
64 Letter to parents, 22/2/1917, SLV, MS 9686.
65 Letter to mother, 1/8/1916, AWM, PR00643, File 3/11.
66 On multiple wounding, see AG Butler, *The Official History*, vol. 2, p. 442.
67 Letter to mother, 3/4/1918, SLV, MS 11651, 1844/7.
68 Letter to parents, 13/1/1918, UMA, 81/81.
69 Letter to Mr and Mrs Worth, 31/5/1915, ML, MSS 6989/1/4; NAA, B2455/1, WORTH W.
70 ibid. Also see Letter from Nurse Nettie Hoey, 16/7/1916, AWM, PR00585.
71 Undated letter to Dot in Eric's war diary, 22/2/1918, in Patrick Wilson (ed.) *So Far from Home*, p. 144.
72 Letter to Jim Keast, 6/9/1916, AWM, PR00643.
73 Undated letter to Dot in Eric's war diary, 22/2/1918, in Patrick Wilson (ed.) *So Far from Home*, p. 144.
74 Letter to Charles Goddard, 3/11/1916, SLV, MS 13106, Box 3777/4.
75 Michael Roper, 'Between Manliness and Masculinity', p. 347; Martin Crotty, *Making the Australian Male*, pp. 221–30.
76 *Our Empire*, 18/12/18, p. 6.
77 Undated letter to Nello (after mid-1918) SLV, MS 10163.
78 Letter to father, 19/8/1916, AWM, PR88/161.
79 Letter from Richard Capel to his cousin Lyle, 3/12/17, AWM, PR00658.
80 Letter to Rose Keast, 1/8/1916, AWM, PR00643, File 3/11.
81 Letter to Rose Keast, 16/8/1916, AWM, PR00643, File 3/11.
82 *Coo-eee!*, vol. 1, no. 5, March 1917, p. 1.
83 *Harefield Park Boomerang*, no. 18, December 1917, unpaginated.
84 See Charles Baker's diary, 17/8/1918, ML, MSS 1608.
85 Interview with Mary Reddrop, 23/9/2004.
86 Diary of James Henry Roberts, published as Mary Reddrop (ed.) *Jim's Story*, p. 107.
87 VE Jones to his father, 2/5/1915, AWM, PR00360.
88 *Albury Daily News*, Friday

11/6/1915, p. 3.
89 Anonymous to unknown recipient, 21/6/1917, AWM, PR87/184.
90 Letter to wife, 15/11/1916, AWM, PR84/332, Folder 1.
91 *Avoca Free Press*, 11/8/1915, p. 2; Randall Family Papers, SLV, MS 11287.
92 Diary, 4/8/1916, NLA, MS 3962.
93 Letter to mother 1/8/1916, AWM, PR00643, File 3/11.
94 Photographic postcard, 7/1/1917, AWM, P04166.008.
95 Jenny Hartley, '"Letters are Everything These Days"', p. 186.
96 Letter to Jim Keast, 6/9/1916, AWM, PR00643.
97 Letter to sister, 29/9/1916, AWM, PR00643, File 3/11.
98 Letter to mother, 16/8/1916, AWM, PR00643, File 3/11.
99 Letter to mother, 15/10/1916, NLA, MS 929.
100 Letter to family, 9/3/1916, AWM, 2DRL/490.
101 Letters to mother, 28/5/1916 & 10/8/1916, SLV, MS 12541, Box 3407.
102 About 25 per cent of the AIF who enlisted before June 1915 were British-born, see LL Robson, 'The Origin and Character of the First AIF', p. 744.
103 Letter to parents, 31/8/1915, AWM, 1DRL/0047/1.
104 Letter to Mr Antill, 9/9/1916, AWM, 1DRL/0047/1, Folder 2.
105 Diary of Charles A Baker, 18/8/1918, ML, MSS 1608.
106 William Tooney to daughter, 22/2/1918, AWM, PR02027.
107 Letter to Charles Goddard, 6/10/1916, SLV, MS 13106, Box 3777/4.

CHAPTER 2

1 Record of Evidence, 21/3/29, NAA, B73/58, Box 80, M15005.
2 *Argus*, 4/12/1916, p. 8.
3 *Age*, 4/12/1916, p. 8.
4 Base Records to Richard Hargreaves, 10/11/1916, NAA, B2455, HARGREAVES JA.
5 Interview with Joan Wishart, 9/8/2004.
6 *West Wimmera Mail*, 25/1/1918, p. 4
7 See veteran's sister to Repatriation Department, 23/2/1930, NAA, B73/37, Box 127, M74937.
8 AG Butler, *The Official History*, vol. 3, p. 903–04.
9 *Age*, 12/7/1915, p. 11.
10 AG Butler, *The Official History*, vol. 3, p. 903–04.
11 See Memoirs of ET Chalk, AWM, PR85/428 and Memoirs of Raymond E Membrey, AWM, PR02022.
12 AG Butler, *The Official History*, vol. 3, p. 903–04 and 880–83.
13 *Karoolian*, September 1918, p. 3.
14 Bart Ziino, 'Journeys to War', pp. 11 and 78.
15 Diary of Charles A Baker, 18/9/1918, ML, MSS 1608.
16 *Karoolian*, September 1918, p. 4.
17 William Gamble, *Reminiscences of William Gamble*, p. 51.
18 WJ Voss, *Light of the Mind*, p. 62.
19 *Optimist*, April 1936, p. 4.
20 Ticket to the Anzac Buffet, undated, AWM, 3DRL/7028.
21 *Sydney Morning Herald*, 16/5/1917, p. 12.
22 *Argus*, 3/12/1918, p. 7.
23 *Warrnambool Standard*, 7/10/1919, p.3. Also see *West Wimmera Mail*, 25/1/1918, p. 4.
24 *Warrnambool Standard*, 28/10/1919, p.5.
25 Letter to mother, 9/2/1919, UMA, 88/109.
26 Senator Lt. Col. Bolton, 19/7/1917, *Australian Parliamentary Debates*, vol. 82, 1917, p. 278.
27 *Tassie Digger*, April 1921, p. 30.
28 Application, CSWM, Fanny Eager, 7/12/1917, NLA, MS 2864, Box 14, File 3.
29 Application, CSWM, Louisa

Lynch, 30/10/1917, NLA, MS 2864, Box 14, File 3.
30 *Reveille*, 29/11/1930, p. 10.
31 *Duckboard*, 1/9/1927, p. 3.
32 Interview with William Gamble by Patsy Adam Smith, 3/4/1979, SLV, TMS 238.
33 ibid.
34 Letter to Roland Simpson, 21/11/1918, AWM, PR00733.
35 Application, CSWM, Louisa Hogan, 9/7/1917, NLA, MS 2864, Box 14, File 3.
36 Letter to Repatriation Department, 8/9/1919, NAA, B73/54, Box, 142, M65376.
37 Police Interview with Miss Bennett, 21/3/1920, Criminal Trial Proceedings, PROV, VPRS 30/P, Unit 1884, Set 3, 1920, Case 208.
38 *Our Empire*, 18/6/1920, p. 15.
39 See *Soldier*, 6/7/1917, p. 8; Report on the Soldiers' Club, NLA, MS 2864, Box 14, File 1.
40 *Our Empire*, 18/7/1919, p. 7.
41 Statement of mother, 12/5/1930, NAA, B73/82, Box 63, M39997.
42 Bryan S Turner, 'Disability and the Sociology of the Body', p. 262.
43 ARCS, Victoria, Caulfield Branch, *Red Cross Record*, vol. 1, no. 6, 1/5/1917, p. 7.
44 Statement of mother, 12/5/1930, NAA, B73/82, Box 63, M39997.
45 *Argus*, 3/5/1915, p. 6.
46 Interview with Beverley Broadbent, 6/10/2004.
47 Interview with Margaret Cramond, 29/9/2004.
48 Tanja Luckins, *The Gates of Memory*, pp. 109–27.
49 *Rutherglen Sun*, 28/5/1918, p. 3. Also see John McQuilton, *Rural Australia and the Great War*, p. 134.
50 Application, CSWM, Frances Parker, 25/7/1918, NLA, MS 2864, Box 14, File 3; NAA, B2455 PARKER STEPHEN CHARLES.
51 Richard White, 'War and Australian Society', p. 415.
52 PROV, VPRS 283/P0002, Unit 31, Case 1920/508.
53 *Truth*, 16/4/1921, p. 8. Also see PROV, VPRS 283/P0000, Unit 249, 1917/1.
54 JHL Cumpston, *Venereal Disease in Australia*, p. 38. Also see 'Statistics on Venereal Disease', NAA, AWM 41, 519, Part 1.
55 Department of Trade and Customs Committee, *Report on Venereal Diseases*, p. 6.
56 Letter to Minister for Defence, 7/4/1918, NAA, MP 367/1/, 580/1/908.
57 Solicitor AE Jones to Department of Defence, 16/1/1917, NAA, MP 367/1/, 580/1/908.
58 *Australia To-Day*, 21/11/1917, p. 85.
59 *Census of the Commonwealth of Australia*, June 1933, Statistician's Report, 1940, p. 399. and p. 163. The inclusion of returned men in 'general population' data makes accurate comparisons difficult.
60 See Alistair Thomson, *Anzac Memories*, p. 110.
61 ARCS, NSW, *Annual Report*, 1921–22, p. 20.
62 *Truth*, 5/4/1921, p. 4.
63 AG Butler, *The Official History*, vol. 3, pp. 963–64.
64 *Medical Journal of Australia*, 8/12/1923, p. 585.
65 *Australia To-Day*, 21/11/1917, p. 85.
66 Arnold Lawson, *War Blindness at St Dunstan's*, p. 143.
67 *Australia To-Day*, 21/11/1917, p. 85.
68 *Truth*, 27/9/1919, p. 7.
69 *Record*, 20/1/1917, p. 3.
70 *Everylady's Journal*, 6/1/1918, p. 44.
71 *Everylady's Journal*, 6/12/1917, p. 748.
72 *Truth*, 5/4/1921, p. 4.
73 *League*, 31/3/1922, p. 44.
74 Clem Lloyd & Jacqui Rees, *The Last Shilling*, p. 129.
75 Interview with Keith Falconer, 20/10/2004.
76 Albert Facey, *A Fortunate Life*, pp. 283–87.
77 ibid., p. 285.
78 Interview with Joan Wishart,

9/8/2004.
79 Richard White, 'War and Australian Society', p. 416.
80 *Truth*, 11/3/1922, p. 5.
81 South Australian Soldiers' Fund, *Half-Yearly Report for the Year Ending 31 March 1920*, p. 6.
82 *Anzac Bulletin*, no. 102, December 1918, p. 6.

CHAPTER 3

1 Letter, 5/4/1928, SLSA, TSAS, SRG 488, Box 13.
2 Letter to Citizens' Returned Soldiers Benefit Fund, June 1922, City of Sydney Archives, File 2390/22.
3 RH Fetherston, *Report on 1. Australian Army Medical Services Overseas*, p. 9.
4 There are numerous studies on war pensions for disabled soldiers, see Clem Lloyd & Jacqui Rees, *The Last Shilling*; Kate Blackmore, 'War, Health and Welfare'; K Walter Hickel, 'Medicine, Bureaucracy, and Social Welfare'; Stephen Garton, *The Cost of War*. On the 'household economy', see Kerreen Reiger, *Family Economy*; Pat Hudson & WR Lee (eds) *Women's Work and the Family Economy in Historical Perspective*.
5 Stephen Garton, *The Cost of War*, p. 86.
6 This figure is an estimate, based on a sample of ninety-nine repatriation medical files of disabled soldiers provided to me for this project by the Department of Veterans' Affairs.
7 *Recruiting Campaign No. 2 Organiser's Manual*, p. 17.
8 John McQuilton, *Rural Australia and the Great War*, p. 111.
9 *Recruiting Campaign No. 2 Organiser's Manual*, p. 17.
10 *Our Empire*, 18/8/1919, p. 8.
11 See AB Piddington, *The Next Step*; Marilyn Lake, 'Translating Needs into Rights'.
12 *Report of the Royal Commission on the Basic Wage*, pp. 58 & 89.
13 *Australian Soldiers' Repatriation Act 1920*, p. 33–34.
14 *Australian Parliamentary Papers*, vol. 4, 1920–21, pp. 697–706 & 704.
15 Repatriation Commission, *Annual Report*, 1923–24, p. 47.
16 Deborah Stone, *The Disabled State*, p. 117.
17 Letter to the Repatriation Commission, 24/2/1920, in Summary of Evidence, August 1927, NAA, B73/84, Box 72, M36431.
18 See Repatriation Commission, *Annual Report*, 1927–28, p. 25.
19 See Stephen Garton, *The Cost of War*, p. 111.
20 Department of Repatriation, NSW, *Report on Repatriation Activities, 1926–27*, p. 23; *The Civil Re-establishment of the AIF*, p. 17.
21 Repatriation Commission, *Annual Report*, 1924–25, p. 12.
22 Interview with Mavis Floyd, 25/11/2004.
23 Interview with Keith Falconer, 20/10/2004.
24 See *Argus*, 22/5/1919, p. 8; *Register*, 23/3/1921, p. 10.
25 Stephen Garton, *The Cost of War*, p. 86.
26 Interview with Keith Falconer, 20/10/2004.
27 *Worker*, 4/12/1919, p. 20.
28 Commonwealth Bureau of Census and Statistics, *Official Year Book of the Commonwealth of Australia*, 1922, p. 871.
29 ibid., 1925, p. 595, & 1930, p. 440.
30 Partially Blinded Soldiers' Association of Australia, Deputation to Prime Minister, 14/4/1925, NLA, RSL, MS 6609, File 1786B; NAA, K60/17/8, M10679.
31 Letter to Department of Repatriation, 17/10/1924, NAA, B73/84, Box 61, M13968.
32 See NLA, RSL, MS 6609, File 1640B, File 2630B & File 4933B.

33 *Diggers' Gazette*, 9/3/1923, p. 24; Medical Report, 13/12/1922, NAA, B73/82, Box 25, M16395.
34 'Enlistments in the AIF', NAA, AWM 41, 566, Part 1.
35 Royal Commission on National Insurance, Minutes of Evidence, 6/11/1924, NLA, RSL, MS 6609, File 2053B, p. 71.
36 Bobbie Oliver, *War and Peace in Western Australia*, p. 137.
37 A Ellis, 'Blind Soldier's Souvenir', Poetry Card, Adelaide, 1927.
38 See ARCS, NSW, *Annual Report*, 1919–20, p. 29; ARCS, NSW, *Annual Report*, 1920–21, pp. 6–7; *Argus*, 9/5/1925, p. 34.
39 *Summary of Meetings of Conference of St. Dunstan's Delegates*, p. 9.
40 See NAA, P130/1, M8367.
41 *Herald*, 30/3/1922, p. 7.
42 See Jessica Meyer, '"Not Septimus Now"', pp. 122 & 124.
43 *Argus*, 1/4/1921, p. 7.
44 Judith Smart, 'Feminists, Food and the Fair Price', p. 277.
45 Iris Mead to TSAS, 5/4/1928, SLSA, TSAS, SRG 488, Box 13.
46 *Diggers' Gazette*, 21/5/1922, p. 22; *Soldier*, 25/5/1917, p. 30.
47 Iris Mead to TSAS, 5/4/1928, SLSA, TSAS, SRG 488, Box 13.
48 Application, 1/10/1918, NAA, B73/25, Box 1, R12.
49 Undated letter to TSAS, c.1928, SLSA, TSAS, SRG 488, Box 10.
50 Marilyn Lake, *The Limits of Hope*, pp. xv, vxii & 3–24.
51 *Report of the Royal Commission on Soldier Settlement*, p. 8.
52 Marilyn Lake, *The Limits of Hope*, pp. 60 & 54.
53 *Limbless Soldier*, 17/3/1924, p. 1.
54 Marilyn Lake, *The Limits of Hope*, pp. 143–74 & 177–94.
55 WG Sewell to CSB, 9/12/1929, PROV, VPRS 746/P0000, Unit 150.
56 Qualification Certificate, 18/2/1919, PROV, VPRS 10381/P0000, Unit 150.
57 Reference, 7/5/1917, PROV, VPRS 10381/P0000, Unit 150.
58 Inspector's Report, September 1922, PROV, VPRS 10381/P0000, Unit 150.
59 Mary Watson to CSB, 28/11/1922, PROV, VPRS 10381/P0000, Unit 150.
60 See *Report of the Royal Commission on Soldier Settlement*, pp. 16–18.
61 James Inman to CSB, 26/10/1921, PROV, VPRS 746/P0000, Unit 150. Inman gave up his block in 1923.
62 *Report of the Royal Commission on Soldier Settlement*, pp. 16, 23 & 48.
63 Repatriation Commission, *Annual Report*, 1924–25, p. 3.
64 *Limbless Soldier*, September 1931, p. 6.
65 See Henry Stone employment records, Noel Butlin Archives, Australian National University, CSR Ltd Records, 142/3063; CSR Ltd Staff Summary Book, Z109/557, 1918.
66 Margaret Cramond, Gwen Summers, Diane Nicholas, Mary Reddrop, Joan Wishart.
67 Interview with Margaret Cramond, 29/9/2004.
68 Qualification Certificate of Harold Wallace, 28/2/1920, PROV, VPRS 747/P0000, Unit 90.
69 Interview with Betsy Burchett, 3/11/2004.
70 George Goodwin to TSAS, 9/11/1926, SLSA, TSAS, SRG 488, Box 11.
71 See ARCS, NSW, *Annual Report*, 1925–26, p. 13.
72 ARCS, NSW, *Annual Report*, 1921–22, p. 24.
73 ARCS, NSW, *Annual Report*, 1925–26, p. 13–14.
74 ARCS, NSW, *Annual Report*, 1927–28, p. 17.
75 ARCS, NSW, *Annual Report*, 1922–23, p. 26.
76 Edwina Gleadle to TSAS, 2/12/1932, SLSA, TSAS, SRG 488, Box 11.

77 Thomas Reid to TSAS, 14/9/1926 & 21/2/1927, SLSA, TSAS, SRG 488, Box 15.
78 John McMaster to TSAS, 4/11/1926, SLSA, TSAS, SRG 488, Box 14.
79 ARCS, Victoria, *Annual Report*, 1926–27, p. 11.
80 See case of LG, SLSA, TSAS, SRG 488, Box 11.
81 Application, CSWM, Violet Fraser, 15 April 1920, NLA, MS 2864, Box 14, File 3.
82 ARCS, NSW, *Annual Report*, 1927–28, pp. 13 & 67.
83 ED Millen, Minister for Repatriation, *What Australia is Doing for Her Returned Soldiers*, p. 5.
84 ARCS, Victoria, *Annual Report*, 1925–26, p. 8.
85 Application, CSWM, Sarah Storey 13/4/1920, NLA, MS 2864, Box 14, File 3.
86 EH to TSAS, 26/6/1938 & 11/5/1936, SLSA, TSAS, SRG 488, Box 8.
87 For example, see ARCS, NSW, *Annual Report*, 1927–28, p. 89.
88 *Daily Telegraph*, 29/6/1920, p. 7.
89 *Smith's Weekly*, 17/7/1920, p. 23.
90 Repatriation Commission, *Annual Report*, 1926–27, p. 5.

CHAPTER 4

1 ARCS, NSW, *Annual Report*, 1926, p. 13.
2 Record of Evidence, 21/3/1929, NAA, B73/58, Box 80, M15005.
3 *RSA Magazine*, September, 1918, p. 51.
4 John Raftery & Sandra Schubert, *A Very Changed Man*, p. 72.
5 See Melanie Oppenheimer, *Red Cross VAs*.
6 'Press Censorship Conference, Melbourne, 1918', NAA, MP367/1, 437/1/115, Part 2, p. 277.
7 Lady Munro-Ferguson to Mrs Matheson, 3/8/1920 & 9/8/1920, NLA, FM Pharo Papers, MS 6669, Folder 2.
8. Lady Munro-Ferguson to No. 11 AGH Caulfield, 4/8/1920, NLA, FM Pharo Papers, MS 6669, Folder 2.
9 Secretary, Soldiers' Wives Committee to Repatriation Commission, 12/10/October 1921, NAA, A2487, 1922/7622.
10 On 'emotional labour', see Bruce Scates, 'The Unknown Sock Knitter', p. 31.
11 *Repatriation*, 25/4/1919, p. 2.
12 Arnold Lawson, *War Blindness at St Dunstan's*, p. 131.
13 *Soldier*, 22/4/1924, p. 33; Kerreen Reiger, *The Disenchantment of the Home*.
14 *Everylady's Journal*, 5/7/1919, p. 377.
15 Loftus Hills, *The Returned Sailors and Soldiers' Imperial League of Australia*, p. 89.
16 Letter from State War Council Hobart to Comptroller of Repatriation, 19/3/1918, NAA, A2483/1, B18/2757.
17 *Our Empire*, 18/5/1921, p. 3.
18 Interview with Keith Falconer, 20/10/2004.
19 Interview with Margaret Cramond, 29/9/2004.
20 Interview with Mary Reddrop, 23/9/2004.
21 See NAA, B73/39, Box 10, M30862.
22 Undated newsclipping, NAA, AWM 164. Charles Eyde Berg died on 30/5/1936.
23 Repatriation Department Memo, 1918, NAA, A2487, 1922/14074.
24 See Joy Damousi, *The Labour of Loss*, pp. 47–48.
25 ARCS, NSW, *Annual Report*, 1927–28, p. 66.
26 ibid.
27 Interview with Mavis Floyd, 25/11/2004.
28 Interview with Beverley Broadbent, 6/10/2004.
29 Interview with Margaret Cramond,

29/9/2004.
30 Interview with Mary Reddrop, 23/9/2004.
31 Interview with Mavis Floyd, 25/11/2004.
32 Interview with Diane Nicholas, 12/10/2004.
33 Interview with Joan Wishart, 9/8/2004.
34 Interview with Gwen Summers, 28/10/2004.
35 Interview with Margaret Cramond, 29/9/2004.
36 Joy Damousi, *The Labour of Loss*, p. 85.
37 Randall Family Papers, SLV, MS 11287, MSB 401. In the British context, see Joanna Bourke, *Dismembering the Male*, p. 32; Lesley Hall, *Hidden Anxieties*, p. 117–18.
38 *Our Empire*, 18/5/1920, p. 2.
39 Medical Report, 26/4/1915, NAA, C138/18, Box 57275, M47319.
40 File note, 1931, NAA, B73/37, Box 127, M74937.
41 Letter to Department of Repatriation, 23/2/1930, NAA, B73/37, Box 127, M74937.
42 File note 1931, NAA, B73/37, Box 127, M74937.
43 *Age*, 20 January 1919, p. 4. See Marina Larsson, 'An Iconography of Suffering'.
44 Private note to AG Butler 14/12/1923, NAA, AWM 41, 520.
45 Inspector-General of the Insane to Hospital for the Insane at Sunbury 27/8/1925, PROV, VPRS 7471/P0001, Unit 2.
46 Inspector-General of the Insane to Deputy Commissioner of Repatriation, Melbourne, 7/9/1925, PROV, VPRS 7471/P0001, Unit 2.
47 On the official rejection of such cases, see Clem Lloyd & Jacqui Rees, *The Last Shilling*, p. 235.
48 Record of Evidence, Mrs D Brown, 12/3/1929, NAA, B73/32, M12490.
49 Record of Evidence, May Brown, 23/3/1923, NAA, B73/32, M12490.
50 Medical Report, 23/5/1935, NAA, B73/0, Box, 12, H15303.
51 Medical Report, 29/1/1935, NAA, B73/0, Box, 12, H15303.
52 *RSA Magazine*, June 1919, p. 21.
53 Interview with Joyce Muir, 5/4/2005.
54 Interview with Jean Ingram, 12/11/1937, NAA, B73/0, Box 2, M2785. Also see Judith Allen, *Sex and Secrets*, 'Heroes at Home', pp. 130–56; Elizabeth Nelson, 'Homefront Hostilities'.
55 Application, CSWM, Emily Whealey, 22/3/1920, NLA, MS 2864, Box 14, File 3.
56 Application, CSWM, Maud Perks, 17/1/1918, NLA, MS 2864, Box 14, File 3.
57 See Elizabeth Nelson, 'Civilian Men and Domestic Violence'.
58 Interview with Joan Wishart, 9/8/2004.
59 Medical Report, 30/11/1929, NAA, B73/25, Box, 107, M2321.
60 Medical Report, 31/1/1929, NAA, B73/25, Box, 107, M2321.
61 Interview with Jean Ingram, 12/11/1937, NAA, B73/0, Box 2, M2785.
62 Marilyn Lake, *The Limits of Hope*, p. 145.
63 Inspector's Report, 28/5/1926, File of George McMahon, PROV, VPRS 10381/P0000, Unit 170.
64 Interview with Beverley Broadbent, 6/10/2004.
65 Inspector's Report, 29 May 1928, File of Frank Ingamells, PROV, VPRS 746/P0000, Unit 150.
66 ibid.
67 Attachment to letter from Blinded Soldiers' Association to Prime Minister, March 1932, NAA, A461, 0394/1/1.
68 See United Returned Soldiers' Fund, *The Work it is Doing*; Stephen Garton, *The Cost of War*, p. 204.
69 See Application, CSWM, Bertha Rea, 4/3/1920, NLA, MS 2864, Box 14, File 3.
70 Bruce Scates, 'The Unknown Sock

Knitter', p. 39; Jay Winter, *Sites of Memory*, pp. 30, 47.
71 Sailors, Soldiers and Nurses Relatives' Association Constitution, NLA, RSL, MS 6609, File 492B.
72 Friendly Union of Soldiers' Wives, Mothers and Sisters, *Seventh Annual Report*, 1922, NLA, RSL, MS 6609, Folder 492B.
73 ibid.
74 Katie Holmes, *Spaces in Her Day*, p. 2.
75 AG Butler, *The Official History*, vol. 3, p. 828.

CHAPTER 5

1 ARCS, NSW, *Annual Report*, 1937, p. 10.
2 Letter, 4/8/1929, PROV, VPRS 7539/P0001, Unit 2.
3 Inspector-General of the Insane to Elizabeth Moffatt, 30/7/29, PROV, VPRS 7539/P0001, Unit 2.
4 Letter to President, RSSILA Melbourne, 22/6/1931, PROV, VPRS 7532/P0001, Unit 4.
5 The international and Australian historiography on shell shock is vast, see Joanna Bourke, 'Shell Shock and Australian Soldiers'; Stephen Garton, 'Freud Versus the Rat'; Michael Tyquin, *Madness and the Military*; Joanna Bourke, 'Effeminacy, Ethnicity'; George Mosse, 'Shell Shock as a Social Disease'; Jay Winter, 'Shell Shock and the Cultural History of the Great War'; Peter Leese, *Shell Shock*; Paul Lerner, *Hysterical Men*; Jessica Meyer, '"Gladder to be Going Out than Afraid"'. Two recent books have explored families' involvement in the institutionalisation of shell-shocked soldiers, see Peter Barham, *Forgotten Lunatics*, pp. 167–80 & 340–54, and Michael Tyquin, *Madness and the Military*, pp. 139–41. The literature on families and civilian mental patients includes Mark Finnane, 'Asylums, Families and the State'; David Wright, 'Family Strategies'; Peregrine Horden & Richard Smith (eds) *The Locus of Care*; David Wright, *Mental Disability in Victorian England*; Roy Porter & David Wright (eds) *The Confinement of the Insane*.
6 See PROV, VPRS 7528/P0001 Unit 2 & PROV, VPRS 7525/P0001, Unit 1
7 *Duckboard*, 1/4/1924, p 9.
8 ibid.
9 Official statistics indicates that between 2500 and 3300 returned soldiers received pensions for 'war neuroses' annually after the war, and that between 330 and 530 were pensioned as 'mentals under restraint'. AG Butler, *The Official History*, vol. 3, p. 965. There is no data on the number of returned soldiers in private mental hospitals.
10 AG Butler, *The Official History*, vol. 3, p. 142.
11 ARCS, NSW, *Red Cross Record*, 1 January 1920, p. 39–40.
12 DC to Inspector-General of the Insane, 16/7/1930, PROV, VPRS 7532/P0001, Unit 4.
13 Medical file note, 10/10/1930, NAA, B73/39, Box 88, M33048.
14 See NAA, B73/60, Box 50, M49903.
15 File note, June 1928, PROV, VPRS 7532/P0001, Unit 3.
16 *Report of the Inspector-General of the Insane*, 1917, p. 31.
17 See Catharine Coleborne, '"His Brain Was Wrong, His Mind Astray"'.
18 On 'preference', see Clem Lloyd & Jacqui Rees, *The Last Shilling*, pp. 277–78; Stephen Garton, *The Cost of War*, pp. 74–117. In the New Zealand context, see John Weaver & David Wright, 'Shell Shock and the Politics of Asylum Committal'.
19 AWM 41, 295, Notes of AG Butler, 11/12/1935.
20 *Sun News-Pictorial*, 23/2/1923, p. 6.
21 Letter from RSSILA, 11/11/1919,

NLA, RSL, MS 6609, File 963. In the UK context, see Fiona Reid, 'Distinguishing Between Shell-Shocked Veterans and Pauper Lunatics'.
22 PROV, VPRS 7512/P0001, Unit 1, Registers of Military Patients.
23. Repatriation Commission, *Annual Report*, 1920–21, p. 193.
24 Letter to Medical Superintendent, Mont Park, 30/1/1920, PROV, VPRS 7472/P0001, Unit 2.
25 Legacy Melbourne, *Weekly Bulletin*, 7/9/1926, Legacy Archives, Melbourne; ARCS Victoria to Inspector-General of the Insane, 30/4/1924, PROV, VPRS/7527, P0001, Unit 1.
26 AG Butler, Notes of interview, 11/12/1935, NAA, AWM 41, 295.
27 WH to Inspector-General of the Insane, 23/8/1928, PROV, VPRS 7527/P0001, Unit 1.
28 Inspector-General of the Insane to Medical Superintendent, Royal Park, 8/6/1928, PROV, VPRS 7539/P0001, Unit 2.
29 Interview with Beverley Broadbent, 6/10/2004.
30 MacLeod and Watsonia Progress Association to Inspector-General of the Insane, 9/3/1918 & 17/4/1928, PROV, VPRS 7532/ P0001, Unit 3.
31 Interview with Betsy Burchett, 3/11/2004.
32 Interview with Gwen Summers, 28/10/2004.
33 See Stephen Garton, 'Freud Versus the Rat'.
34 RH Fetherston, *Report*, p. 80; Repatriation Commission, *Annual Reports*, 1920–21 & 1921–22.
35 AG Butler, *The Official History*, vol. 3, p. 60.
36 Interview with Joan Wishart, 9/8/2004.
37 *Argus*, 15/8/1924, p. 7.
38 Fred W Jacoby to RSSILA Federal Congress, 29/10/1924, NLA, RSL, MS 6609, File 1976B.
39 President, National Council of Women WA to RSSILA Federal Conference, 29/10/1924, NLA, RSL, MS 6609, File 1976B.
40 Repatriation Commission, *Annual Report*, 1927–28, p. 25.
41 Letter to Department of Repatriation, 20/7/1929, NAA, B73/52, Box 136, M72110.
42 Record of Evidence, 16/6/1929, NAA, B73/52, Box 136, M72110.
43 Letter to Repatriation Department, 20/7/1929, 1373/52, Box 136, M72110.
44 Letter to Repatriation Department, 23/10/1930, NAA, B73/50, Box 14, M60352.
45 Letter to Repatriation Department, 24/10/1930, NAA, B73/50, Box 14, M60352.
46 ibid.
47 Letter to Repatriation Department, 23/10/1930, NAA, B73/50, Box 14, M60352.
48 Letter to Repatriation Department, March 1931, NAA, B73/50, Box 14, M60352.
49 Letter to Inspector-General of the Insane, 4/8/1929, PROV, VPRS 7539/P0001, Unit 2.
50 See Catharine Coleborne, 'Families, Patients and Emotions'.
51 *Report of the Inspector-General of the Insane*, 1925, p. 32. The amount of this fee varied from year to year.
52 Inspector-General of the Insane to Reginald Mackie, 9/12/1927, PROV, VPRS 7527/P0001, Unit 1.
53 Reginald Mackie to Inspector-General of the Insane 9/3/1928, PROV, VPRS 7527/P0001, Unit 1.
54 See Memo from Deputy Inspector-General of the Insane to Medical Superintendent Mont Park, 14/8/1928, PROV, VPRS 7532/ P0001, Unit 3.
55 Edwina Leonard to Medical Superintendent, Mont Park, 4/3/1929, PROV, VPRS 7527/ P0001, Unit 1.
56 Medical Superintendent, Mont Park, handwritten note, 5/3/1929,

PROV, VPRS 7527/P0001, Unit 1.
57 Such communications may have been recorded in patients' case files which appear to be unavailable in the Victorian Public Records Office.
58 See Geelong Branch, RSSILA to Inspector-General of the Insane, 31/1/1928, PROV, VPRS 7539/P0001, Unit 2.
59 See NAA, B73/32, M12490.
60 Miss Bell to Mont Park Hospital 4/10/1918, PROV, VPRS 7532/P0001, Unit 1.
61 See letter from Mrs W, 28/8/1923, PROV, VPRS 7539/P0001, Unit 1.
62 Medical Superintendent, Hospital for the Insane, Ballarat to Inspector-General of the Insane, 6/5/1919, PROV, VPRS 7523/P0001, Unit 1.
63 See NAA, B73/56, Box 17, M56846.
64 Interview with Betsy Burchett, 3/11/2004.
65 Draft Letter from Inspector-General of the Insane, Victoria to Deputy Commissioner for State Repatriation, 30/8/1921, PROV, VPRS 7532/P0001, Unit 1. On attendants see PROV, VPRS 7527/P0001, Unit 1, 1925 File.
66 Lunacy Department Memo, 14 January 1926, PROV, VPRS 7527/P0001, Unit 1. On supply of basic items see PROV, VPRS 7527/P0001, Unit 1, 1924 File.
67 Deputy Commissioner for Repatriation to Inspector-General of the Insane, 15 July 1924, PROV, VPRS 7527/P0001, Unit 1.
68 FT to Inspector-General of the Insane, 9/4/1924, PROV, VPRS 7527/P0001, Unit 1.
69 See File Note, 19/8/1931, NAA, B73/32, M12490.
70 ibid.
71 *Age*, undated newsclipping from 1925, PROV, VPRS 7527/P0001, Unit 1.
72 *Sun News-Pictorial*, February 1923, newscutting, PROV, VPRS 7532/P0001, Unit 1, 1923 File.
73 President, National Council of Women WA to RSSILA Federal Conference, Adelaide, 29/10/1924, NLA, RSL, MS 6609, File 1976B.
74 President, Housewives' Association, WA to RSSILA Federal Conference, Adelaide, 4/11/1924, NLA, RSL, MS 6609, File 1976B.
75 Fred W Jacoby to President, RSSILA Federal Congress, 29/10/1924, NLA, RSL, MS 6609, File 1976B, quoting Harry Gregory MHR, 21/1/1924.
76 *Truth*, 17/2/1923, p. 5.
77 Desegregation was proposed in all states, see NLA, RSL, MS 6609, File 963 & 1976B; *Our Empire*, 18/6/1921, p. 4.
78 Repatriation Commission, *Annual Report*, 1920–21, p. 15.
79 *Herald*, 30/3/1922, p. 7.
80 ibid.; *Sun*, 26/2/1923, p. 6.
81 See NAA, B73/37, Boxes 126 & Box 127, M74903.
82 Letter to Department of Repatriation, December 1926, NAA, B73/37, Boxes 126 & Box 127, M74903.
83 Memo from Dr B, 7/1/1938, NAA, B73/37, Boxes 126 & Box 127, M74903.

CHAPTER 6

1 *Register*, 8/1/1921, p. 6.
2 Letter to Department of Repatriation, 28/3/1923, quoted in medical report 16/5/1923, NAA, B73/25, R2321.
3 ibid. My italics.
4 Medical report, 16/5/1923, Letter 16/5/1926, NAA, B73/25, Box 107, R2321.
5 *Optimist*, April 1938, p. 7.
6 *Repatriation*, August 1920, p. 12.
7 *Optimist*, September 1933, p. 15.
8 *Argus*, 28/6/1917, p. 4.
9 Henry A Ellis, *How Shall I be Saved from Consumption?*, p. 97.
10 AG Butler, *The Official History*, vol. 3, p. 828.

11 There is an extensive historiography on tuberculosis, see Linda Bryder, *Below the Magic Mountain*; AJ Proust (ed.) *History of Tuberculosis in Australia, New Zealand and Papua New Guinea*; David S Barnes, *The Making of a Social Disease*; Katherine Ott, *Fevered Lives*; Michael Roe, *Life Over Death*; Thomas Dormandy, *The White Death*; Alison Bashford, 'Cultures of Confinement'. Tubercular ex-servicemen after the First World War are discussed in Robin Walker, 'The Struggle Against Pulmonary Tuberculosis', pp. 457–58; Michael Roe, *Life Over Death*, pp. 76–79; Joy Damousi, *The Labour of Loss*, pp. 91–92.
12 Alison Bashford, 'At the Border', p. 351; Claudia Thame, 'Health and the State', pp. 85–86.
13 Claudia Thame, 'Health and the State', p. 86.
14 Medical report, 1/6/1916, NAA, B73/25, Box 107, M2321.
15 See Matthew Smallman-Raynor & Andrew D Cliff, 'War and Disease'.
16 *Medical Journal of Australia*, 16/2/1924, p. 29; Repatriation Commission, *Annual Report*, 1926–27.
17 *Bedford Call*, 1922, p. 3, SLSA, TSAS, SRG 488, Box 6.
18 *Medical Journal of Australia*, 3/10/1914, p. 323.
19 See Katherine Ott, *Fevered Lives*, pp. 17 & 53–64.
20 *Medical Journal of Australia*, 22/10/1921, p. 342.
21 Committee Concerning the Causes of Death and Invalidity in the Commonwealth, *Report on Tuberculosis*, p. 23.
22 Henry A Ellis, *How Shall I be Saved?*, p. 15. My italics.
23 ARCS, NSW, *Red Cross Record*, 1/5/1928, p. 25.
24 Extract from the booklet *The Medical Examination of Intending Immigrants to Australia*, NAA, A1/15, 1921/21464.
25 Vera Bax to WH Kelley, MP, 17/5/1917, NAA, MP 367/1, 513/8/32.
26 Fetherston, Director-General, AAMS to Brigadier-General, 3rd Military District 11/5/1917, NAA, MP 367/1, 513/8/32.
27 Military institutions for tubercular soldiers included MacLeod Sanatorium (Melbourne) Bodington (Blue Mountains, near Sydney) Bedford Park (Adelaide), Stanthorpe (Queensland), Woorooloo (Western Australia), see Australian Army Medical Services Report, 16/8/1917, NAA, MP 367/1, 513/8/32.
28 *The Civil Re-establishment of the AIF*, p. 21.
29 *Medical Journal of Australia*, 17/1/1925, p. 55.
30 *RSA Magazine*, September 1918, p. 51.
31 *Optimist*, April 1938, p. 7.
32 *Argus*, 12/9/1921, p. 10.
33 Harold Kenworthy to his father, 12/4/1926, AWM, PR00120.
34 William J Robinson, *Eugenics, Marriage and Birth Control*, p. 159.
35 *Tassie Digger*, January 1921, p. 28.
36 Lawrason Brown, *Rules for Recovery*, pp. 164 & 162.
37 *Everylady's Journal*, 6/5/1918, p. 297.
38 ibid.
39 See medical reports, 22/11/1923, 30/4/1929, NAA, B73/25, M2321.
40 RSSILA to Commissioner for Pensions, 18/2/1920, NLA, RSL, MS 6609, File 1339.
41 Letter to TSAS, 7/12/1926, SLSA, TSAS, SRG 488, Box 13.
42 Town Clerk's Department Paper, 22/4/1929, City of Sydney Archives, File 1838/29.
43 *Optimist*, no. 6, March 1928, p. 7.
44 Interview with Beryl Nelson, 27/4/2005.
45 *Argus*, 18/9/1920, p. 27.
46 *Optimist*, November 1937, pp. 1–2.
47 Interview with Beryl Nelson, 27/4/2005.

48 *Optimist*, February 1933, p. 2.
49 *Optimist*, March 1933, p. 12.
50 Medical Reports 30/6/1927, 1/1/1932, NAA, B73/25, Box 107, M2321.
51. *Tassie Digger*, January 1921, p. 12.
52 Matron Burns to TSAS, 9/8/1927, SLSA, TSAS, SRG 488, Box 1A.
53 TSAS to Matron of Angorichina, 19/8/1927, SLSA, TSAS, SRG 488, Box 1A.
54 ARCS, NSW, *Annual Report*, 1923–24, p. 28.
55 Col. Cuscaden, AAMC, Minute Paper, 4/5/1917, NAA, MP 367/1, 513/8/32.
56 Interview with Beryl Nelson, 27/4/2005.
57 *Optimist*, May 1938, p. 15.
58 ARCS, NSW, *Red Cross Record*, 1/5/1928, p. 25.
59 Minister in Charge of Repatriation to RSSILA, 30/7/1929, NLA, RSL, MS 6609, File 4185B.
60 TSAS to Matron of Angorichina, 12/9/1927, SLSA, TSAS, SRG 488, Box 1A.
61 *Bedford Call*, 1923, p. 13.
62 Anti-Tuberculosis Association of New South Wales, *Your Baby*, p. 30.
63 Letter to TSAS, 26/6/1934, SLSA, TSAS, SRG 488, Box 11.
64 Letter to TSAS, 20/7/1935, SLSA, TSAS, SRG 488, Box 9.
65 Newscutting from unknown source, 26/11/1924, in SLSA, TSAS, SRG 488, Box 1A.
66 Mrs Dewhurst to TSAS, 26/4/1929, SLSA, TSAS, SRG 488, Box 12.
67 Minister for Repatriation to RSSILA, 30/7/1929, NLA, RSL, MS 6609, File 4185B.
68 *Optimist*, February 1933, p. 1.
69 AG Butler, *The Official History*, vol. 3, p. 829.
70 TSAS to Mrs Gardener, 15/6/1929, SLSA, TSAS, SRG 488, Box 9.
71 Tubercular Soldiers' Association, Minutes, 12/8/1926, SLSA, TSAS, SRG 488, Box 3A.
72 ARCS, NSW, *Red Cross Record*, 5/12/1924, p. 32.
73 See Cynthia Connolly, 'Pale, Poor, and "Pretubercular" Children'.
74 ARCS, National Division, *Annual Report*, 1930, p. 44.
75 ARCS, NSW, *Annual Report*, 1926–27, p. 43.
76 ARCS, NSW, *Annual Report*, 1934–35, p. 65.
77 ARCS, NSW, *Annual Report*, 1927–28, p. 66, & 1926–27, p. 43
78 ARCS, NSW, *Red Cross Record*, 1/5/1928, p. 25.
79 *Sydney Morning Herald*, 11/9/1929, p. 14.
80 *Optimist*, July 1933, p. 1.
81 *Optimist*, June 1933, p. 15.
82 Interview with Beryl Nelson, 27/4/2005.
83 ibid.
84 *Optimist*, March 1930, p. 13.
85 See *Optimist*, March 1926, p. 14.
86 *Optimist*, April 1933, p. 16.
87 See *Tassie Digger*, January 1921, p. 12.
88 *Optimist*, July 1933, p. 1.
89 *Optimist*, September 1933, p. 15.
90 *Mufti*, 1/8/1934, p. 14.

CHAPTER 7

1 *Duckboard*, 1/5/1926, p. 31 (first and last stanzas).
2 *Age*, 26/4/1935, p. 9; *Herald*, 30/4/1935, p. 8.
3 *Herald*, 26/4/1935, p. 4.
4 *Herald*, 27/4/1935, p. 8.
5 *Age*, 26/4/1935, p. 9; *Herald*, 26/4/1935, p. 4.
6 *Sydney Morning Herald*, 26/4/1934, p. 9.
7 *Argus*, 26/4/1936, p. 9.
8 *Sydney Morning Herald*, 10/8/1927, p. 14.
9 Interview with Beverley Broadbent, 6/10/2004.
10 State Recruiting Committee of South Australia, *Honour, Opportunity, Cash*, Recruiting Leaflet, South Australia, undated, AWM, 5/5/9.
11 In the British context, see Joanna

Bourke, *Dismembering the Male*, pp. 31 & 251. Also see Clem Lloyd & Jacqui Rees, *The Last Shilling*, pp. 241–62; Stephen Garton, *The Cost of War*, pp. 95–97.
12 *Reveille*, 30/6/1931, p. 2.
13 *Census of the Commonwealth of Australia*, 30/6/1933, vol. 3, ch. 21, pp. 397 & 399.
14 Medical reports 1916 & 1929, NAA, C138/18, Box 57096, N4088.
15 Form 71, 28/12/1924, NAA, B73/81, Box 9, H30781.
16 *Reveille*, 31/3/1931, p. 78.
17 AJ Withers to AG Butler, 4/6/1940, NAA, AWM 41, 230.
18 *Mufti*, 1/7/1939, p. 17.
19 AG Butler, *The Official History*, vol. 3, pp. 963–65. The 1933 census showed that there were 226 438 returned soldiers alive in that year.
20 RSSILA, *Biennial Report*, 1937, NLA, RSL, MS 6609, Box 394, p. 3.
21 *Census of the Commonwealth of Australia*, 30 June 1933, Statistician's Report, 1940, p. 398; AG Butler was a sceptic, see *The Official History*, vol. 3, pp. 816–19.
22 See Barry Smith, 'Australian Public Health During the Depression'.
23 CB Schedvin, *Australia and the Great Depression*, p. 47.
24 ibid.; Commonwealth Bureau of Census and Statistics, *Official Year Book of the Commonwealth of Australia*, 1935, p. 395 & 1940, p. 720.
25 *Age*, 6/7/1932, p. 6.
26 See Judy Mackinolty (ed.) *The Wasted Years?*; CB Schedvin, *Australia and the Great Depression*; David Potts, 'A Positive Culture of Poverty'; Joanne Scott & Kay Saunders, 'Happy Days are Here Again?'; David Potts, *The Myth of the Great Depression*.
27 *Brisbane Courier*, 15/4/1931, p. 3.
28 Letter to President RSSILA, 22/6/1931, PROV, VPRS 7532/P0001, Unit 4.
29 See NAA, A461/9, 13/1/5; *Herald*, 1/10/1930, p. 8; NAA, MP33/1, QLD 1930/137.
30 'Report of the Interdepartmental Committee', 1/2/1932, City of Sydney Archives, File 2494/30.
31 ibid.
32 Interview with Margaret Cramond, 29/9/2004.
33 Interview with Joan Wishart, 9/8/2004.
34 *Herald*, 5/11/1932, p. 1.
35 *Census of the Commonwealth of Australia*, 30/6/1933, Part XVII, pp. 1087–88.
36 *Whiz-Bang*, September 1930, p. 8.
37 *Sydney Morning Herald*, 17/1/1931, p. 14.
38 Repatriation Commission, *Annual Report*, 1936–37, p. 8.
39 Medical note, 11/11/1936, NAA, B73/56, Box 181, M61006.
40 Clem Lloyd & Jacqui Rees, *The Last Shilling*, p. 244.
41 Repatriation Commission, *Annual Report*, 1937–38, p. 7; War Pensions Entitlement Appeal Tribunal, *Annual Reports*, 1930–36.
42 Letter to Repatriation Department, Brisbane, 18/11/1937, NAA, J26/10, Box 3453, M16065.
43 AG Butler, *The Official History*, vol. 3, pp. 963–64.
44 Repatriation Commission, *Annual Report*, 1931–32, p. 6. The 22.5 per cent drop in the pensions of disabled soldiers' wives was amended to 10 per cent by the *Financial Relief Act* in mid-1933. See Clem Lloyd & Jacqui Rees, *The Last Shilling*, p. 248.
45 *Sydney Morning Herald*, 16/3/1932, p. 6.
46 *Sydney Morning Herald*, 8/4/1931, p. 7.
47 See cases in Limbless Soldiers' Association, 'Re Pensions for New Wives and Children', 1936, NLA, RSL, MS 6609, File 7664B.
48 Clem Lloyd & Jacqui Rees, *The Last Shilling*, p. 246.
49 See Repatriation Commission, *Service Pensions Handbook*, 1937; Clem Lloyd & Jacqui Rees, *The Last Shilling*, p. 252.

50 Repatriation Commission, *Annual Report*, 1935–36, p.6.
51 *Mufti*, 1/12/1935, p. 4.
52 Letter to the Inspector-General of the Insane, 3/10/1927, PROV, VPRS 7527/P0001, Unit 1.
53 ibid. Underlining is in the original.
54 ibid.
55 Letter to Repatriation Department, 16/2/1936, NAA, B73/30, Box 136, M40019.
56 Summary of Evidence, 15/9/1932, NAA, B73/0, Box 2, M2785.
57 Interview with Beverley Broadbent, 6/10/2004.
58 AG Butler, *The Official History*, p. 966.
59 *Mufti*, 10/10/1934, p. 25.
60 Limbless Soldiers' Association, 'Re Pensions for New Wives and Children', 1936, NLA, RSL, MS 6609, File 7664B.
61 File note 17/3/1937, NAA, B73/0, Box 12, H15303.
62 Interview with Joyce Muir, 5/4/2005.
63 Interview with Beverley Broadbent, 6/10/2004.
64 ARCS, NSW, *Red Cross Record*, 1/3/1929, p. 8.
65 *Mufti*, 1/9/1934, p. 6.
66 *Mufti*, 1/3/1938, p. 16. Also see Stephen Garton, *The Cost of War*, pp. 204–06.
67 Victor Whatley to Returned Soldiers' Association, 14/7/1934, AWM, PR 86/270.
68 AH Banfield to Victor Whatley, 9/8/1934, AWM, PR 86/270.
69 Victor Whatley to Returned Soldiers' Association, 14/7/1934, AWM, PR 86/270.
70 ARCS, NSW, *Annual Report*, 1935–36, p. 7.
71 ARCS, NSW, *Annual Report*, 1929–30, p. 11.
72 *Sir Samuel McCaughey Memorial to the Fallen and Disabled Soldiers of Australia*, p. 27.
73 Interview with Mavis Floyd, 25/11/2004.
74 See Wendy Lowenstein, *Weevils in the Flour*; David Potts, *The Myth of the Great Depression*, pp. 90–109.
75 ARCS, NSW, *Annual Report*, 1934–35, p. 9.
76 *Census of the Commonwealth of Australia*, 30 June 1933, Statistician's Report, 1940, pp. 163 & 399; Richard White, 'War and Australian Society', p. 414. The specific divorce rate among disabled soldiers is not available.
77 Catherine Maxwell to Director, AWM, 29/11/1936, NAA, AWM 93, 2/5/19C, Part II.
78 ARCS, NSW, *Red Cross Record*, 1/3/1929, p. 8.
79 *Reveille*, 1 March 1937, p. 10.
80 ARCS, National Division, *Annual Report*, 1930–31, p. 26.
81 *Reveille*, October 1936, p. 14.
82 Inspector-General of the Insane to Mont Park Hospital, 16/9/1930, PROV, VPRS 7471/P0001, Unit 3.
83 Letter to Inspector-General of the Insane, 16/11/1931, PROV, VPRS 7539/P0001, Unit 3.
84 *Herald*, 11/11/1927, p. 5; Marilyn Lake, *The Limits of Hope*, p. 220.
85 Record of Evidence 23/12/1936, NAA, B73/38, M52658.
86 Inspector's Report, 17/9/1923, File of JE Love, PROV, VPRS 749/P0000, Unit 200.
87 See File of Thomas L Fielder, PROV, VPRS 10381/P0000, Unit 200.
88 Interview with Keith Falconer, 20/10/2004.
89 ibid; NAA, B73/46, Box 90, R4232.
90 Repatriation Commission, *Annual Report*, 1921–22, p. 37.
91 Graeme Davison, '"Our Youth is Spent"', p. 51.

CHAPTER 8

1 *Reveille*, 1/6/1934, p. 17.
2 NAA, P130/1, M8367.
3 Letter, 21/4/1926, AWM, PR00120.

4 *Hobart Mercury*, 23/8/1926, p. 1.
5 Details supplied by Mercia Kenworthy, received 15/8/1940, NAA, AWM 164.
6 Bart Ziino, *A Distant Grief*.
7 Kenneth J Doka, 'Disenfranchised Grief', p. 4.
8 Vanderlyn R Pine, 'Death, Loss and Disenfranchised Grief', p. 14.
9 Some recent books explore postwar death, see Pat Jalland, *Changing Ways of Death*, pp. 106–26. After the Second World War, see Joy Damousi, *Living with the Aftermath*, pp. 164–91 & 193. The war death literature is extensive, see David Cannadine, 'War and Death'; George Mosse, *Fallen Soldiers*; Jay Winter, *Sites of Memory*; Jonathan Vance, *Death So Noble*; KS Inglis, *Sacred Places*; Joy Damousi, *The Labour of Loss*; Tanja Luckins, *The Gates of Memory*; Bart Ziino, *A Distant Grief*; Daniel J Sherman, *The Construction of Memory in Interwar France*; Pat Jalland, *Australian Ways of Death*.
10 AG Butler, *The Official History*, vol. 3, p. 965.
11 *Reveille*, 1/4/1937, p. 3. Also see *Reveille*, 29/11/1930, p. 27; *Reveille*, 1/11/1936, p. 4.
12 See *Census of the Commonwealth of Australia, 30th June 1933, Part XVII – War Service*, p. 1086.
13 *Optimist*, March 1934, p. 6.
14 *Optimist*, November 1934, p. 10. On life expectancy, see *Census of the Commonwealth of Australia, Australian Life Tables, 1932–34*, p. 9. See discussion of 'premature death' in the previous chapter.
15 See *Reveille*, 1/6/1934, p. 17; 1/7/1934, pp. 16–17.
16 *Sydney Morning Herald*, 10/8/1928, p. 12.
17 See Papers of Alexander Pullar Cameron, SLV, MS 10714.
18 Tasmanian RSSILA to National RSSILA, 13/11/1922, NLA, RSL, MS 6609, File 1432B.
19 See Pat Jalland, *Australian Ways of Death*, pp. 325–28.
20 Interview with Diane Nicholas, 12/10/2004.
21. NAA, B73/54, Box 144, R65449.
22 Beverley Raphael, *The Anatomy of Bereavement*, p. 30.
23 *Medical Journal of Australia*, 24/2/1945, p. 197.
24 Record of Evidence, 5/3/1931, NAA, B73/0, Box 172, M68183.
25 Coroner's Inquest Evidence, 1931, NAA, B73/0, Box 172, M68183.
26 See case file of FK, SLSA, TSAS, SRG 488, Box 13.
27 ARCS, NSW, *Annual Report*, 1930–31, p. 28; TSAS Minute Book, 8/1/1925, SLSA, TSAS, SRG 488, Box 3A.
28 Letter to Department of Repatriation 1/2/1931, NAA, B73/46, Box 90, R4232.
29 N Fletcher to Director AWM, 12/11/1936, NAA, AWM 93, 2/5/19C, Part II.
30 See NAA, B73/77, Box 112, M62091.
31 See Joy Damousi, *Living with the Aftermath*, p. 193; NAA, B73/77, Box 112, M62091.
32 Letter to TSAS, October 1936, SLSA, TSAS, SRG 488, Box 13.
33 Interview with Diane Nicholas, 12/10/2004.
34 Legacy Club Melbourne, *Bulletin*, 19/2/1929, vol. 3, 1928–29.
35 Mark Lyons, *Legacy*, pp. 82 & 52.
36 KS Inglis, *Sacred Places*, p. 180.
37 ibid., p. 182.
38 See *Tassie Digger*, July 1921, pp. 4–5.
39 *Bega District News*, 22/5/1924.
40 Bart Ziino, 'Claiming the Dead', p. 145.
41 *Unveiling of the War Memorial at the University*, Brisbane, 1925, p. 3.
42 See AWM, A02814.
43 Minutes, Executive Sub-Committee, National War Memorial of Victoria, 16 July 1929, PROV, VPRS 2498, P/0000, Unit 1.

44 See Ambrose Pratt & John Barnes, *The National War Memorial of Victoria*, p. 16.
45 Catherine Moriarty, 'Private Grief and Public Remembrance', p. 125.
46 *Warrnambool Standard*, 26/4/1928, p. 5.
47 Jay Winter, *Sites of Memory*, p. 223; Tanja Luckins, *The Gates of Memory*, p. 143.
48 Joy Damousi, *The Labour of Loss*, 26–45; Tanja Luckins, *The Gates of Memory*, pp. 183–208.
49 For example, see Anzac Day coverage, *Sydney Morning Herald*, 26/4/1935.
50 Jay Winter, *Sites of Memory*, p. 80.
51 *Brisbane Courier*, 27/4/1925, p. 8.
52 Kathy Charmaz, 'Grief and Loss of Self', p. 236.
53 Pat Jalland, *Australian Ways of Death*, p. 325; Philippe Ariès, *The Hour of Our Death*, p. 583.
54 Pat Jalland, 'Changing Ways of Grieving', p. 10.
55 Pat Jalland, *Australian Ways of Death*, p. 305.
56 *Sydney Morning Herald*, 26/4/1924, p. 15.
57 Tanja Luckins, *The Gates of Memory*, p. 143.
58 Interview with Betsy Burchett, 3/11/2004.
59 Funeral arrangements for Ambrose Kerin, May 1920, UMA, 82/44, Book 7, p. 44.
60 See UMA, 82/44.
61 Interview with Beverley Broadbent, 6/10/2004.
62 Interview with Diane Nicholas, 12/10/2004.
63 Ric Throssell, *My Fathers' Son*, p. 141. Throssell's suicide was officially accepted.
64 Interview with Beverley Broadbent, 6/10/2004.
65 Kenneth J Doka, 'Disenfranchised Grief', p. 6.
66 Interview with Betsy Burchett, 3/11/2004.
67 *Optimist*, November 1934, p. 10.
68 See NAA, MP 367/1, 446/10/4917.
69 Department of Defence to St Arnaud Sub-Branch, RSSILA, 30 October 1936, NAA, B1535, 746/8/1322.
70 NAA, MP 367/1, 446/10/4917; *Reveille*, 1/6/1934, p. 17.
71 Interview with Betsy Burchett, 3/11/2004.
72 See Headstones for Soldiers' Graves, 1926–27, NAA MP367/1, 446/10/5306; Bart Ziino, *A Distant Grief*, pp. 149–50.
73 Erection of Headstones, June 1922 to May 1925, NAA, MP367/1, 446/10/3759.
74 Headstones for Soldiers' Graves, 1926–27, NAA, MP367/1, 446/10/5306.
75 *Reveille*, 1/6/1936, p. 29.
76 Bruce Scates, 'The Unknown Sock Knitter', p. 40.
77 Donald Cameron to Minister of Defence, 29/4/1927, NAA, MP 367/1, 446/10/4917.
78 See NAA, MP 367/1, 446/10/4917.
79 Peter Soutar to Imperial War Graves Commission, 27/5/1935, NAA, B1535, 746/8/910.
80 Application for In Memoriam Badge, 6/11/1926, NAA, B2455/1 CAMERON A P.
81 *Age*, 24/4/1937, p. 7.
82 *Sydney Morning Herald*, 23/3/1928, p. 12.
83 Michael McKernan, *Here is Their Spirit*, p. 144.
84 Letter to AWM, 13/11/1936, NAA, AWM 93, 2/5/19C, Part II.
85 Letter to AWM, 28/11/1936, NAA, AWM 93, 2/5/19C, Part II.
86 Letter to AWM, 25/11/1936, NAA, AWM 93, 2/5/19C, Part II.
87 Letters to AWM, 23/3/1928 & 31/5/1928, NAA, AWM 93, 2/5/19C, Part I.
88 Letter to Minister for Repatriation, 3/12/1936, NAA, AWM 93, 2/5/19C, Part II.
89 Letter to AWM, 28/11/1936, NAA, AWM 93, 2/5/19C, Part II.

90 Letter to AWM, 16/7/1940, NAA, AWM 93, File 2/5/35, Part 1.
91 See 'slip sent' at top of Catterall letter 21/9/1934, NAA, AWM 93, File 2/5/19C, Part 1.
92 Letter to AWM, 22/10/1941, NAA, AWM 164.
93 Letter to AWM, 12/11/1936, NAA, AWM 93, 2/5/19C, Part II.
94 Letter to AWM, received 20/11/1940, NAA, AWM 164.
95 Letter to AWM, 12/11/1936, NAA, AWM 93, 2/5/19C, Part II.
96 ibid.
97 AWM to RSSILA, 19/3/1941, NAA, AWM 93, 12/8/11.
98 Michael McKernan, *Here is Their Spirit*, p. 229. The supplementary rolls were closed in 1967.
99 See NAA, AWM 261.
100 Peter Stanley, *Rosemary and Wattle*, p. 2.
101 Interview with Diane Nicholas, 12/10/2004.
102 George Mosse, *Fallen Soldiers*, p. 80.
103 Jay Winter, *Sites of Memory*, pp. 5 & 95.

CONCLUSION

1 *West Wimmera Mail*, 18/5/1917, p. 1.
2 Inspector-General of the Insane to Chairman, Repatriation Commission, 7/8/1925, PROV, VPRS 7521/P0001, Unit 1.
3 Letter to Deputy Commissioner, Repatriation Department, 23 September 1966, NAA, B73/62, Box 249, M115094.
4 Emily K Abel, *Hearts of Wisdom*, p. 274.
5 Interview with Betsy Burchett, 13/12/2005.
6 See *Vietnam Veterans Counselling Service Victoria Newsletter*, March 2005, p. 7; *Vetaffairs*, December 2005, p. 7.
7 *Medical Journal of Australia*, vol. 183, no. 3, 1/8/2005, pp. 146–50.

bibliography

PRIMARY SOURCES

INTERVIEWS
Beverley Broadbent, 6 October 2004.
Betsy Burchett, 3 November 2004.
Margaret Cramond, 29 September 2004.
Keith Falconer, 20 October 2004.
Mavis Floyd, 25 November 2004.
Joyce Muir, 5 April 2005.
Beryl Nelson, 27 April 2005.
Diane Nicholas, 12 October 2004.
Mary Reddrop, 23 September 2004.
Gwen Summers, 28 October 2004.
Joan Wishart, 9 August 2004.
Alan Preskett, President of the Tubercular Soldiers' Aid Society, 31 January 2005.

PERSONAL PAPERS

Australian War Memorial Archives
Anonymous PR87/184.
Antill, Robert 1DRL 0047/1.
Capel, Richard PR00658.
Edwards, Roland PR02057.
Evans, HF 2DRL 490.
Hocking, FR PR88/161.
Hoey, Nettie PR00585.
Inglis, Ken PR00944.
Jones, Vyner PR00360.
Keast, James Astrubale PR00643.
Kenworthy, Harold PR00120.
Lynch, Clive PR84/332.
Mayne, WC 3DRL 0866.
Palmer, John Henry PR03407.
Simpson, Roland PR00733.
Tooney, William PR02027.
Whatley, Victor PR86/270.

Mitchell Library
Baker, Charles A MSS 1608.
Green, J MSS 1838.
Worth, William MSS 6980/1/4.

National Library of Australia
Booth, Mary MS 2864.
Donnell, Anne MS 3962.
Peach, William E MS 929.
Pharo, FM MS 6669.

State Library of Victoria
Beament, Eric MS 9686.
Bourke, W 'Perco' MS 10163.
Cameron, Alexander Pullar, MS 10714.
Foxcroft, AJ MS 96/3.
Gamble, William MS 11989.
Goddard, Charles James, MS 13106.
Nicholas, Philip, MS 12068.
Poppins, Ernest, MS 11651.
Randall Family Papers, MS 11287.
Ross, John Lindsay, MS 12541.

University of Melbourne Archives
Derham, Alfred Plumley 67/6.
Lord, Jim 88/109.
Jones, Ray 81/81.

PUBLISHED COLLECTIONS OF LETTERS AND MEMOIRS

Chandler, Mary J (ed.) (1988) *'Dear Homefolks': Letters Written by LG Chandler During the First World War*, TV Printing, Mildura.
Facey, Albert (1981) *A Fortunate Life*, Fremantle Arts Centre Press, Fremantle.
Hinckfuss, Harold (1982) *Memories of a Signaller: The First World War, 1914–1919*, Dominion, Hedges & Bell, Melbourne.
McKay, Lyn (ed.) (1989) *Diary 1916–18: Private A Richer 59th Battalion*, Genealogical Society of Victoria, Ballarat.
Reddrop, Mary (ed.) (1982) *Jim's Story: With the 37th Battalion AIF*, Spectrum Publications, Melbourne.
Voss, WJ (1935) *Light of the Mind*, Chapman & Hall, London.
Wilson, Patrick (ed.) (2002) *So Far from Home: The Remarkable Diaries of Eric Evans, An Australian Soldier During World War 1*, Kangaroo Press, Sydney.

ORGANISATIONAL RECORDS

Australian Red Cross Society
Australian Red Cross Society, New South Wales Division, *Annual Report*, 1914–39.
Australian Red Cross Society, New South Wales Division, *Red Cross Record*, 1914–39.
Australian Red Cross Society, Victorian Division, *Annual Report*, 1914–39.
Australian Red Cross Society, Caulfield Branch, *Red Cross Record*, 1916–39.
Note: The Australian Red Cross was founded in August 1914. During and after the war, it was officially known as the Australian Branch of the British Red Cross Society, but was often referred to as the Australian Red Cross Society. In 1927, it formally gained independence under that name.

Australian War Memorial
AWM 25 Department of Defence, Written Records, 1914–18 War.
AWM 131 Roll of Honour Circulars, 1914–18 War.
AWM 164 Roll of Honour Circulars, 1914–18 War, Supplementary Series.
AWM 261 Supplementary Roll of Honour Cards.
AWM 38 Records of CEW Bean, Official Historian.
AWM 41 Records of AG Butler, Historian of Australian Army Medical Services.
AWM 93 Australian War Memorial Registry Files.

Other
Colonial Sugar Refining Company, CSR Ltd Records 142/3063; CSR Ltd Staff Summary Books, Noel Butlin Archives, Z109/557, 1918.
Limbless Soldiers' Association of South Australia, Minute Books, State Library of South Australia, SRG 316.
Mulqueen Funerals, Papers, University of Melbourne Archives, 82/44.
Returned Servicemen's League, RSL Collection, National Library of Australia, MS 6609.
Tubercular Soldiers' Aid Society, TSAS Collection, State Library of South Australia, SRG 488.
Victorian Shrine of Remembrance Committee Papers, Victorian Public

Records Office, VPRS 2498.

COMMONWEALTH GOVERNMENT AGENCY RECORDS

National Archives of Australia

AUSTRALIAN IMPERIAL FORCE
B2455 Personnel Dossiers.

DEPARTMENT OF DEFENCE
B1535, MP367/1 Correspondence Files.

DEPARTMENT OF REPATRIATION
A2483, A2487, A2489 Correspondence Files.

REPATRIATION MEDICAL CASE FILES
B73 Victoria; C138 New South Wales; J26 & J30 Queensland; K60 Western Australia; D363 South Australia; P107 & P130 Tasmania.

VICTORIAN STATE GOVERNMENT AGENCY RECORDS

Public Records Office of Victoria

DEPARTMENT OF LUNACY
VA 2864, Lunacy Department, VPRS 7471, Outward Letter Books.
VA 2846, Mont Park Hospital for the Insane, VPRS 7472, Outward Letter Books.
VA 2845, Royal Park Hospital for the Insane, VPRS 7481, Asylum Records.
VA 2864, Lunacy Department, VPRS 7512, Registers of Military Patients.
VA 2844, Ballarat Hospital for the Insane, VPRS 7523, Correspondence Files.
VA 2841, Ararat Hospital for the Insane, VPRS 7525, Correspondence Files.
VA 2846, Mont Park Hospital for the Insane, VPRS 7527, Military Mental Hospital Correspondence Files.
VA 2839, Yarra Bend Hospital for the Insane, VPRS 7528, Correspondence Files.
VA 2846, Mont Park Hospital for the Insane, VPRS 7532, Correspondence Files.
VA 2845, Royal Park Hospital for the Insane, VPRS 7539, Royal Park Receiving House Correspondence Files.

CLOSER SETTLEMENT BOARD
VA 2266, Closer Settlement Board, VPRS 746, Advances Files – Geelong Division.
VA 2266, Closer Settlement Board, VPRS 747, Advances Files – Eastern Division.
VA 2266, Closer Settlement Board, VPRS 10381, Soldier Settlement Advances Files.

SUPREME COURT OF VICTORIA
VA 2549, Supreme Court of Victoria, VPRS 283, Divorce Case Files, Melbourne.

LOCAL GOVERNMENT RECORDS

City of Sydney Archives

File 940 Minutes of the Lord Mayor's Patriotic Fund I.
File 941 Minutes of the Lord Mayor's Patriotic Fund II.
File 1838/29 Application by TB Sailors' and Soldiers' Association for Erection of Kiosks.
File 2390/22 Public Meeting re Unemployed Returned Soldiers.

COMMONWEALTH GOVERNMENT PUBLICATIONS

Legislation
War Pensions Act 1914
Australian Soldiers' Repatriation Fund Act 1916
Australian Soldiers' Repatriation Act 1917
Australian Soldiers' Repatriation Act 1920

Reports, monographs, pamphlets
Australian Department of Defence, Deputy Chief Censor (1917) *Rules for Censorship of the Press.*
Census of the Commonwealth of Australia, 30th June 1933, Part XVII – War Service (1937) Government Printer, Canberra.
Cumpston, JHL (1919) *Venereal Disease in Australia*, Government Printer,

Melbourne.
Department of Trade and Customs Committee Concerning Causes of Death and Invalidity in the Commonwealth (1916) *Report on Venereal Diseases*, Government Printer, Melbourne.
Fetherston, RH (1919) *Report on 1. Australian Army Medical Services Overseas. 2. The Medical Services of Great Britain and the Allies. 3. Re-education and Re-establishment of War Cripples in America, Europe, and India*, Department of Defence, Melbourne.
Millen, ED (1918) *What Australia is Doing for Her Returned Soldiers*, HJ Green, Melbourne.
Official Year Book of the Commonwealth of Australia, 1914–1939.
Repatriation Commission, *Annual Report*, 1920–1939.
Repatriation Commission (1937) *Service Pensions Handbook: To Explain the Provisions of the Australian Soldiers' Repatriation Act 1920–1936 Relating to Service Pensions*, Government Printer, Canberra.
Repatriation, Government Printer, Melbourne, 1919–1920.
Report of the Royal Commission on the Assessment of War Service Disabilities (1925) Government Printer, Melbourne.
Report of the Royal Commission on the Basic Wage (1920) Government Printer, Melbourne.
Rules for Censorship of the Press Revised to 30th June 1918 (1918) HJ Green Government Printer, Melbourne.
The Civil Re-establishment of the AIF – A Summary of the Work of the Department of Repatriation (1918) Government Printer, Melbourne.
War Pensions Entitlement Appeal Tribunal, *Annual Report*, 1929–1939.

STATE GOVERNMENT PUBLICATIONS

Fitzpatrick, William (1917) *The Repatriation of the Soldier: Vocational Training, Employment, Afforestation, Land Settlement*, Victorian State War Council, Melbourne.
New South Wales State Recruiting Committee (c.1914–1918) 'Free Tour to Great Britain and Europe' AWM RCO 2289, 5/5/3, William Brooks & Co Ltd, Sydney.
New South Wales State Recruiting Committee (c.1914–1918) 'A Golden Rule, Put Your Best Foot Forward and Join the AIF', AWM RCO 2291, 5/5/3.
Recruiting Campaign No. 2 Organiser's Manual (1917) Director-General of Recruiting, Victoria.
Report of the Inspector-General of the Insane (1914–1939) Department of Lunacy, Government Printer, Melbourne.
Report of the Royal Commission on Soldier Settlement (1925) HJ Green Government Printer, Melbourne.

OFFICIAL HISTORIES

Butler, AG (1930) *The Official History of the Australian Army Medical Services in the War of 1914–18*, vol. 1, Australian War Memorial, Melbourne.
—— (1940) *The Official History of the Australian Army Medical Services in the War of 1914–18*, vol. 2, *The Western Front*, Australian War Memorial, Canberra.
—— (1943) *The Official History of the Australian Army Medical Services in the War of 1914–18*, vol. 3, *Special Problems and Services*, Australian War Memorial, Canberra.

NEWSPAPERS

Age, Argus, Bendigo Advertiser, Brisbane Courier, Daily Telegraph, Herald, Hobart Mercury, Register [Adelaide], *Record* [South Melbourne], *Sun*

News-Pictorial, Sydney Mail, Sydney Morning Herald, Albury Daily News, Warrnambool Standard, Western Australian, West Wimmera Mail.

MAGAZINES AND JOURNALS

Anzac Bulletin, Aussie, Australia To-Day, Bulletin, Coo-eee!, Crosslight, Diggers' Gazette, Duckboard, Everylady's Journal, Harefield Park Boomerang, Karoolian, Observation Post, League, Whiz-Bang, Returned Sailors and Soldiers' Annual, Limbless Soldier, Medical Journal of Australia, Optimist, Mufti, Our Empire, Reveille, RSA Magazine, Smith's Weekly, Soldier, Southward-Ho!, Bedford Call, Tassie Digger, Truth , Worker.

BOOKS

Anti-Tuberculosis Association of New South Wales (1938) *Your Baby*, Academy, Sydney.

Brown, Lawrason (1916) *Rules for Recovery from Tuberculosis*, Lea & Febiger, New York.

Ellis, Henry A (1923) *How Shall I be Saved from Consumption?*, George Allen & Unwin Ltd, London.

Hills, Loftus (c.1927–1939) *The Returned Sailors and Soldiers' Imperial League of Australia: Its Origin, History, Achievements and Ideals*, RSSILA, Melbourne.

Lawson, Arnold (1922) *War Blindness at St Dunstan's*, Oxford Medical Publications, London.

McMurtrie, Douglas (1919) *The Disabled Soldier*, MacMillan, New York.

Piddington, AB (1921) *The Next Step: Family Income*, Macmillan & Co, Melbourne.

Pratt, Ambrose & John Barnes (1934) *The National War Memorial of Victoria: An Interpretative Appreciation of the Shrine of Remembrance*, WD Joynt, Melbourne.

Scott, Ernest (1937) *Australia During the War*, 2nd edn, Angus & Robertson, Sydney.

Sir Samuel McCaughey Memorial to the Fallen and Disabled Soldiers of Australia: Bequest for the Technical Education of Soldiers' Children (1928) AIF Canteen Funds Trust, Melbourne.

Summary of Meetings of Conference of St. Dunstan's Delegates Representing the War-Blinded Men of the Empire Held (1929) St. Dunstan's, London.

SECONDARY SOURCES

UNPUBLISHED THESES

Blackmore, Kate (1994) 'War, Health and Welfare: The Great War and its Aftermath', PhD Thesis, School of History, Philosophy and Politics, Macquarie University.

Larsson, Marina (1995) 'An Iconography of Suffering: VD in Australia 1914–1918', MA Thesis, Department of History, University of Melbourne.

Lindstrom, RG (1997) 'The Australian Experience of Psychological Casualties in War 1915–1939', PhD Thesis, Department of History, Victoria University.

Nelson, Elizabeth (2004) 'Homefront Hostilities: The First World War and Domestic Violence in Victoria', PhD Thesis, History Department, University of Melbourne.

Thame, Claudia (1974) 'Health and the State: The Development of Collective Responsibility for Health Care in Australia in the First Half of the Twentieth Century', PhD Thesis, Australian National University.

Ziino, Bart (1999) 'Journeys to War: Experiences of Australian Recruits in the Great War', MA Thesis, History Department, University of Melbourne.

BOOKS, BOOK CHAPTERS AND JOURNAL ARTICLES

Abel, Emily K (2000) *Hearts of Wisdom: American Women Caring for Kin*, Harvard University Press, Cambridge, Massachusetts.

Allen, Judith (1990) *Sex and Secrets: Crimes Involving Australian Women Since 1880*, Oxford University Press, Melbourne.

Ariès, Philippe (1981) *The Hour of Our Death*, trans. Helen Weaver, Alfred A Knopf, New York.

Barham, Peter (2004) *Forgotten Lunatics of the Great War*, Yale University Press, London.

Barnes, David S (1995) *The Making of a Social Disease: Tuberculosis in Nineteenth Century France*, University of California Press, Berkeley.

Bartlett, Peter & David Wright (eds) (1999) *Outside the Walls of the Asylum: The History of Care in the Community 1750–2000*, The Athlone Press, London.

Bashford, Alison (2002) 'At the Border: Contagion, Immigration, Nation', *Australian Historical Studies*, 33(120): 344–58.

—— (2003) 'Cultures of Confinement: Tuberculosis, Isolation and the Sanatorium', in Carolyn Strange & Alison Bashford (eds) *Isolation: Places and Practices of Exclusion*, Routledge, London, 133–49.

Bourke, Joanna (1995) 'Shell Shock and Australian Soldiers in the Great War', *Sabretache*, 36: 3–10.

—— (1996) *Dismembering the Male: Men's Bodies, Britain and the Great War*, Reaktion Books, London.

—— (1998) 'The Battle of the Limbs: Amputation, Artificial Limbs and the Great War in Australia', *Australian Historical Studies*, 110(29): 49–67.

—— (2000) 'Effeminacy, Ethnicity and the End of Trauma: The Sufferings of "Shell-Shocked" Men in Great Britain, 1914–1939', *Journal of Contemporary History*, 35(1): 57–70.

Bryder, Linda (1988) *Below the Magic Mountain*, Oxford University Press, New York.

Cannadine, David (1981) 'War and Death, Grief and Mourning in Modern Britain', in Joachim Whaley (ed.) *Mirrors of Mortality: Studies in the Social History of Death*, Europa Publications, London, 187–242.

Charmaz, Kathy (1997) 'Grief and Loss of Self', in Kathy Charmaz, Glennys Howarth & Allan Kellehear (eds) *The Unknown Country: Death in Australia, Britain and the USA*, Macmillan, London, 229–41.

Cochrane, Peter (1990) 'Deliverance and Renewal: The Origins of the Simpson Legend', *Journal of the Australian War Memorial*, 16: 18–29.

—— (1992) *Simpson and the Donkey: The Making of a Legend*, Melbourne University Press, Melbourne.

Cohen, Deborah (2001) *The War Come Home: Disabled Veterans in Britain and Germany 1914–1939*, University of California Press, Berkeley.

Coleborne, Catharine (2006) 'Families, Patients and Emotions: Asylums for the Insane in Colonial Australia and New Zealand, c.1880–1910', *Social History of Medicine*, 19(3): 425–42.

—— (2006) '"His Brain Was Wrong, His Mind Astray": Families and the Language of Insanity in New South Wales, Queensland and New Zealand, 1880s–1910', *Journal of Family History*, 31(1): 45–65.

Connolly, Cynthia (2004) 'Pale, Poor, and "Pretubercular" Children: A History of Pediatric Antituberculosis Efforts in France, Germany and the United States, 1899–1929, *Nursing Inquiry*, 11(3): 138–147.

Crotty, Martin (2001) *Making the Australian Male: Middle-Class*

Masculinity 1870–1920, Melbourne University Press, Melbourne.

Damousi, Joy & Marilyn Lake (eds) (1995) *Gender and War: Australians at War in the Twentieth Century*, Cambridge University Press, Melbourne.

—— (1999) *The Labour of Loss: Mourning, Memory and Wartime Bereavement in Australia*, Cambridge University Press, Melbourne.

—— (2001) *Living with the Aftermath: Trauma, Nostalgia and Grief in Post-war Australia*, Cambridge University Press, Melbourne.

Davison, Graeme (1995) '"Our Youth is Spent and Our Backs are Bent": The Origins of Australian Ageism', in David Walker & Stephen Garton (eds) *Ageing*, Special Issue of *Australian Cultural History*, 14: 40–62.

Dawes, JNI & LL Robson (1997) *Citizen to Soldier: Australia Before the Great War, Recollections of the First AIF*, Melbourne University Press, Melbourne.

Doka, Kenneth J (ed.) (1989) *Disenfranchised Grief: Recognising Hidden Sorrow*, Lexington Books, Lanham, Maryland.

Dormandy, Thomas (1999) *The White Death: A History of Tuberculosis*, New York University Press, New York.

Ferguson, Philip M (2001) 'Mapping the Family: Disability Studies and the Exploration of Parental Response to Disability' in Gary L Albrecht, Katherine D Seelman & Michael Bury (eds) *Handbook of Disability Studies*, Sage Publications, California, 373–95.

Finnane, Mark (1981) *Insanity and the Insane in Post-Famine Ireland*, Croom Helm, London.

—— (1985) 'Asylums, Families and the State', *History Workshop Journal*, 20: 134–48.

Garton, Stephen (1996) *The Cost of War: Australians Return*, Oxford University Press, Melbourne.

—— (1998) 'Freud Versus the Rat: Understanding Shell Shock in World War 1', *Australian Cultural History*, 16: 45–59.

Gerber, David (ed.) (2000) *Disabled Veterans in History*, University of Michigan Press, Ann Arbor.

Gilding, Michael (1991) *The Making and Breaking of the Australian Family*, Allen & Unwin, Sydney.

Grayzel, Susan (1999) *Women's Identities at War: Gender, Motherhood, and Politics in Britain and France During the First World War*, University of North Carolina Press, Chapel Hill.

Hall, Lesley (1991) *Hidden Anxieties: Male Sexuality, 1900–1950*, Polity Press, Cambridge.

Hanna, Martha (2003) 'A Republic of Letters: The Epistolary Tradition in France During World War I', *American Historical Review*, 108(5): 1338–61.

Hickel, K Walter (2001) 'Medicine, Bureaucracy, and Social Welfare: The Politics of Disability Compensation for American Veterans of World War I', in Paul K Longmore & Lauri Umansky (eds) *The New Disability History: American Perspectives*, New York University Press, New York, 236–67.

Higonnet, Margaret, Jane Jenson, Sonya Michel & Margaret Weitz (eds) (1987) *Behind the Lines: Gender and the Two World Wars*, Yale University Press, New Haven.

Holmes, Katie (1995) *Spaces in Her Day: Australian Women's Diaries of the 1920s and 1930s*, Allen & Unwin, Sydney.

Horden, Peregrine & Richard Smith (eds) (1998) *The Locus of Care: Families, Communities, Institutions and the Provision of Welfare Since Antiquity*, Routledge, London.

Hudson, Pat & WR Lee (eds) (1990) *Women's Work and the Family Economy in Historical Perspective*,

Manchester University Press, Manchester.
Inglis, Ken (1987) 'Passing Away' in Bill Gammage & Peter Spearritt (eds) *Australians 1938*, Fairfax, Syme & Weldon, Sydney, 234–53.
—— (1998) *Sacred Places: War Memorials in the Australian Landscape*, Melbourne University Press, Melbourne.
Jalland, Pat (2002) *Australian Ways of Death: A Social and Cultural History 1840–1918*, Oxford University Press, Melbourne.
—— (2005) 'A Secular and Private Grief: Katherine Susannah Prichard Confronts Death and Bereavement', *History Australia*, 2(2): 42/1–42/15.
—— (2005) 'Changing Ways of Grieving in 20th Century Australia', *Dialogue*, 24(3): 4–18.
—— (2006) *Changing Ways of Death in Twentieth-Century Australia: War, Medicine and the Funeral Business*, University of New South Wales Press, Sydney.
Kienitz, Sabine (2002) 'Body Damage: War Disability and Constructions of Masculinity in Weimar Germany', in Karen Hagemann & Stefanie Schüler-Springorum (eds) *Home/Front: The Military, War and Gender in Twentieth-Century Germany*, Berg, Oxford, 181–04.
Koven, Seth (1994) 'Remembering and Dismemberment: Crippled Children, Wounded Soldiers and the Great War in Great Britain', *American Historical Review*, 99(4): 1167–202.
Lake, Marilyn (1987) *The Limits of Hope: Soldier Settlement in Victoria 1915–1938*, Oxford University Press, Melbourne.
—— (2004) 'Translating Needs into Rights: Race, Manhood and the Family Wage', *Tasmanian Historical Studies*, 9: 34–42.
Larsson, Marina (2004) 'Restoring the Spirit: The Rehabilitation of Disabled Soldiers in Australia After the Great War', *Health and History*, Special Issue: Military Medicine, 6(2): 45–59.
—— (2008) 'Writing about Wounds: Australian Soldiers' Hospital Letters 1914–18' in Claire Woods & Judith Timoney (eds) *Writings of War*, Lythrum Press, Adelaide, 2008, 82–97.
—— (2009) 'A Disenfranchised Grief: Postwar Death and Memorialisation in Australia after the First World War', *Australian Historical Studies*, March 2009.
Laugesen, Amanda (2007) 'Australian Soldiers and Print Culture During the Great War' in ME Hammond & Shafquat Towheed (eds) *Publishing and the First World War*, Palgrave Macmillan, Basingstoke, 93–110.
Leese, Peter (2002) *Shell Shock: Traumatic Neuroses and the British Soldiers of the First World War*, Palgrave Macmillan, London.
Lerner, Paul (2003) *Hysterical Men: War, Psychiatry, and the Politics of Trauma in Germany, 1890–1930*, Cornell University Press, London.
Lloyd, Clem & Jacqui Rees (1994) *The Last Shilling: A History of Repatriation in Australia*, Melbourne University Press, Melbourne.
Lomas, Janet (2000) '"Delicate Duties": Issues of Class and Respectability in Government Policy Towards the Wives and Widows of British Soldiers in the Era of the Great War', *Women's History Review*, 9(1): 123–47.
Longmore, Paul K (2003) *Why I Burned My Book and Other Essays on Disability*, Temple University Press, Philadelphia.
—— & Lauri Umansky (eds) (2001) *The New Disability History: American Perspectives*, New York University Press, New York.
Lowenstein, Wendy (1978) *Weevils in the Flour: An Oral Record of the 1930s*

Depression in Australia, Hyland House, Melbourne.

Luckins, Tanja (2004) *The Gates of Memory: Australian People's Experiences and Memories of Loss and the Great War*, Curtin University Books, Fremantle.

Lyons, Mark (1978) *Legacy: The First Fifty Years*, Legacy, Melbourne.

Lyons, Martyn (2003) 'French Soldiers and Their Correspondence: Towards a History of Writing Practices in The First World War', *French History*, 17(1): 79–95.

—— & Lucy Taksa (1992) *Australian Readers Remember: An Oral History of Reading 1890–1930*, Oxford University Press, Melbourne.

McCalman, Janet (1993) *Journeyings: The Biography of a Middle-Class Generation 1920–1990*, Melbourne University Press, Melbourne.

McGill, Jeff (2001) *Campbelltown: World War One 1914–1918*, Campbelltown and Airds Historical Society, Sydney.

McKernan, Michael (1991) *Here is Their Spirit: A History of the Australian War Memorial*, University of Queensland Press in Association with the Australian War Memorial, Brisbane.

—— (2001) *This War Never Ends: The Pain of Separation and Return*, University of Queensland Press, Brisbane.

—— & M Browne (eds) (1988) *Australia, Two Centuries of War and Peace*, Australian War Memorial/ Allen & Unwin, Canberra.

MacKinolty, Judy (ed.) (1981) *The Wasted Years? Australia's Great Depression*, Allen & Unwin, Sydney.

McQuilton, John (2001) *Rural Australia and the Great War: From Tarrwingee to Tangambalanga*, Melbourne University Press, Melbourne.

Meyer, Jessica (2004) '"Gladder to be Going Out than Afraid": Shell Shock and Heroic Masculinity in Britain 1914–1919', in Pierre Purseigle & Jenny McLeod (eds) *Uncovered Fields: Perspectives in First World War Studies*, Brill, Leiden, 195–210.

—— (2004) '"Not Septimus Now": Wives of Disabled Veterans and Cultural Memory of the First World War in Britain', *Women's History Review*, 13(1): 117–38.

Morton, Desmond & Glenn Wright (1987), *Winning the Second Battle: Canadian Veterans and the Return to Civilian Life 1915–1930*, University of Toronto Press, Toronto.

Mosse, George (1990) *Fallen Soldiers*, Oxford University Press, New York.

—— (2000) 'Shell Shock as a Social Disease', *Journal of Contemporary History*, 35(1): 101–08.

Nelson, Elizabeth (2003) 'Civilian Men and Domestic Violence in the Aftermath of the First World War', *Journal of Australian Studies*, 76: 99–108.

Oliver, Bobbie (1995) *War and Peace in Western Australia: The Social and Political Impact of the Great War 1914–1926*, University of Western Australia Press, Perth.

Oliver, Michael (1990) *The Politics of Disablement*, Macmillan Education, London.

Oppenheimer, Melanie (1999) *Red Cross VAs: A History of the VAD Movement in New South Wales*, Ohio Productions, Walcha, NSW.

Ott, Katherine (1996) *Fevered Lives: Tuberculosis in American Culture Since 1870*, Harvard University Press, Cambridge, Massachusetts.

Panchasi, Roxanne (1995) 'Reconstructions: Prosthetics and the Rehabilitation of the Male Body in World War 1 France', *Differences*, 7(3): 109–40.

Porter, Roy & David Wright (eds) 2003, *The Confinement of the Insane: International Perspectives, 1800–1965*, Cambridge University Press, Cambridge.

Potts, David (1990) 'A Positive Culture

of Poverty Represented in the Memories of the 1930s Depression', *Journal of Australian Studies*, 26: 3–14.
—— (2006) *The Myth of the Great Depression*, Scribe Publications, Melbourne.
Priestly, Mark (ed.) (2001) *Disability and the Life Course: Global Perspectives*, Cambridge University Press, Cambridge.
Proust AJ (ed.) (1991) *History of Tuberculosis in Australia, New Zealand and Papua New Guinea*, Brolga Press, Canberra.
Purseigle, Pierre (ed.) (2005) *Warfare and Belligerence: Perspectives in First World War Studies*, Brill, Leiden.
—— & Jenny McLeod (eds) (2004) *Uncovered Fields: Perspectives in First World War Studies*, Brill, Leiden.
Raftery, John (2003) *Marks of War: War Neurosis and the Legacy of Kokoda*, Lythrum Press, Adelaide.
—— & Sandra Schubert (1995) *A Very Changed Man: Families of World War Two Veterans Fifty Years After War*, School of Human Resource Studies, University of South Australia, Adelaide.
Raphael, Beverley (1983) *The Anatomy of Bereavement*, Basic Books, New York.
Reid, Fiona (2007) 'Distinguishing Between Shell-Shocked Veterans and Pauper Lunatics: The Ex-Services' Welfare Society and Mentally Wounded Veterans after the Great War', *War in History*, 14(3): 347–71.
Reiger, Kerreen (1980) *The Disenchantment of the Home: Modernising the Australian Family 1880–1940*, Oxford University Press, Melbourne.
—— (1989) '"Clean and Comfortable and Respectable": Working-Class Aspirations and the Australian Royal Commission on the Basic Wage', *History Workshop*, 27: 86–105.
—— (1991) *Family Economy*, McPhee Gribble, Melbourne.
Reznick, Jeffrey (2004) *Healing the Nation: Soldiers and the Culture of Caregiving in Britain During the Great War*, Manchester University Press, Manchester.
Robson, Lloyd (1970) *The First AIF: A Study of Its Recruitment*, University of Melbourne Press, Melbourne.
—— (1973) 'The Origin and Character of the First AIF, 1914–18: Some Statistical Evidence', *Historical Studies*, 15(61): 737–49.
Roe, Michael (1999) *Life Over Death: Tasmanians and Tuberculosis*, Tasmanian Historical Research Association, Hobart.
Roper, Michael (1991) *Manful Assertions: Masculinities in Britain Since 1800*, Routledge, London.
—— (2004) 'Maternal Relations: Moral Manliness and Emotional Survival in Letters Home During the First World War', in Stefan Dudink, Karen Hagemann & John Tosh (eds) *Masculinities in Politics and War: Gendering Modern History*, Manchester University Press, Manchester, 295–315.
—— (2005) 'Between Manliness and Masculinity: The "War Generation" and the Psychology of Fear in Britain, 1914–1950', *Journal of British Studies*, 44(2): 343–62.
Rothman, Sheila M (1994) *Living in the Shadow of Death: Tuberculosis and the Social Experience of Illness in American History*, Johns Hopkins University Press, Baltimore.
Saunders, Kay (1998) '"Specimens of Superb Manhood": The Lifesaver as National Icon', *Journal of Australian Studies*, 56: 96–105.
Scates, Bruce (2001) 'The Unknown Sock Knitter: Voluntary Work, Emotional Labour, Bereavement and the Great War', *Labour History*, 81: 29–50.
Schedvin, CB (1970) *Australia and the Great Depression: A Study of*

Economic Development in the 1920s and 1930s, Sydney University Press, Sydney.

Sherman, Daniel J (1999) *The Construction of Memory in Interwar France*, University of Chicago Press, Chicago.

Sieder, Reinhard J (1988) 'Behind the Lines: Working-Class Family Life in Wartime Vienna', in Richard Wall & Jay Winter, *The Upheaval of War: Family, Work and Welfare in Europe, 1914–1918*, Cambridge University Press, Cambridge, 109–38.

Smallman-Raynor, Matthew & Andrew D Cliff (2003) 'War and Disease: Some Perspectives on the Spatial and Temporal Occurrence of Tuberculosis in Wartime', in Matthew Gandy & Alimuddin Zumla (eds) *The Return of the White Plague: Global Poverty and the 'New' Tuberculosis*, Verso, London, 70–94.

Smart, Judith (1995) 'Feminists, Food and the Fair Price: The Cost of Living Demonstrations in Melbourne, August–September 1917', in Joy Damousi & Marilyn Lake (eds) *Gender and War: Australians at War in the Twentieth Century*, Cambridge University Press, Melbourne, 274–96.

Smith, Barry (1998) 'Australian Public Health During the Depression of the 1930s', *Australian Cultural History*, 16: 96–106.

Stanley, Peter (1993) *Rosemary and Wattle: The Roll of Honour, Hall of Memory and the Tomb of the Unknown Australian Soldier*, Australian War Memorial, Canberra.

Stone, Deborah (1984) *The Disabled State*, Temple University Press, Philadelphia.

Summerfield, Penny (1998) *Reconstructing Women's Wartime Lives: Discourse and Subjectivity in Oral Histories of the Second World War*, Manchester University Press, Manchester.

Thomson, Alistair (1994) *Anzac Memories: Living With the Legend*, Oxford University Press, Melbourne.

—— (1994) 'Embattled Manhood: Gender, Memory and the Anzac Legend', in Kate Darian-Smith & Paula Hamilton (eds) *Memory and History in Early Twentieth-Century Australia*, Oxford University Press, Melbourne, 158–73.

—— & Robert Perks (eds) (1998) *The Oral History Reader*, Routledge, London.

Throssell, Ric (1989) *My Father's Son*, William Heinemann, Melbourne.

Tyquin, Michael (1993) *Gallipoli: The Medical War, The Australian Army Medical Services in the Dardanelles Campaign of 1915*, University of New South Wales Press, Sydney.

—— (2006) *Madness and the Military: Australia's Experience of the Great War*, Australian Military History Publications, Sydney.

Vance, Jonathan (1997) *Death So Noble: Memory, Meaning and the First World War*, University of British Columbia Press, Vancouver.

Walker, Robin (1983) 'The Struggle Against Pulmonary Tuberculosis in Australia 1788–1950', *Historical Studies*, 20(80): 439–60.

Wall, Richard & Jay Winter (1988) *The Upheaval of War: Family, Work and Welfare in Europe, 1914–1918*, Cambridge University Press, Cambridge.

Weaver John & David Wright (2005) 'Shell Shock and the Politics of Asylum Committal in New Zealand, 1916–22', *Health & History*, 7(1): 17–40.

Whalen, Robert Weldon (1984) *Bitter Wounds: German Victims of the Great War, 1914–1939*, Cornell University Press, London.

White, Richard (1986) 'Motives For Joining Up: Self-Sacrifice, Self-Interest and Social Class', *Journal of the Australian War Memorial*, 9: 3–16.

—— (1988) 'War and Australian Society' in Michael McKernan & M Browne (eds) *Australia, Two Centuries of War and Peace*, Australian War Memorial/Allen & Unwin, Canberra, 391–423.

Winter, Jay (1995) *Sites of Memory, Sites of Mourning: The Great War in European Cultural History*, Cambridge University Press, Cambridge.

—— (2000) 'Shell Shock and the Cultural History of the Great War', *Journal of Contemporary History*, 35(1): 7–12.

Wright, David (1998) 'Family Strategies and the Institutional Confinement of "Idiot" Children in Victorian England', *Journal of Family History*, 23(2): 190–208.

—— (2001) *Mental Disability in Victorian England: The Earlswood Asylum, 1847–1901*, Oxford University Press, Oxford.

Ziino, Bart (2003) 'Claiming the Dead: Great War Memorials and Their Communities', *Journal of the Royal Australian Historical Society*, 89(2): 145–61.

index

ageing *see* carers and caregiving, disabled soldiers
Aiken, Harry 21
alcoholism 78, 123, 141–42, 165, 191, 238
Antill, Robert 58
Anzac Buffet, Hyde Park 70–71, 72
Anzac Day
    1930s shift in meaning 248
    commemorations 15–16, 235, 236, 250
    disabled soldiers' deaths and 206, 247–250
    disabled soldiers' participation in 15–16, 206–7, 247
    lack of acknowledgment of families 16, 22
    local ceremonies 255
    private experiences of 249–250
    wartime dead 16, 247–50, 255
Anzac Fellowship of Women 255
Anzac hostels 77, 95–96
    Brighton, Melbourne 129
    Glenelg, Adelaide 124, 125
    Graythwaite, Sydney 123
    Tasmania 127

Anzac legend 21–22, 25, 53, 184, 248, 265, 270, 272
Ardill Brice, Dr Katie 145
Armistice 18, 69, 237
Arnall, Harry 256
arrival in Australia *see* welcome home
artificial limbs 46, 132, 134–5
Australian Imperial League of Sailors' and Soldiers' Womenfolk 146
Australian Red Cross Society *see also* charity and charities
    After-Care Department 113, 114, 116, 192, 225
    as 'fictive kin' 146
    commentary on disabled soldiers 227
    Furlough House 145–46, 227
    nerve homes 90
    preventoria (Shuna & Juong) 198–99
    provision of support 113, 114, 43
    Ramsgate Home 130
    rest homes 62
    sheltered industries 103
    and support of mental hospital patients 156
    voluntary aids 57, 86, 122

Australian Soldiers' Repatriation Act 19–20, 24, 95, 114, 190, 197, 216, 242, 267, 276, 270
Australian War Memorial *see* war memorials

Baker, Charles 59
Bean, CEW 258
Bennett, Timothy 78
Blevins, Vincent 46
blindness 72–73, 83, 103
body, scholarship on 22
Boer War 40, 149
Bourke, William 51
British-born soldiers 58
Broadbent family 79–80, 132, 144, 157, 223, 251–52, 253, 275–76
Brown, John Godber (father of Betsy Burchett) 112, 158, 168–70, 253, 254, 270, 273, 276
Burchett, Betsy *see* Brown, John Godber
Butler, AG 148, 151, 180
burnt-out soldiers 206–33
  RSSILA campaign for 211

Cameron, Alexander 240, 257
carers and caregiving 120–48, 176–77
  ageing of carers 207, 220–22
  archives 23
  as 'dependants' 24, 92, 104, 106–07, 118–19, 267
  benefits of 270
  by children 130, 223
  by extended family 129–30, 222, 268
  by friends 129
  by men (fathers) 129, 130, 221, 268
  by women (wives, mothers) 21, 55–56, 75, 77, 80, 84, 86, 122, 126–28, 139, 141, 188, 190, 198, 217–18, 220–22, 268, 269
  caring for carers 145–47
  home treatment by 77, 121, 127, 188
  propping up repatriation system 147, 148, 267, 268
  personal cost of 80, 122, 145, 147–48, 227, 268, 269
casualty lists 31, 38–39, 238
Caulfield Repatriation Hospital *see* hospitals, repatriation

censorship
  of correspondence 46
  of newspapers 39, 69
Centre for Soldiers' Wives and Mothers 113, 115, 117, 145
Chandler, Les 44
charity and charities
  see also specific organisations
  attitude of Repatriation Department towards 116, 204–05
  attitude towards disabled soldiers 113–14, 243, 270
  application for 90–91, 113, 115, 116–17
  dependence on 92, 112–17
  during 1930s Depression 224–26, 225
  stigma associated with 113, 117–18
  propping up repatriation system 114, 116, 267–69, 270
children of disabled soldiers
  childhood illnesses of 116, 143
  and Children's Health Bureau 224
  living with a disabled father 132–34, 193–94, 223–24, 270
  families' relinquishment of 243
  Soldiers' Children Education Scheme 225
class, social 93, 112, 117–18, 127, 164, 167, 269
Clayton, William 40
Cochrane, Peter 39
Cramond, Margaret *see* Plane, Alfred

Davey, Wilfred (father of Gwen Summers) 133, 159, 273, 280
deafness 48, 49, 73, 100
death *see also* grief, mourning, war memorials
  bodies 235, 236, 240
  cemeteries 254–58
  during war 25, 74, 227, 235, 240
  economic consequences of 241–45
  emotional consequences of 241
  fear of 75, 133–34
  funerals 235, 250, 253–54
  graves and headstones 254–58
  in memoriam notices 235, 238, 257–58
  of disabled soldiers 19, 77, 144, 234–64, 268

officially rejected 242, 254
premature 211, 223, 238
public commentary on 238–39
statistics on 18, 211, 237
Department of Defence 254, 257
Department of Repatriation *see*
 Repatriation Department
Department of Veterans' Affairs 271
Depression, Great 1930s 206–33
 economic impact of 205, 211, 212–20, 224–26
 prosperity during 213–14
 statistics 211
 unemployment during 211–12, 212–14, 225
 see also pensions
Derham, Alfred 21, 38, 43
disability
 see also disabled soldiers
 anxiety about 24, 31, 32, 38, 45, 50, 68
 as a loss 78–79
 definition of 20
 humour and 46, 77, 134–35, 270
 patriotism and 52, 53, 79, 80
 positive experiences of 131
 social model of 272
 statistics on 18–19, 19, 66, 210–11, 222
 terminology 19
 types of 19, 66–67, 95, 209–10, 231–32
disabled soldiers
 age and marriage statistics 31, 102, 209, 214
 ageing of 206–07, 209–10, 220–22, 228, 232
 as 'forgotten men' 208–09, 232–33
 life expectancy of 238
 newspaper reports on 24, 39, 53, 65, 72, 85–86, 89
disenfranchised grief 236, 244, 249, 250, 264
 see also grief
divorce 81, 82, 227
Doka, Kenneth 236
domestic violence 268, 139–40
 attitude of Repatriation Department towards 142
Donnell, Anne 54–55
dreams 38
drug addiction 78

Eager, Reginald 74–75
Eckhardt, William 58
economic effects of disability 90–119, 189–90
 debt 90–91, 106, 231
 dependence on family 75, 106–07, 113
 income of wives and relatives 105, 106–07
 prosperity 111–12
 strategies to manage 93–94, 103–08
 wives' economic management 91, 93, 104–05
 see also charity and charities, pensions, Soldier Settlement Scheme
Edwards, Roland 45–46
embodiment 20
emotional labour 121, 125
 see also carers and caregiving
employment
 attitude of employers 102, 158, 212, 213
 government policy on 100–02, 212
 home-based businesses 106–07
 impact of disability on 79, 100–02, 158, 213, 242
 of disabled soldiers 100–03
 self-esteem and 117–18, 130, 214
 sheltered industries 103
 statistics on 100
 types of jobs 225
 unemployment 91, 118, 125–26, 212–14, 218–20, 226
 see also Depression, Great 1930s
enlistment
 families' discussions about 31, 34–35
 reasons for and against 31–35
 statistics on 32
 see also recruitment
eugenics 84, 160–61, 184, 198–99
Evans, Eric 50
Evans, Harold 57–58
extended family 103, 129, 224–25, 243, 268
 see also carers and caregiving

Facey, Albert 87
facial disfigurement 45–46, 68–69, 73, 76, 77, 100
Falconer, Frank (father of Keith

Falconer) 86, 98–99, 128, 230–31, 277
family
  absence of 75, 153, 175, 228
  as a site of repatriation 21, 120–48, 267, 268
  breakdown 21, 144, 243, 268 *see also* divorce
  caregiving *see* carers and caregiving
  centred history 22–23, 266–67
  definition of 20
  dependence on 59, 224–25, 148, 266, 267, 268, 270
  relationships 120–48
  support organisations for 144–47, 196–202, 257
farewelling Australia 35–36
feigned illness 41
Fielder, Thomas 230
Financial Emergency Act 1931 217, 226
Floyd, Mavis *see* Mackay, John Gordon
fortune tellers 38
Friendly Union of Soldiers' Wives and Mothers 146, 257
Fryer, John 246

Gamble, William 68–69, 76
Garton, Stephen 92
gas, effects of 40, 80, 117, 120
Goddard, Charles 30, 42, 43, 45, 50, 60
grief
  after disabled soldiers' deaths 236, 244, 245, 257, 264
  disability and 78–79
  disenfranchised 236, 244, 249, 250, 264
  in memoriam badges 257
  in response to wartime death 25, 74–75, 235, 264
Guy, Walter (Wally) 239

Hancock, Claude 255
Hargreaves, John (father of Joan Wishart) 62–64, 87–88, 133, 213–14, 280
Healy, Frank 238
Henley, Timothy 127
Hinckfuss, Harold 35
Hobbes, Narelle 49–50
Hocking, Fred 51

Hogan, Frederick 77
hospitals, mental *see* mental hospitals
hospitals, military *see* military hospitals
hospitals, repatriation *see* repatriation hospitals
hospital ships
  Karoola 61, 67
  Kyarra 66
  voyage home 67, 88
Housewives' Association 172

Imperial War Graves Commission 255
Ingamells, Frank 144
Inman, James 110

Jacoby, Fred 172–73
Jalland, Pat 249
Jones, Ray 40, 48
Jones, Vyner 53

Keast, Jim 29, 38, 43, 46, 52, 55, 57
Kenworthy, Harold 187, 234–35
Kerin, Ambrose 251

Lake, Marilyn 142
Legacy 156, 225, 244–45, 273–74
letters (to and from the wounded) 41–60, 65
  archive 44
  censorship of 46
  from wives and mothers 55–56
  heroic narratives in 50–53
  inclusion of photographs in 55, 56
  inclusion of wound trophies in 54, 55
  as narratives of survival 54–57
  optimism in 44–48
  postal delays and 42, 43, 46
  silences in 48–50
  submission to newspapers 53
  therapeutic value of 52–53
  written by nurses 48–50
lifespan history 26–27
limblessness 46, 47, 51, 80, 81, 82, 83, 84, 85, 97, 108–09, 132, 144, 253
  see also artificial limbs, Plane, Alfred
Limbless Soldiers' Association 113
Long, Bernard 17
Lord, Jim 44–45, 74
Luckins, Tanja 80
Lynch, Clive 54

Lynch, James 75
Lyons, Martyn 42

Mackay, John Gordon (father of Mavis Floyd) 31–32, 98, 130–31, 132, 226, 277–78
Maddern, Fanny 257–58
Marks, Walter (father of Beryl Nelson) 278–79, 190, 193–94, 201, 202
marriage 34, 74, 78, 81–88, 115–16, 118, 137, 178, 217–18, 221, 227, 244
see also divorce
masculinity 24, 50–51, 85, 106–07, 117, 130, 131, 159–60, 191, 203–04
see also Repatriation Department, ideology of manly independence
McMahon, George 143
mental hospitals
abandonment of soldiers to 153, 228
archives 153
assessment for admission to 161–67
attendants 156
Broughton Hall 155
Bundoora Convalescent Home 156, 158, 163, 167, 168, 212
campaigns against desegregation 172–75
campaigns to improve conditions 172–73
Claremont Mental Hospital 172, 173
complaints about 170–172, 173–74
during the 1930s Depression 221, 228
family advocacy 149–77
fear of civilian institutions 161, 163
Kew Mental Hospital 157, 163, 167
Mont Park Mental Hospital 150, 153, 154, 156, 157, 167, 168, 170, 221, 228
private 164–65
Royal Park Mental Hospital 87, 138, 150, 153, 162, 164
segregation policy of 155–57, 174–75
treatment of soldiers in 149–77
trial leave from 167, 168
visits to 167, 168–70
Waley Convalescent Home 90
mental illness *see* mental hospitals, shell shock
Mental Soldiers' Parents of Western Australia 173
Mental Treatment Act 1915 156
military hospitals 43, 57–58, 73, 86

Bishop's Knoll Hospital 52
Harefield Park Hospital 47
Keswick Military Hospital 125, 251
King George's Hospital 58
magazines of 52
Norfolk War Hospital 57
photographs taken in 47, 55–56
Weymouth Convalescent Depot 55
mourning 249, 250–54
see also grief
Muir, Gerald (father of Joyce Muir) 139, 223, 273, 278
Muir, Joyce *see* Muir Gerald
Munro-Ferguson, Lady 124

National Council of Women 172
Nelson, Beryl *see* Marks, Walter
Nicholas, Diane *see* Nicholas, Philip
Nicholas, Philip (father of Diane Nicholas) 132–33, 240, 244, 252, 262, 279
nurses 40, 48–50, 54–55, 86, 127, 240

O'Brien, Hugh 55
oral history 25–26, 65, 266, 273–74

pacifism 26
Palmer, Henry 41
paralysis 49
parents 31, 34, 51, 62–63, 74–75, 76, 78, 116, 220–21
absence of 80, 129
letters to and from 41–60
see also carers and caregiving, grief, Sailors' and Soldiers' Fathers Association
Parker, Stephen 80–81
patriotic funds 90, 94, 113, 116
patriotism 52, 53, 79, 80
Peach, William 40, 57
pensions
1930s cuts to 208, 217–19
1930s tightening of assessment for 215–20
1932 call to give up 214
after death 118, 242–43
amount of 35, 36, 95, 96
assessment of 19–20, 26, 96–98, 114–15, 161–62, 189–90, 216–17
experiences of system 90, 94–100, 217

family wage model 95, 106–07, 118–19
for war death 100, 227
rejection of 98, 115, 118, 215–16, 218, 228, 243–44
see also Repatriation Department
service pension 218–19
statistics on 18–19, 83, 95, 215, 216
Plane, Alfred (father of Margaret Cramond) 80, 276, 111–12, 128–29, 132, 134–35, 213
Poppins, Ernest 48
postal system *see* letters
pregnancy 115–16
Prentice, Bertie 85
pseudonyms 7

Randall, William 54
recruitment
   pamphlets 35, 36–37
   posters 32–33
   rallies 32
repatriation (as a concept) 23, 267
Red Cross Society *see* Australian Red Cross Society
Reddrop, Mary *see* Roberts, James
rehabilitation 74, 84–85, 118
Repatriation Department 21
   anger at 98–99, 216, 243–44, 252
   archives 23, 24, 92, 266
   attitude to charities 91, 116, 199
   attitude to disabled soldiers 91, 92, 97, 155, 231–32
   attitude to families 23, 84–85, 89, 91, 99, 104, 114, 118, 126, 137–38, 204–05, 224, 268
   attitude to family caregiving 104–05, 121, 122, 126, 127, 145, 148
   benefits provided by 73, 94, 187
   expectations of 67, 73–74, 94, 103–04
   funeral grant 251, 254
   ideology of 'manly independence' 24, 74, 91, 92, 116, 117, 118–19, 122, 126, 148, 205, 233, 265–66, 268, 269, 271
   see also pensions, *Australian Soldiers' Repatriation Act*
repatriation hospitals 123, 222, 236
   Caulfield Repatriation Hospital 62, 63, 125, 251, 253, 251, 259
   Keswick Repatriation Hospital 125, 251
   Randwick Repatriation Hospital 75, 234
Rose Hall Convalescent Home 113
see also Anzac hostels
return home *see* welcome home
Returned and Services League (RSL) 273–74
Returned Sailors' and Soldiers' Imperial League of Australia (RSSILA)
   children and 223–24
   Children's Health Bureau 224
   disabled soldiers and 147, 155, 164, 171, 188, 201, 211, 248, 254,
   disabled soldiers' deaths and 236, 251–52, 253, 255
   families and 126–27, 167, 195
   women's clinic 145
Roberts, James (Jim) (father of Mary Reddrop) 52–53, 129, 132, 273, 279
Roper, Michael 41
Ross, Lindsay 41, 58
Rouhan, Patrick 178–79

Sailors and Nurses Relatives' Association 146
Sailors' and Soldiers' Fathers Association 99, 146, 147, 171
Sailors' and Soldiers' Mothers' Association 146
Second World War 19, 26, 262, 268, 272
self-inflicted wounds 40–41
severely disabled 77, 103, 129
see also Anzac hostels
sexual impairment 50, 73, 135–36, 187
shell shock
   absence of veterans' organisation 173–74
   attitude of Repatriation Department to 159, 174
   causes of 159
   civilian mental illness and 151, 157, 160, 166
   concealment of 141, 158
   definition of 138, 152
   diagnosis of 140, 161–62
   experiences of 40, 48, 62–63, 78, 120, 139, 149–77
   impact on families of 73, 78, 90, 270, 133, 138–142, 149–77, 221
   marriage and 81–82, 83, 86
   masculinity and 51, 159–60
   mental depression and 141, 268
   statistics on 151, 156, 162

index   319

stigma against 157–61, 244
symptoms of 138, 139, 152
violence and 78, 170, 175–76 *see also* domestic violence
see also mental hospitals
Shrine of Remembrance *see* war memorials
Soldier Settlement Scheme
  attitude of Closer Settlement Board 144
  disabled soldiers and 108–10, 118, 229, 142–45
  during 1930s Depression 228–32
  failure of settlers 110, 144, 229–31, 253
  statistics on 108, 228–29
  successful disabled settlers 112, 230
  support of wives 108–10, 142–43
  wives' health 142–43, 144
Soldiers' Children Education Scheme 225
Soutar, Peter 257
'Spanish' influenza 66
spiritualism 38
Starke, William 255
stoicism 79–80
Stone, Henry 111
suicide
  of disabled soldiers 117, 149, 231, 241, 243, 252
  of parents of disabled soldiers 80
  pensions after 118
  statistics on 241
Summers, Gwen *see* Davey, Wilfred

TB Women's Association 201
telegrams 30, 42, 43, 45, 50, 69
Throssell, Hugo 252
Tooney, William 29–30, 59
trade unions 102
Tubercular Soldiers' Aid Society 197–98, 200–02, 203–04
  archives of 192
  commentary on tuberculosis 190–91
  families and 113, 115, 196, 202
  magazine, the *Optimist* 191, 203–04
  provision of support by 106–07, 198, 243
Tubercular Soldiers' Association 197, 201, 202
tuberculosis 178–205
  anxiety about 184–85
  attitude of Repatriation Department to 181, 192, 196–97, 204–05

belief in 'wartime tuberculosis' 195, 203
children and 190, 195–96, 198
description of 182–84
economic effects of 107–08
employment and 179, 189
invalidism and 190–91
phthisiophobia (fear of tuberculosis) 189–92, 202
statistics on 179, 192, 205
stigma about 200–01
transmission within families 179, 180, 186–88, 192–96, 203–04, 268
treatment of 185–86, 191–92

unemployment *see* employment

Vawser, Percy 28, 259
venereal disease 82, 136–38, 165–66, 268
Vietnam War 22, 26, 272
Voss, WJ 69

war disability *see* disability
war memorials 235, 236, 245–47
  Australian War Memorial 22, 235, 258–64
  Shrine of Remembrance, Melbourne 139, 206, 247
  University of Queensland War Memorial 246
  Western Australian State War Memorial 247
Watson, John 109–10
welcome home
  anticipation 67–68
  arrival 68–69
  community ceremonies 73
  meeting family 62–63, 69–73
  official ceremonies 61–62
  photographs of 65, 70–71
Whatley, Victor 225
white feathers 32
widows 75, 242, 244
Winter, Jay 23, 248
Wishart, Joan *see* Hargreaves, John
Worth, William 49–50
wounded soldiers
  letters to and from families 41–60
  statistics on 18–19, 40, 66
wound trophies 54, 55

Ziino, Bart 67, 235

www.ingramcontent.com/pod-product-compliance
Lightning Source LLC
Chambersburg PA
CBHW031723230426
43669CB00007B/220